The Gen X Series

MATHS OLYMPIAD 5

Useful for Maths Olympiads Conducted at School, National & International Levels

Author
Shraddha Singh

Peer Reviewer
Jyotsna Gopikrishnan

Strictly According to the Latest Syllabus of Maths Olympiad

V&S PUBLISHERS

Published by:

F-2/16, Ansari road, Daryaganj, New Delhi-110002
☎ 23240026, 23240027 • *Fax:* 011-23240028
✉ info@vspublishers.com • 🌐 www.vspublishers.com

 Online Brandstore: amazon.in/vspublishers

Regional Office : Hyderabad
5-1-707/1, Brij Bhawan (Beside Central Bank of India Lane)
Bank Street, Koti, Hyderabad - 500 095
☎ 040-24737290
✉ vspublishershyd@gmail.com

Follow us on:

BUY OUR BOOKS FROM: | AMAZON | | FLIPKART |

© Copyright: *V&S Publishers*
ISBN 978-93-579405-4-2
New Edition

DISCLAIMER

While every attempt has been made to provide accurate and timely information in this book, neither the author nor the publisher assumes any responsibility for errors, unintended omissions or commissions detected therein. The author and publisher makes no representation or warranty with respect to the comprehensiveness or completeness of the contents provided.

All matters included have been simplified under professional guidance for general information only, without any warranty for applicability on an individual. Any mention of an organization or a website in the book, by way of citation or as a source of additional information, doesn't imply the endorsement of the content either by the author or the publisher. It is possible that websites cited may have changed or removed between the time of editing and publishing the book.

Results from using the expert opinion in this book will be totally dependent on individual circumstances and factors beyond the control of the author and the publisher.

It makes sense to elicit advice from well informed sources before implementing the ideas given in the book. The reader assumes full responsibility for the consequences arising out from reading this book.

For proper guidance, it is advisable to read the book under the watchful eyes of parents/guardian. The buyer of this book assumes all responsibility for the use of given materials and information.

The copyright of the entire content of this book rests with the author/publisher. Any infringement/transmission of the cover design, text or illustrations, in any form, by any means, by any entity will invite legal action and be responsible for consequences thereon.

Publisher's Note

General Trade and Mass Appeal books across various genres have helped **V&S Publishers** to gain widespread popularity. In a short span of 10 years, we have successfully published more than 1000 titles across 9 languages in our 50 subject categories. Being into the publishing business for about 40 years, we have always been a dynamic publishing house, with a massive distribution network, across India; including E-commerce platforms.

Understanding the need of inculcating knowledge and developing a spirit of healthy competition amongst students to make them ready for the world outside schools and colleges; we created Olympiad Series under the **GEN X SERIES Imprint** which, owning to its rich content and unique representation became popular amongst students, in no time. The motivation is not to improve marks in terms of numbers, but is to make sure that the students are already prepared to face competitive environment with respect to college admissions and cracking various entrance examinations, while ensuring their conceptual clarity.

Published for classes 1-10 across subjects English, Mathematics, Science, Computers, General Knowledge, the books are unlike any other in the market and are written in a guidebook pattern and exhaustively include examples and Multiple-Choice Questions.

Here, we present the latest Edition of **MATHS OLYMPIAD CLASS 5**.

Unique Features of the book are as follows:

- Authored by Subject Matter Experts' and Peer reviewed by School Principals and HOD's for the respective subjects
- Books based on principles of Applied Psychology and Bloom's Taxonomy
- Suited for Olympiad Examinations held at School level, National level & International Level irrespective of organizing body.
- The only Olympiad Book in India written in Guidebook Pattern with Concise Theory, images and illustrations.
- Exhaustively include Examples, MCQs, Subjective Questions, and HOTS with Answer Keys & Solutions.
- Multiple Model Papers for thorough practice also given inside the book with solutions.
- OMR sheets appended at the end of the book for simulating exam environment.

Besides, we are also planning to launch an App very soon for the Olympiad preparation which further testifies our constant endeavor to keep up with student demands. We have made sure to closely follow syllabus patterns of not only Olympiad conducting bodies but also education boards & organizations like CBSE and NCERT, to make sure that our books prove useful to students; helping them to boost their academic performance in schools as well.

P.S. While every care has been taken to ensure the correctness of the content, if you come across any error, howsoever minor, do not hesitate to discuss with teachers while pointing that out to us in no uncertain terms.

We wish you All the Best!

DISTINCTIVE

WHY OLYMPIADS?
Olympiads are just like competitive exams; conducted by various bodies at national and international levels. The aim is to experience a competitive examination at the school level and also to help students to discover their interest acrss subjects like English, Mathematics, Science and General Knowledge.

WHY V&S OLYMPIADS?
We at V&S Publishers aim to build an avid-reading student audience. Hence, our resolve is to follow an innovative pedagogic pattern which would help students to navigate through the book with utmost ease and comfort. Crisp theory practical examples and illustrations keep our book interactive and comprehensive.

01 LEARNING OBJECTIVES
They list the whole chapter as subtopics, helping the teachers to guide children in a step-by-step manner.

02 DID YOU KNOW
Enhance your knowledge by getting acquainted with some amazing facts across various subjects like science, Mathematics and English.

03 MULTIPLE CHOICE QUESTIONS
MCQs act as an excellent learning aid, helping you to understand and work on your mistakes.

04 THINGS TO REMEMBER
A quick recap of the chapter in a summarized format helps in faster revision along with conceptual clarity.

05 HOTS
The High Order Thinking Questions aim to help the student to solve Application-based questions and gain practical understanding of the subject.

FEATURES

SUBJECTIVE QUESTIONS
06
Help to place the knowledge gained in orderly fashion by using **"WH"** questions, mostly in the form of bullet points.

ACHIEVER'S SECTION
07
Offers a quick revision of the book along with some new facts for the students to discover.

A SET OF OMR SHEETS
08
To allow the student to practice question in an exam-like format which would help them to get the "feel" of how Olympiad exams take place.

MODEL TEST PAPERS
09
Two model test papers are provided at the end of each book, which help the student to test the knowledge which they have gained after thorough reading of all chapters.

ANSWER KEY & SOLUTIONS
10
Detailed Answer Key along with explanations aid the pupil to indentify, understand the mistakes they make during the course of Olympiad preparation.

COMPLEMENT SCHOOL SYLLABI

The syllabi across all Olympiad examination closely follow the pattern of academic books. Hence, they not only provide a competitive examination experience, but also help to revise topics for school examinations as well, while strengthening conceptual precision.

ENHANCEMENT OF ANALYTICAL & LOGICAL REASONING

Practicing analytical ability questions, not only helps in developing intellectual ability but also plays a vital role in building critical thinking ability which helps an individual to think about a question or a crisis like situation in day to day life; from all aspects and directions.

Note to Parents

Dear Parents,

Olympiad examinations come with a plethora of advantages. First and foremost among such advantages is the application of knowledge studied, in the form of multiple-choice questions. It helps the child not only to step away from rote learning, but also helps them to exhibit their competencies across various subjects.

In addition to this, Olympiads help the student to understand the importance of revision and practice, and to imbibe upon these practices; which also prove useful in academic performance of the child.

The Olympiads are conducted across multiple subjects, and help the child to recognize their field of interest, thereby encouraging the students to make a career in the field where they can excel the most.

However, cognitive development of a child is not just limited to the four walls of classroom. Following steps can be encouraged by you, to ensure their ward is able to grasp various concepts with ease or lesser difficulty:

- **Eat a balanced diet:** Ensure intake of vitamins and minerals to keep you active. Include fruits and super foods like millet in your diet to ensure healthy functioning of organs. Huge intake of junk food should be avoided.
- **Indulge in outdoor activities:** Outdoor games break the monotony of life. Play your heart out in greenery to keep yourself alert, active and fit.
- **Sleep well:** A sound sleep of 7-8 hours refreshes the brain and makes it ready to understand new topics with more clarity. A sleep derived person faces difficulty in doing even the simplest tasks of day to day life.
- **Reduce your Screen time:** More screen time leads to not only weakening of eyesight but decreases concentration span. Regulated Screen time should be encouraged
- **Do not hesitate to raise a hand:** Having a doubt in class? Do not hesitate to ask your parents or teachers. This ensures more Conceptual Clarity and hence leads to Application based understanding of various subjects and topics.
- **Teach and Learn:** No need to do rote-learning. Once you understand a topic teach or explain it to your friends, siblings and parents. It brings clarity and ensures the child does his revision this way.
- **Keep smiling:** A positive attitude promotes a growth mindset and encourages the child to be more inquisitive and try to learn something new, everyday!

HAPPY LEARNING!

Contents

SECTION 1 : MATHEMATICAL REASONING

1. Number System — 9
2. Roman Numbers — 21
3. Operations on Numbers — 29
4. Decimals and Fractions — 38
5. Algebra — 53
6. LCM and HCF — 57
7. Ratio and Proportion — 69
8. Measurement — 79
9. Temperature — 88
10. Money — 95
11. Area, Perimeter and Volume — 102
12. Geometrical Shapes and Angles — 111

SECTION 2: LOGICAL REASONING

1. Series and Pattern — 129
2. Analogy — 135
3. Odd One Out — 140
4. Coding and Decoding — 143
5. Number Ranking and Alphabet Test — 153
6. Direction Sense Test — 161
7. Mirror and Water Images — 168
8. Data Handling — 177

SECTION 3 : ACHIEVERS' SECTION

Key Charts — 192
Model Test Paper – 1 — 197
Model Test Paper – 2 — 202

ANSWER KEYS (Access Content Online on Dropbox) — 207
APPENDIX — 214

SECTION 1
MATHEMATICAL REASONING

Number System

Learning Objectives : In this chapter, students will learn about:
- ✓ Number System
- ✓ Numerals
- ✓ Fractions
- ✓ Rules of Divisibility
- ✓ Imaginary Numbers
- ✓ Types of Numbers
- ✓ Place Value
- ✓ Number Sense
- ✓ Number Names
- ✓ Integers

CHAPTER SUMMARY

Number System
Numbers are used heavily in our daily routine. They can be used for counting, measuring, and comparing things. It can be used to talk about number of dolls a girl has or the number of chocolates a kid has left in his box.

The number system that we use in our everyday life is called decimal system. This is because there are 10 digits (0, 1, 2, 3, 4, 5, 6, 7, 8, and 9). Numbers are written using these digits.

Number Sense
Number sense refers to a student's fluidity and elasticity with numbers. He/She has sense of what number mean, understands symbolic representation, is able to perform mental math, understands their relationships to one another and can use those numbers in real world problems.

Formation of numbers from given digits
The greatest and smallest numbers, without repetition, can be formed using any number of digits by arranging them in the descending and ascending order respectively.

For example, if we form a 4-digit number from the digits, 9, 2, 7 and 3, then

Greatest number = 9732
Smallest number = 2379

When repetition of digits is allowed, then the greatest number can be formed by writing the greatest digit as many times as the number is required. Similarly, the smallest number can be formed by writing the smallest digit as many times as required.

Greatest number (with repetition) = 9999
Smallest number (with repetition) = 2222

Types of Numbers
Now let us see how classification of numbers is done.

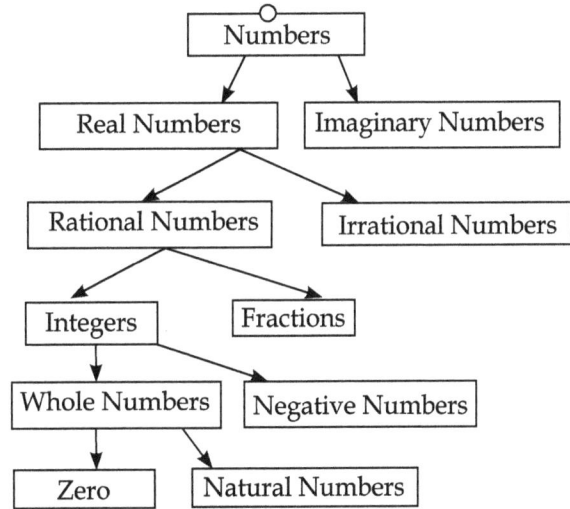

Real Number
Set of all numbers that can be represented on the number line are called real numbers. e.g.

$4, -8, 0, \dfrac{9}{11}$ etc.

$-\infty \;\; \underset{-6\;-5\;-4\;-3\;-2\;-1\;\;0\;\;1\;\;2\;\;3\;\;4\;\;5}{\vdash\!\!\!\vdash\!\!\!\vdash\!\!\!\vdash\!\!\!\vdash\!\!\!\vdash\!\!\!\vdash\!\!\!\vdash\!\!\!\vdash\!\!\!\vdash\!\!\!\vdash\!\!\!\vdash} \;\; +\infty$

Rational Numbers
A number that can be represented in the form p/q, where p and q are integers and q is not

zero. Example : 2/3, 1/10, 8/3 etc. They can be finite decimal numbers, whole numbers, integers, fractions.

Irrational Numbers

A number that cannot be represented in the form p/q, where p and q are integers and q ≠ zero. An infinite non recurring decimal is an irrational number. Example : √2, √5 , √7 and π(pie)=3.1428

The rational numbers are classified into integers and fractions

Integers

The set of numbers on the number line, with the natural numbers, zero and the negative numbers are called integers, I = {….., – 3, – 2, – 1, 0, 1, 2, 3, …….}

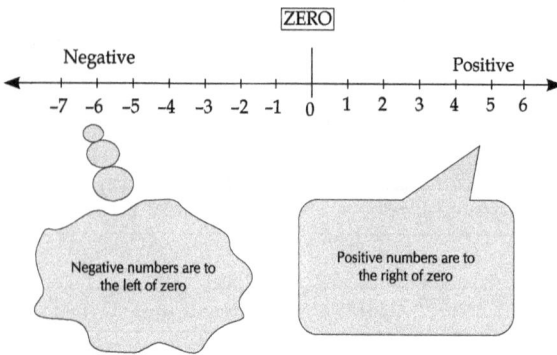

Fractions

A fraction denotes part or parts of an integer. For example 1/6, represents 1/6th part of the whole.

Types of Fraction

1. **Common Fractions** : The fractions where the denominator is not 10 or a multiple of it. Example : 2/3, 4/5 etc.
2. **Decimal Fractions** : Decimals are a form of expressing or representing fractional numbers. The decimal 0.5 represents the fraction 5/10. The decimal 0.25 represents the fraction 25/100. Decimal fractions always have a denominator based on a power of 10.
   Example : 7/10, 9/100, etc.

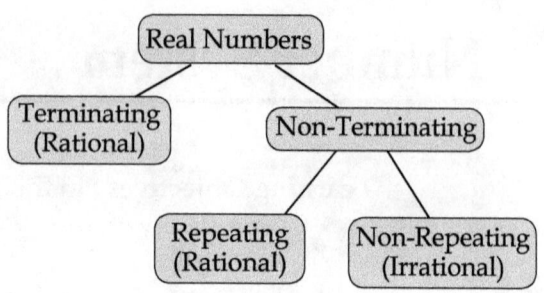

Any rational number (that is, a fraction in lowest terms) can be written as either a terminating decimal or a repeating decimal. Just divide the numerator by the denominator. If you end up with a remainder of 0, then you have a terminating decimal. Otherwise, the remainders will begin to repeat after some point, and you have a repeating decimal.

3. **Proper Fractions :** The fractions where the numerator is less than the denominator. Its value is always less than 1
   Example : 3/4, 2/5 etc.
4. **Improper Fractions :** The fractions where the numerator is greater than the denominator. Its value is always greater than 1.
   Example : 4/3, 5/3 etc.
5. **Compound Fraction :** A fraction of a fraction is called a compound fraction
   Example : 3/5 of 7/9 = 3/5 × 7/9 = 21/45
6. **Complex Fractions :** The combination of fractions is called a complex fraction.
   Example : (3/5)/ (2/9)
7. **Mixed Fractions :** A fraction which consists of two parts, an integer and a fraction.
   Example : $3\frac{1}{2}$, $6\frac{3}{4}$
   Q.1. Express 27/8 as a mixed fraction.
   Ans. Divide the numerator by denominator; note the multiplier, whatever remainder is left divide it with the original denominator. For 27/8, 24/8 = 3, and remainder left is 3, therefore $3^{3/8}$ is the mixed fraction.

Q.2. Express 35 7/17 as an improper fraction.

Ans. Here we need to multiply the denominator with the non-fraction part and add it to numerator and denominator will remain the same.

For 35 7/17 = = 602/17

Integers

The integers are classified into negative numbers and whole numbers

Natural Numbers : The counting numbers 1, 2, 3, 4, 5……. are known as natural numbers, N = {1, 2, 3, 4, 5…..}. The natural numbers along with zero make the set of the whole numbers.

Whole Numbers : The set of all positive numbers and 0 are called whole numbers, W = {0, 1, 2, 3, 4…….}.

Negative Numbers : These are the negative of natural numbers and lies on the left of zero on the number line, {…..–3, –2, –1}

Even Numbers : The numbers divisible by 2 are even numbers. e.g., 2, 4, 6, 8, 10 etc. Even numbers can be expressed in the form $2n$, where n is an integer other than 0.

Odd Numbers : The numbers not divisible by 2 are odd numbers. e.g. 1, 3, 5, 7, 9 etc. Odd numbers are expressible in the form $(2n + 1)$, where n is an integer.

Prime Numbers : The numbers that have only two factors, unity and the number itself are called prime numbers. e.g. {2, 3, 5, 11, 13, 17, 19}.

Composite Numbers : A composite number has other factors besides itself and unity .e.g. 8, 72, 39 etc. A real natural number that is not a prime number is a composite number.

Did you know?

- The only even prime number is 2
- 1 is neither a prime nor a composite number.
- If p is a prime number then for any whole number a, $ap - a$ is divisible by p.
- 2, 3, 5, 7, 11, 13, 17, 19, 23, 29 are first ten prime numbers (should be remembered)
- Two numbers are supposed to be co-prime if their HCF is 1, e.g. 3 & 5, 14 & 29 etc. are coprime numbers.
- A number is divisible by ab only when that number is divisible by each one of a and b, where a and b are co prime.
- To find a prime number, check the rough square root of the given number and divide the number by all the prime numbers lower than the estimated square root.
- All prime numbers can be expressed in the form $6n - 1$ or $6n + 1$, but all numbers that can be expressed in this form are not prime.

Prime Factors : The composite numbers can be expressed in factors, wherein all the factors are prime. To get prime factors we divide the number by prime numbers till the remainder is a prime number. All composite numbers can be expressed as prime factors, for example prime factors of 150 are 2,3,5,5.

A composite number can be uniquely expressed as a product of prime factors.

e.g. $12 = 2 \times 6 = 2 \times 2 \times 3 = 2^2 \times 3^1$
$20 = 4 \times 5 = 2 \times 2 \times 5 = 2^2 \times 5^1$ etc.

Perfect Number : If the sum of the divisor of N excluding N itself is equal to N, then N is called a perfect number. *e.g.* 6, 28, 496.

Imaginary Numbers

Numbers that when squared give a negative result. If you square a real number you always get a positive, or zero, result. For example 2×2 = 4, and (–2) × (–2) = 4 also, so "imaginary" numbers can seem impossible, but they are still useful.

An imaginary number is denoted by bi, where
- b is a real number.
- i is the imaginary unit, $i = \sqrt{-1} = i$

Example : Is zero a rational number?

Answer : Zero can be written in the form p/q $\left(\dfrac{0}{1}\right)$, where p and q are integers and q (=1) is not equal to 0. Therefore, zero is a rational number.

Example : Find six rational number between 3 and 4.

Sol.

Step 1 : $\dfrac{3+4}{2} = \dfrac{7}{2}$

Step 2 : $\dfrac{\dfrac{7}{2}+4}{2} = \dfrac{\dfrac{7+8}{2}}{2} = \dfrac{15}{2 \times 2} = \dfrac{15}{4}$

Step 3 : $\dfrac{3+\dfrac{7}{2}}{2} = \dfrac{\dfrac{6+7}{2}}{2} = \dfrac{\dfrac{13}{2}}{2} = \dfrac{13}{2 \times 2} = \dfrac{13}{4}$

Step 4 : $\dfrac{\dfrac{15}{4}+4}{2} = \dfrac{\dfrac{15+16}{4}}{2} = \dfrac{31}{4 \times 2} = \dfrac{31}{8}$

Step 5 : $\dfrac{3+\dfrac{15}{4}}{2} = \dfrac{\dfrac{12+15}{4}}{2} = \dfrac{\dfrac{27}{4}}{2} = \dfrac{27}{4 \times 2} = \dfrac{27}{8}$

Step 6 : $\dfrac{\dfrac{13}{4}+4}{2} = \dfrac{\dfrac{13+16}{4}}{2} = \dfrac{\dfrac{29}{4}}{2} = \dfrac{29}{4 \times 2} = \dfrac{29}{8}$

Hence, six rational numbers between 3 and 4 are:

$$\dfrac{13}{4}, \dfrac{27}{8}, \dfrac{7}{2}, \dfrac{29}{8}, \dfrac{15}{4}, \dfrac{31}{8}$$

You can notice that by calculating averages between two numbers we get a number which is exactly between these two numbers. This way you can go on calculating infinite number of numbers.

Example : Find five rational numbers between 3/5 and 4/5.

Sol. Step 1 : $\dfrac{\dfrac{3}{5}+\dfrac{4}{5}}{2} = \dfrac{7}{10}$

Step 2 : $\dfrac{\dfrac{3}{5}+\dfrac{7}{10}}{2} = \dfrac{13}{20}$

Step 3 : $\dfrac{\dfrac{7}{10}+\dfrac{4}{5}}{2} = \dfrac{3}{4}$

Step 4 : $\dfrac{\dfrac{3}{5}+\dfrac{13}{20}}{2} = \dfrac{5}{8}$

Step 5 : $\dfrac{\dfrac{3}{4}+\dfrac{4}{5}}{2} = \dfrac{31}{40}$

Hence, five rational numbers between $\dfrac{3}{5}$ and $\dfrac{4}{5}$ are $\dfrac{7}{10}, \dfrac{13}{20}, \dfrac{3}{4}, \dfrac{5}{8}, \dfrac{31}{40}$

Comparison of Numbers : If one number has more digits than the other, then it is greater of the two. For example 8542 is greater than 984.

- If two numbers have the same number of digits, then the number with bigger digit on the extreme left is greater. For example 5732 is greater than 2884.
- If two numbers have the same number of digits and the extreme left digits are also the same, then compare the next digits to the right and so on. For example 8342 is greater than 8217.

Note : Count the digits first, then check Th, then 'H', then 'T', then O. Symbols used for 'is greater than' and 'is less than' are > and < respectively.

Numerals

Numbers can be written using different symbols. The numbers represented by particular symbols are known as the digits of the system. The numerals formed by the digits 0, 1, 2, 3, 4, 5, 6, 7, 8 and 9 are known as Hindu-Arabic numbers. These are called international numbers.

Number system is a way of counting and naming numbers. Number is an idea where the symbols used to represent the numbers are called numerals.

Number Names (7 and 8 digit Numbers)

10 ones = 1 ten
100 ones = 1 Hundred
100 is a three digit numeral.
1000 ones = 1 thousand
10000 ones = ten thousand
100000 ones = 1 Lakh
1000000 ones = 10 Lakh
1,00,00,000 ones = 1 Crore

1,00,00,000 is the smallest number of eight digits. We know 9999999 is the greatest of seven digits. 1,00,00,000 is the successor of 9999999.

Place Value

Place value of a digit depends on its position in the number. As the digit moves to the left, its value increases. The place value of each digit in 9999 is as follows.

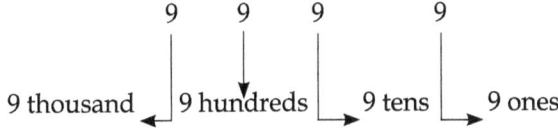

Expanded form of 9999 = 9000 + 900 + 90 + 9
= 9 thousands + 9 hundreds + 9 tens + 9 ones

Rules of Divisibility

A number is divisible by 2 if the unit's digit is 0 or divisible by 2. *e.g.* 8,16,32 etc.

Divisibility by 3 : A number is divisible by 3 if the sum of digits in the number is divisible by 3. *e.g.* 49185

4 + 9 + 1 + 8 + 5 = 27, and since 27 is divisible 3, 49185 is divisible by 3.

Divisibility by 4 : A number is divisible by 4 if the numbers formed by the last two digits is divisible by 4.

e.g. 6032 is divisible by 4.

Divisibility by 5 : A number is divisible by 5 if the unit's digit in the number is 0 or 5. e.g. 525 and 110 are divisible by 5.

Divisibility by 9 : A number is divisible by 9 is the sum of its digits is divisible by 9.

Divisibility by 10 : A number is divisible by 10 if the unit's digit is 0.

Divisibility by 11 : A given number is divisible by 11 if the difference of the sum of the digits at odd places and sum of the digits at even places is either zero or divisible by 11.

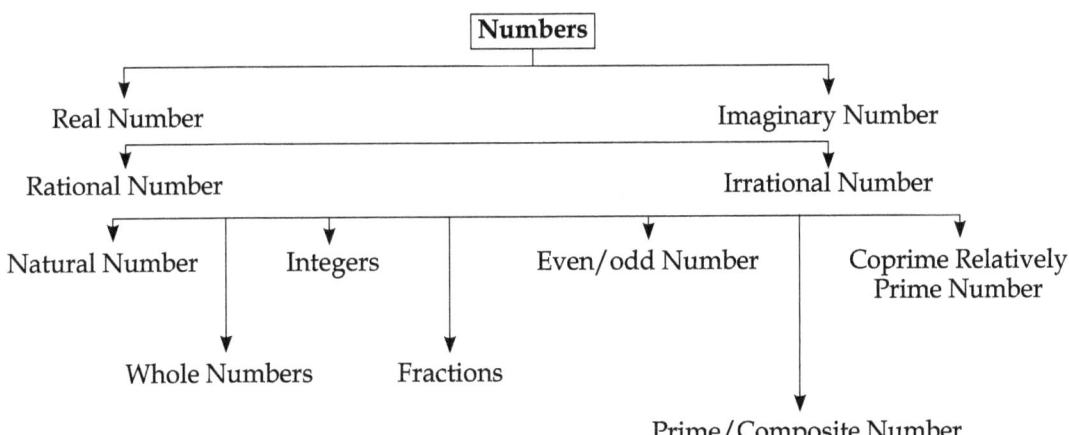

Number System

> **TRIVIA**
> Google's name is inspired from the mathematical word googol, which is a very large number 10 to the power 100 (1 followed by 100 zeros).

Example : State if following statements are true or false:
(a) Every natural number is a whole number.
(b) Every integer is a whole number.
(c) Every rational number is a whole number.

Sol.
(a) As natural number is all numbers starting from 1 and the whole number includes zero as well so this statement is true. On the other hand every whole number is not natural number as zero is not a natural number.
(b) Only positive integers are whole numbers. Hence this statement is false.
(c) Rational numbers are not whole numbers as they are not complete. Hence this statement is false.

Example : Write the following in decimal form and comment on their kind of decimal expression.

(a) $\dfrac{36}{100} = 0.36$, we get zero as remainder in the end so it is a terminating decimal.

(b) $\dfrac{1}{11} = 0.09090909$, we don't get zero as remainder and the quotient keeps on repeating, so this is a non-terminating recurring decimal.

(c) $4\dfrac{1}{8} = 4.125$, terminating decimal.

Example : Express the following in the form p/q, where p and q are integers and q is not 0.

(a) $0.\overline{6} = \dfrac{6}{9} = \dfrac{2}{3}$

(b) $0.\overline{47} = \dfrac{47}{99}$

(c) $0.00\overline{1} = \dfrac{1}{900}$

Put 9 for every non-zero digit in the denominator and zero for zero in the denominator.

A fraction in lowest terms with a prime denominator other than 2 or 5 (*i.e.* co-prime to 10) always produces a repeating decimal. The period of the repeating decimal, $1/p$, where p is prime, is either $p - 1$ (the first group) or a divisor of $p - 1$ (the second group).

Examples of fractions of the first group are :

- 1/7 = 0.142857; 6 repeating digits
- 1/17 = 0.0588235294117647; 16 repeating digits
- 1/19 = 0.052631578947368421; 18 repeating digits
- 1/23 = 0.0434782608695652173913; 22 repeating digits
- 1/29 = 0.0344827586206896551724137931; 28 repeating digits
- 1/97 = 0.01030927 83505154 63917525 77319587 62886597 93814432 98969072 16494845 36082474 22680412 37113402 06185567; 96 repeating digits

Example : What property should a rational number satisfy to have terminating decimal expression?

Sol. If the denominator is either 2 or 5 as its factor then the result will be terminating decimal. As 10 is the product of 2 and 5 to have terminating decimal, 2 or 5 are required. If there is a prime number other than 2 or 5 in the denominator then the decimal can or cannot be terminating.

Example : Which number is represented on the given abacus?

Sol.

The spike corresponding to ones place has 8 beads.

∴ Digit at ones place = 8

The spike corresponding to tens place has 0 beads.

∴ Digit at tens place = 0

The spike corresponding to hundreds place has 9 beads.

∴ Digit at hundreds place = 9

The spike corresponding to thousands place has 4 beads.

∴ Digit at thousands place = 4

The spike corresponding to ten thousands place has 7 beads.

∴ Digit at ten thousands place = 7

The spike corresponding to lakhs place has 8 beads.

∴ Digit at lakhs place = 8

Thus, the number represented on the given abacus is 8,74,908.

Example : Write the difference between the Roman numerals MDCXXIV and MCCCXL in Hindu Arabic numeral?

Sol. We know that,
I stands for 1, V stands for 5, X stands for 10, L stands for 50, C stands for 100, D stands for 500 and M stands for 1000

∴ MDCXXIV = 1000 + 500 + 100 + 10 + 10 + 5 − 1

= 1625 − 1
= 1624

and MCCCXL = 1000 + 100 + 100 + 100 + 50 − 10

= 1350 − 10
= 1340

Required difference = MDCXXIV − MCCCXL

= 1624 − 1340
= 284

Thus, the difference between the Roman numerals MDCXXIV and MCCCXL, in Hindu-Arabic numeral, is 284.

Example : Which number should be filled in the box to complete the given number line?

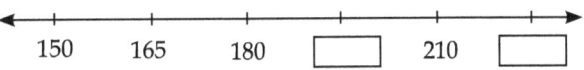

Sol. Distance between points 150 and 165
= (165 − 150) units = 15 units

It is known that the distance between any two consecutive points on a number line is equal.

∴ Distance between any two consecutive points on the given number line = 15 units.

To obtain the first missing value, add 15 to 180

∴ First missing value = 180 + 15 = 195

To obtain the second missing value, add 15 to 210

∴ Second missing value = 210 + 15 = 225

Example : What is the difference between the largest and the smallest 5-digit numbers formed by the digits 0, 9, 3, 7, 2 using each digit only once?

Sol. The smallest number formed by the digits 0, 9, 3, 7, 2, using each digit only once, is 02379.

But, 0 cannot be the first digit of a number. So, the positions of 0 and 2 are interchanged.

So, the smallest number formed by the given digits is 20379.

The largest number formed by the digits 0, 9, 3, 7, 2, using each digit only once, is 97320.

Required difference = Largest number – Smallest number

$$= 97320 - 20379$$
$$= 76941$$

Thus, the difference between the largest and the smallest numbers formed by the digits 0, 9, 3, 7, 2, using each digit only once, is 76941.

Example : What is the correct descending order of the numbers 82931, 82382, 89231, 8293 and 81392?

Sol. Writing the given numbers in place value table.

Ten thous. (T Th)	Thous. (T)	Hundreds (H)	Tens (T)	Ones (O)
8	2	9	3	1
8	2	3	8	2
8	9	2	3	1
	8	2	9	3
8	1	3	9	2

Arranging numbers in descending order means arranging them in decreasing order.

It can be observed that 8293 is the smallest among the given numbers.

The numbers 82931, 82382, 89231 and 81392 have the same digit i.e. 8 at the Ten thousands place.

The digits at the Thousands place of these numbers are 2, 2, 9 and 1 respectively.

As 1 < 2 < 9, therefore, 89231 is the greatest and 81392 is the smallest among these numbers.

Also, 82931 and 82382 have 9 and 3 respectively at the Hundreds place.

As 9 > 3, therefore 82931 is greater than 82382.

Thus, the correct descending order of the given numbers is, 89231, 82931, 82382, 81392 and 8293.

Example : Which of the following numbers is the greatest?

97,342 or 97,432 or 9,734 or 94,723.

Sol. Writing the given numbers in the place value table as :

Ten thous. (T Th)	Thous. (Th)	Hundreds (H)	Tens (T)	Ones (O)
9	7	3	4	2
9	7	4	3	2
		9	7	3	4
9	4	7	2	3

It can be observed from the table that 9,734 is the smallest number among all.

Now, comparing digits at various places. It can be observed that 97,342 as well as 97,432 and 94,723 have the same digit at the Ten thousands place i.e. 9.

Also, 97,342 and 97,432 have the same digit i.e. 7 at the Thousands place while 94,723 has 4 at the Thousands place. As 7 > 4, 97,342 and 97,432 are greater than 94,723.

97,342 and 97,432 have 3 and 4 respectively at the Hundreds place. As 4 > 3, 97,432 is greater than 97,342.

Thus, 97,432 is the greatest among the given numbers.

MUST REMEMBER

- The numbers divisible by 2 are even numbers.
- The numbers not divisible by 2 are odd numbers.
- The numbers that have only two factors, unity and the number itself are called prime numbers.
- Place value of a digit depends on its position in the number. As the digit moves to the left, its value increases.

MULTIPLE CHOICE QUESTIONS

1. What is the predecessor of the greatest six-digit number?
   (a) 100000 (b) 100001
   (c) 999998 (d) 999999

2. What is the difference between the place values of 5's in the number 4598351?
   (a) 499950 (b) 49995
   (c) 49950   (d) 0

3. 9,87,61,230 ☐ 9,87,16,230
   Which of the following signs can be placed in the box between the two numbers?
   (a) > (b) <
   (c) = (d) None of these

4. 10000001 is the successor of _____
   (a) 10000002 (b) 10000000
   (c) 9999999   (d) None of these

5. How many three-digit numbers can be formed with the digits 3, 0 and 7 without repetition?
   (a) 6 (b) 5
   (c) 4 (d) 3

6. Which are the respective greatest and the smallest numbers amongst 321987, 319240, 321978 and 321970?
   (a) 319240 and 321987
   (b) 321987 and 319240
   (c) 321987 and 321970
   (d) 319240 and 321978

7. What is the difference between the greatest and smallest 5-digit numbers formed by using all the digits 3, 0, 9, 1 and 5?
   (a) 93951 (b) 84951
   (c) 81720 (d) 79172

8. Which of the following numbers is equal to 3 crore?
   (a) 3 million   (b) 30 million
   (c) 300 million (d) 3000 million

9. How can the number fifty million twenty-one thousand two hundred thirty six be written using commas according to Indian system of numeration?
   (a) 50,021,236   (b) 5,00,21,236
   (c) 50,00,21,236 (d) 500,021,236

10. How can the numbers 10 million, 1 billion and 216 thousand be arranged in descending order?
    (a) 216 thousand, 10 million, 1 billion
    (b) 10 million, 216 thousand, 1 billion
    (c) 1 billion, 10 million, 216 thousand
    (d) 216 thousand, 1 billion, 10 million

11. 2,357,822 ☐ 2,357,799
    (a) < (b) >
    (c) = (d) None of these

12. The number 35 million ends with how many zeroes?
    (a) Four (b) Five
    (c) Six   (d) Seven

13. Which one of the following numbers is prime?
    (a) 18 (b) 19
    (c) 20 (d) 21

14. Which one of the following numbers is prime?
    (a) 26 (b) 27
    (c) 28 (d) 29

15. Which one of the following numbers is composite?
    (a) 67 (b) 69
    (c) 71 (d) 73

16. Which one of the following numbers is composite?
    (a) 101 (b) 103
    (c) 105 (d) 107

17. The number 24 is to be written as a product of its prime factors. Which one of the following is correct?

(a) 24 = 3 × 8
(b) 24 = 4 × 6
(c) 24 = 2 × 3 × 4
(d) 24 = 2 × 2 × 2 × 3

18. The number 90 is to be written as a product of its prime factors. Which one of the following is correct?
    (a) 90 = 2 × 5 × 9
    (b) 90 = 2 × 3 × 3 × 5
    (c) 90 = 3 × 5 × 6
    (d) 90 = 2 × 3 × 15

19. The place value of 5 in 780756 is
    (a) Five ones   (b) Five tens
    (c) 5 tenths   (d) Five hundreds

20. Match the following numbers in list I with the corresponding place value of number 5.

Unit-I	Unit-II
(a) 750	1. 500
(b) 17510	2. 50
(c) 124605	3. 5
(d) 50630	4. 50000

        a b c d   a b c d
    (a) 1 2 3 4   (b) 2 1 3 4
    (c) 1 2 3 4   (d) 3 1 2 4

HOTS

1. Adding a number to 22 thousand gives 25 thousands 3 hundreds and 2 tens. The number is ____.
   (a) 3340   (b) 3320
   (c) 3680   (d) 3660

2. Navneet spends 1.33 hours studying for Computer, 4.67 hours studying for Maths and 0.4 hours studying for Hindi. How much total time does Navneet spends studying?
   (a) Six and four thousandth hour
   (b) Six and four tenths hour
   (c) Six hours
   (d) Six and four hundredth hours

3. Sum of a number of two digits and the number obtained by reversing the digits of the first number is 10 more than 100. If the difference of the digits is 4, then the number is
   (a) 22   (b) 64
   (c) 73   (d) 81

4. Sum of place values of 6 in 62616 is
   (a) 666   (b) 180
   (c) 60606 (d) 6006

5. Housing Board built 200 flats. A painter is engaged to serially number each flat individually from 1 to 200. How many times will he be required to write zero?
   (a) 12   (b) 18
   (c) 19   (d) 22

SUBJECTIVE QUESTIONS

1. Write the following in the standard form.
   A. 50,00,000 + 2,00,000 + 10,000 + 500 + 30 + 4
   B. 6,00,00,000 + 70,00,000 + 9,00,000 + 50,000 + 3,000 + 900 + 40

   Solution:
   A. 50,00,000
       +2,00,000
       + 10,000
       + 500
       + 30
       +4
       ─────────
       52,10,534

   B. 6,00,00,000
       + 70,00,000
       + 9,00,000
       + 50,000
       + 3,000
       + 900
       +40
       ─────────
       6,79,53,940

2. Write the number names for:
   A. 53,47,88,205
   B. 354,567,780
   C. 22,78,295
   D. 36,542,290

   Solution:
   A. 53,47,88,205 - Fifty three crore forty seven lakh eighty eight thousand two hundred five.
   B. 354,567,780 - Three hundred fifty-four million Five hundred sixty-seven thousand seven hundred eighty.
   C. 22,78,295 – Twenty-two lakh seventy-eight thousand two hundred ninety-five.
   D. 36,542,290 - Thirty-six million five hundred forty-two thousand two hundred ninety.

3. Write the place value of 8 in the following numbers.
   A. 8,34,34,556
   B. 82,45,556
   C. 87,73,46,734
   D. 7,76,83,245

   Solution:
   A. The place value of 8 in the number 8,34,34,556 is 8,00,00,000.
   B. The place value of 8 in the number 82,45,556 is 80,00,000.
   C. The place value of 8 in the number 87,73,46,734 is 80,00,00,000.
   D. The place value of 8 in the number 7,76,83,245 is 80,000.

4. Round off the number 45,23,78,453 to the nearest 10, 100 and 1000.

   Solution:
   A. The number 45,23,78,453 can be rounded off to the nearest 10 as 45,23,78,450.
   B. The number 45,23,78,453 can be rounded off to the nearest 100 as 45,23,78,500.
   C. The number 45,23,78,453 can be rounded off to the nearest 1000 as 45,23,78,000.

5. Gautam is thinking of a four-digit number.
   - The fourth digit is thrice the first digit.
   - The second digit is the second multiple of 2.
   - The third digit is the smallest even number.
   - The first digit is 1 less than second digit

   Find the number.

   Solution:
   Let us try to find the digits one by one.
   1. From second statement, we get 2nd digit as 4 (i.e second multiple of 2).
   2. From third statement, we get 3rd digit as 2.
   3. From fourth statement, we get 1st digit as 3 (1 less than 4).
   4. From first statement, we get 4th digit as 9 (thrice of 1st digit).

   Hence, the number will be 3249.

Roman Numbers

Learning Objectives: In this chapter, students will learn about:
- Rules for writing Roman Numerals
- How to convert to Roman Numerals
- Rules on Roman Numbers

CHAPTER SUMMARY

Roman Numerals

Roman Numerals originated in the ancient Roman Empire and are still in use today in a variety of forms. Roman numerals were adapted from Etruscan numerals. The system of Roman numerals that was used in classical antiquity was somewhat modified in the Middle Ages to produce the system that is used today. This system is based on certain letters which are given numerical values.

Use of Roman numerals can still be seen in our daily life. On the face of some clocks, the hours are indicated by Roman Numerals. These numerals are used to denote different volumes of a book, questions in a question paper or exercise, Class room in a school, etc.

Did you know?

What the numbers 0 1 2 3 4 5 6 7 8 9 are called?

These are Arabic numbers as these numbers came from Arabia. But apart from these numbers, we use some symbols too, which represent mathematical values. These numbers are the Roman numerals.

Unlike Hindu-Arabic numeration system and the regional numeration systems, the Roman numeration system uses only seven symbols namely I, V, X, L C, D and M. The respective values of these symbols are as under.

Roman Numerals	I	V	X	L	C	D	M
Value of the symbols	1	5	10	50	100	500	1000

There is no symbol for zero in the Roman Numeral System. This system is also not a place value system.

The most common Roman numerals are :

Roman Numerals 1–100

1	=	I	26	=	XXVI	51	=	LI	76	=	LXXVI
2	=	II	27	=	XXVII	52	=	LII	77	=	LXXVII
3	=	III	28	=	XXVIII	53	=	LIII	78	=	LXXVIII
4	=	IV	29	=	XXIX	54	=	LIV	79	=	LXXIX
5	=	V	30	=	XXX	55	=	LV	80	=	LXXX
6	=	VI	31	=	XXXI	56	=	LVI	81	=	LXXXI
7	=	VII	32	=	XXXII	57	=	LVII	82	=	LXXXII
8	=	VIII	33	=	XXXIII	58	=	LVIII	83	=	LXXXIII
9	=	IX	34	=	XXXIV	59	=	LIX	84	=	LXXXIV
10	=	X	35	=	XXXV	60	=	LX	85	=	LXXXV
11	=	XI	36	=	XXXVI	61	=	LXI	86	=	LXXXVI
12	=	XII	37	=	XXXVII	62	=	LXII	87	=	LXXXVII
13	=	XIII	38	=	XXXVIII	63	=	LXIII	88	=	LXXXVIII
14	=	XIV	39	=	XXXIX	64	=	LXIV	89	=	LXXXIX
15	=	XV	40	=	XL	65	=	LXV	90	=	XC
16	=	XVI	41	=	XLI	66	=	LXVI	91	=	XCI
17	=	XVII	42	=	XLII	67	=	LXVII	92	=	XCII
18	=	XVIII	43	=	XLIII	68	=	LXVIII	93	=	XCIII
19	=	XIX	44	=	XLIV	69	=	LXIX	94	=	XCIV
20	=	XX	45	=	XLV	70	=	LXX	95	=	XCV
21	=	XXI	46	=	XLVI	71	=	LXXI	96	=	XCVI
22	=	XXII	47	=	XLVII	72	=	LXXII	97	=	XCVII
23	=	XXIII	48	=	XLVIII	73	=	LXXIII	98	=	XCVIII
24	=	XXIV	49	=	XLIX	74	=	LXXIV	99	=	XCIX
25	=	XXV	50	=	L	75	=	LXXV	100	=	C

The seven main symbols and their equivalents are :

I = 1   V = 5   X = 10
L = 50   C = 100   D = 500
M = 1000

For even higher numbers, an overline ($^-$) is drawn above the main symbols to indicate multiples of 1000.

$\overline{V}$ = 5000 $\overline{X}$ = 10,000
$\overline{L}$ = 50,000 $\overline{C}$ = 100,000
$\overline{D}$ = 500,000 $\overline{M}$ = 1,000,000

Rules for Writing Roman Numerals

Using the above said seven symbols, Roman Numerals for all numbers can be formed using certain rules.

Rule 1. Roman numerals read from left to right, larger values to the left and work to the smaller values on the right.

Rule 2. If a lesser symbol is before a greater symbol, the lesser is subtracted from the greater. For example, IV = 5 – 1 = 4.

Rule 3. If a lesser symbol is after a greater symbol, the two values are added. For example, VI = 5 + 1 = 6.

Rule 4. If a symbol is repeated twice or thrice, the value of the numeral is obtained by adding the value of the symbol as many times it repeated.

e.g., III = 1 + 1 + 1 = 3
XXX = 10 + 10 + 10 = 30

Rule 5. I and V can only modify up to an X. For example, 49 is not written as IL, rather you first resolve 40 as XL and then resolve 9 as IX. Put them together and 49 = XLIX.

Rule 6. X and L can only modify up to a C. For example, 490 is not written as XD. First you resolve 400 as CD and then you resolve 90 as XC. Put them together and 490 = CDXC.

Rule 7. C and D can only modify up to an M. For example, 950 is not written as LM, rather you first resolve 900 as CM and then add L for 50. So 950 = CML.

Rule 8. No symbol can be repeated more than thrice. The symbols V, L and D are never repeated.

Basically, in Roman numerals, if I is before another numeral, it means that you should subtract 1 from the number appearing after the I. For example, IX would be equal to 9, since the Roman numeral is indicating 1 less than 10.

VL would be 5 less than 50, which is 45. Basically, whenever a smaller number precedes a larger number, you should subtract the smaller number from the larger one. The important thing to remember with Roman numerals is that they need to be as simple as possible. The Roman numeral should be in the easiest form possible. For example, if you want to say 6, you would say VI. You would not say IIIIX. VI is the easiest possible way of saying 6.

You can also add Roman numerals the same way that you would add regular numbers. For example, L + XXX + X + V = XCV. You would solve this problem by converting your problem into regular numbers first: 50 + 30 + 10 + 5 = 95. Once you know that the numbers equal 95, you just need to convert 95 back into a Roman numeral.

Note : The symbol V can never be written on the left of any greater value symbol.

How to Convert to Roman Numerals?
Break the number into Thousands, Hundreds, Tens and Units and write down each in turn.

Example : Convert 1984 to Roman Numerals. Break 1984 into 1000, 900, 80 and 4, then do each conversion

1000 = M   900 = CM
80 = LXXX   4 = IV
So, 1984 = MCMLXXXIV

Rules on Roman Numbers

1. Only subtract powers of ten (I, X, or C, but not V or L)
   For 95, do not write VC (100 – 5).
   Do write XCV (XC + V or 90 + 5)
2. Only subtract one number from another at a time.
   For 13, do not write IIXV (15 – 1 - 1).
   Do write XIII (X + I + I + I or 10 + 3)
3. Do not subtract a number from one that is more than 10 times greater (that is, you can subtract 1 from 10 [IX] but not 1 from 20—there is no such number as IXX.)
   For 99, do not write IC (C–I or 100-1).
   Do write XCIX (XC + IX or 90 + 9)
4. A bar placed on top of a letter or string of letters increases the numeral's value by 1,000 times.
   XV = 15
   $\overline{XV}$ = 10000 + 5000 = 15,000

How To Remember Roman Symbols?

Think "MeDiCaL XaVIer".
It has the Roman numerals in order from 1000 to 1.

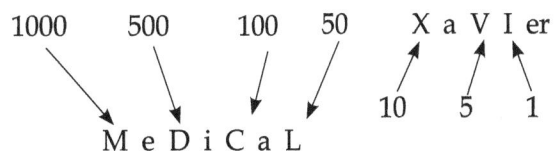

Roman Numbers

How to Remember the Symbols?

Here are some ways to remember some of the Roman representations :

- The easy letters are I, C and M. I is probably a one finger of our hands.

- The Romans spoke a language called Latin, and the Latin for hundred is Centum. So C was an obvious letter for 100.
- We still use cent in English words to mean a hundred, so it's easy to remember. Think of a hundred centimetres in a metre, a hundred years in a century or a hundred cents in a dollar. The Latin for thousand is Mille. So M is the letter for thousand. Think of a thousand years in a millennium or a thousand millimetres in a metre.
- Here is a way to remember that V is five. There are Five fingers in our hand and the shape between any two fingers makes a V shape. If you look at a hand (see figure), you can see that the thumb and little finger make a V.

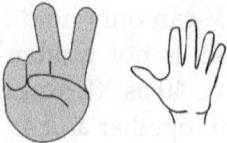

There are ten fingers in both hands, so the two V's make an X.

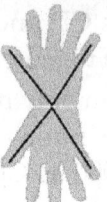

Now for fifty : Fifty is half of a hundred. If you take the symbol for hundred, C, and cut it in half, it looks like an L, which is the letter for fifty.

Five hundred is half of a thousand. If you take the symbol for thousand, M, and cut it in half, it looks like a D (somewhat), which is five hundred.

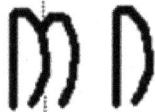

So, now you will be able to remember and use all the Roman numbers.

TRIVIA

Zero is the only number that can't be represented in Roman Numerals.

MUST REMEMBER

- Roman numerals read from left to right, larger values to the left and work to the smaller values on the right.
- If a lesser symbol is before a greater symbol, the lesser is subtracted from the greater. For example, IV = 5 – 1 = 4.
- If a lesser symbol is after a greater symbol, the two values are added. For example, VI = 5 + 1 = 6.
- No symbol can be repeated more than thrice. The symbols V, L and D are never repeated.

MULTIPLE CHOICE QUESTIONS

1. Roman numerals are still commonly used today to :
   (a) Outline and number lists
   (b) Number pages that precede a main body of a book
   (c) Number certain annual sporting events
   (d) All of the above

2. The correct Roman numeral that represents 40 is :
   (a) XXXX   (b) XL
   (c) XLC   (d) XXXVIIIII

3. In the Roman numeral system, whenever a smaller number precedes a larger number, this means one should :
   (a) Subtract the smaller number from the larger one
   (b) Add the smaller number to the larger one
   (c) Subtract the larger number from the smaller one
   (d) Divide the larger number by the smaller one

4. The Roman numeral 'XII' is equal to :
   (a) 60   (b) 128
   (c) 12   (d) 45

5. The Roman numeral ' LXXXIV ' is equal to :
   (a) 84   (b) 108
   (c) 7   (d) 34

6. The Roman numeral ' CXI' is equal to :
   (a) 11   (b) 34
   (c) 111   (d) 12

7. The Roman numeral 'XIV' is equal to :
   (a) 60   (b) 32
   (c) 14   (d) 101

8. Convert MMIV to ordinary numerals.
   (a) 2,004   (b) 2,005
   (c) 2,006   (d) 2,014

9. Write MMMCXXXIV as a number.
   (a) 3034   (b) 3134
   (c) 3334   (d) 3224

10. The Roman numeral ' XLIV ' is equal to:
    (a) 147   (b) 128
    (c) 14   (d) 44

11. The Roman numeral ' CIV' is equal to :
    (a) 108   (b) 44
    (c) 104   (d) 134

12. The Roman numeral ' XLV' is equal to :
    (a) 45   (b) 75
    (c) 12   (d) 66

13. Write 3,396 as a Roman Numeral.
    (a) MMMMMMMCLXXVI
    (b) MMMCXCVI
    (c) MDCXXXVI
    (d) MMMCCCXCVI

14. The Roman numeral ' CXXXIII ' is equal to:
    (a) 19   (b) 12
    (c) 133   (d) 17

15. Convert 2,011 to Roman Numerals.
    (a) MCMXI   (b) MMIX
    (c) MMXI   (d) MMXXI

16. Convert 7,192 to Roman Numerals.
    (a) MMMMMMMXCCII
    (b) MMMMMMMCLXXXXII
    (c) MMMMMMCXCII
    (d) MMMMMMMCXCII

17. The Roman numeral ' LXXV' is equal to :
    (a) 66   (b) 45
    (c) 75   (d) 60

18. Write MDCCCXXXVI as a number.
    (a) 2836   (b) 1,836
    (c) 3336   (d) 3836

19. The Roman numeral 'CXXVIII' is equal to :
    (a) 101   (b) 111
    (c) 128   (d) 4

20. The Roman numeral 'IV' is equal to :
    (a) 9   (b) 147
    (c) 4   (d) 110

21. Convert 1,866 to Roman Numerals.
    (a) MDCCCLXVI
    (b) MCCCCCCCCLXVI
    (c) MDCCCXXXXXVI
    (d) MDCCCXLVI
22. Write DCLXIV as a number.
    (a) 664 (b) 644
    (c) 904 (d) 954
23. Write 524 as a Roman Numeral.
    (a) DXIV (b) DXXIV
    (c) MXXIV (d) MMMIV
24. Convert MMDCCLXXIV to ordinary numerals.
    (a) 2,674 (b) 2,764
    (c) 2,774 (d) 2,776
25. Convert 2328 to a Roman numeral.
    (a) MMCCCXXVIII
    (b) MMCXXXXIIII
    (c) MDCXXXVI
    (d) MDCCCXVIII

HOTS

1. **Statement A:** C = 25.
   Statement B: M > 100.
   (a) Statement A is true.
   (b) Statement B is false.
   (c) Both statements are true.
   (d) Only statement B is true.
2. **Statement A:** In Roman numerals system, the symbol VC does not represent the number 95.
   Statement B: The ascending order of numbers X, VI, VII, IX is X, IX, VI, VII.
   (a) Only B is true (b) Only A is true
   (c) Both are true (d) None of these
3. Kavita Mehra is XII years old. Her brother is X years old. How old will they be when their total age is L years?
   (a) XXIX, XXVI (b) XXVI, XXIV
   (c) XX, XXIII (d) XIX, XXII
4. Select the correct Roman numerals in Column I with Hindu-Arabic numerals in Column II.

Column I	Column II
(a) CCXVIII	318
(b) DCCLXIX	769
(c) MMMCCXCIX	3399
(d) VDCCXLVII	5748

5. What will be the outcome for the given diagram?

   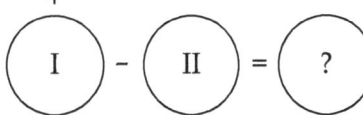

   (a) XIX (b) XII
   (c) XIII (d) XV

SUBJECTIVE QUESTIONS

1. Compare and write the correct symbol (<, >, =) in the blanks.
   (a) CDLV _____ CDXII
   (b) LXIV _____ LXXII
   (c) DCCLXIX _____ DCCXLIX
   (d) MCDXX _____ MCCL

   Solution:
   (a) CDLV = CD + L + V
       = 400 + 50 + 5 = 455
       CDXII = CD + X + II
       = 400 + 10 + 2 = 412
       So, 455 > 412
       Hence, CDLV > CDXII
   (b) LXIV = LX + IV = 60 + 4 = 64
       LXXII = LXX + II = 70 + 2 = 72
       So, 64 < 72
       Hence, LXIV < LXXII
   (c) DCCLXIX = DCC + LX + IX
       = 700 + 60 + 9 = 769
       DCCXLIX = DCC + XL + IX
       = 700 + 40 + 9 = 749
       So, 769 > 749
       Hence, DCCLXIX > DCCXLIX
   (d) MCDXX = M + CD + XX
       = 1000 + 400 + 20 = 1420
       MCCL = M + CC + L
       = 1000 + 200 + 50 = 1250
       So, 1420 > 1250
       Hence, MCDXX > MCCL

2. Remove the letters E and H from the word DELHI. Write the Roman numeral so formed. Also, convert the Roman numeral to its Hindu-Arabic form.

   Solution:
   When you remove the letters E and H from the word DELHI, you get DLI.
   DLI = D + L + I = 500 + 50 + 1 = 551

3. Write the Roman numeral for the years in which
   (a) Your father was born.
   (b) Your mother was born.
   (c) You were born.

   Solution:
   (a) If your father was born in the year 1975, then
       1975 = 1000 + 900 + 70 + 5
       = M + CM + LXX + V
       = MCMLXXV
       Hence, the Roman numeral for the year in which your father was born is MCMLXXV.
   (b) If your mother was born in the year 1980, then
       1980 = 1000 + 900 + 80
       = M + CM + LXXX
       = MCMLXXX
       Hence, the Roman numeral for the year in which your mother was born is MCMLXXX.
   (c) If you were born in the year 2004, then
       2004
       = 2000 + 4
       = MM + IV
       = MMIV
       Hence, the Roman numeral for the year in which you were born is MMIV.

4. Find the product of the Roman numerals IX and XC.

   Solution:
   IX = 10 − 1 = 9 and XC = 100 − 10 = 90
   Now, IX × XC
   = 9 × 90
   = 810
   = DCCCX
   Therefore, IX × XC = DCCCX

5. Find the product of the Roman numerals LIX and XIV.

   Solution:
   LIX = 50 + 10 − 1 = 59
   and XIV = 10 + 5 − 1 = 14
   Now, LIX × XIV
   = 59 × 14
   = 826
   = DCCCXXVI
   Therefore, LIX × XIV = DCCCXXVI

Operations on Numbers 3

Learning Objectives : In this chapter, students will learn about:
- ✓ Addition
- ✓ Subtraction
- ✓ Multiplication
- ✓ Division
- ✓ Operations
- ✓ Order of Operations
- ✓ BODMAS Rule

CHAPTER SUMMARY

Addition
In a math problem it's important to do the operations and that should be in the right order. If you don't, you may end up with the wrong answer. Remember, in mathematics, there can be only one correct answer. The four basic operations on whole numbers are addition, subtraction, multiplication and division.

In this operation two or more numbers are added. The numbers that are added are called addends. The result of addition is called the sum.

Example :
1. Add 1456789, 123458 and 9637067.

   Sol.
   ```
        1456789
      +  123458
      + 9637067
      ---------
       11217314
   ```

2. In the following question replace * with the correct digit.

   Sol.
   ```
        1283 * 9
      +  41 * 56 3
      + 9 * 31 75
      ----------
      * 470 * 07
   ```
   After filling the blanks

   128369
   418563

   + 923175

   1470107

Properties of Addition
1. When we change the order of numbers, the sum remains the same.

   i.e., 13 + 12 = 25 or 12 + 13 = 25

2. When we add 0 to any number, the sum is the number itself

   20 + 0 = 20, 31 + 0 = 31

Subtraction
In this operation the difference between two numbers is found.

Example : Subtract 2456789 from 11083500.

Sol.
```
  11083500
-  2456789
----------
   8626711
```

Example : Find 50342135 – 46380651.

Sol.
```
  50342135
- 46380651
----------
   3961484
```

Properties of Subtraction
1. When we subtract zero from any number, result is the number itself.

   i.e   35 – 0 = 35,   40 – 0 = 40

2. When we subtract a number from itself the result is always zero.

Multiplication

The number to be multiplied is called multiplicand. The number by which we multiply is the multiplier. The result of multiplication is called product. × is the sign of multiplication.

Example :

Sol.
$$
\begin{array}{r}
31429 \\
\times\ 2508 \\
\hline
251432 \\
00000\times \\
157145\times\times \\
62858\times\times\times \\
\hline
78823932
\end{array}
$$

Properties of Multiplication

1. Any number multiplied by 1 is the number itself.
   Example : $2 \times 1 = 2, 6 \times 1 = 6$
2. Any number multiplied by zero is always 0.
   Example : $5 \times 0 = 0, 2 \times 0 = 0$
3. The product of numbers remains same even after changing their order.
   Example : $2 \times 5 = 10$ or $5 \times 2 = 10$

Division

It is the opposite of multiplication. ÷ is the sign of division. If $a \div b = c$ then a is the dividend, b is the divisor and c is the quotient.

Example : Divide 4835678 by 37

$$
\begin{array}{r}
37\overline{)4835678}(130694 \\
\underline{37} \\
113 \\
\underline{111} \\
256 \\
\underline{222} \\
347 \\
\underline{333} \\
148 \\
\underline{148} \\
\times
\end{array}
$$

Properties of Division

1. When we divide any number by 1, the quotient is the number itself.
   Example : Divide 6 by 1.
   $$\frac{6}{1} = 6$$
2. When 0 is divided by any number, the quotient is always 0.
   Example : $\frac{0}{6} = 0$
3. Numbers cannot be divided by 0.

Operations

"Operations" mean things like add, subtract, multiply, divide, squaring, etc. If it isn't a number it is probably an operation.

Now, suppose you have
$$7 + (6 \times 52 + 4)$$
which operation will you do first?

If you calculate them in a wrong order, you will get a wrong answer!

So, some set of rules are followed when doing calculations which tell you the order to follow. This is known as Order of Operations.

TRIVIA

Take any number and multiply it by three. Now add all the digits of that new number together. The sum will always be divisible by three, no matter what number you started with.

Order of Operations

1. Solve things in Brackets first.
   Example:

✓	6 × (5 + 4)	=	6 × 9	=	54	
✗	6 × (5 + 4)	=	30 + 4	=	34	(wrong)

2. Solve Exponents (Powers, Roots) before Multiply, Divide, Add or Subtract.
   Example:

✓	5×4^2	=	5 × 16	=	80	
✗	5×4^2	=	20^2	=	400	(wrong)

3. Solve Multiplication or Division before you Add or Subtract.
   Example:

✓	2 + 5 × 4	=	2 + 20	=	22	
✗	2 + 5 × 4	=	7 × 4	=	28	(wrong)

4. Otherwise just go left to right.
   Example:

✓	30 ÷ 5 × 4	=	6 × 4	=	24	
✗	30 ÷ 5 × 4	=	30 ÷ 20	=	1.5	(wrong)

So, now how Do you remember this All?

BODMAS Rule

This rule is very important and should be followed strictly while solving problems on simplification. Any deviation from this rule will lead to wrong answer. Thus whenever we see brackets or division, multiplication, addition and subtraction operations in any question we must start with the treatment of brackets and then proceed further step by step following the BODMAS Rule. Details of BODMAS Rule are given alongside.

Order	Abbreviated	Meaning	Notation letter used in rule
1	B	Brackets	[ ], { }, ( ),
2	O	Of	of
3	D	Division	÷
4	M	Multiplication	×
5	A	Addition	+
6	S	Subtraction	−

Note: (*i*) Order of the letters which is used in BODMAS is always fixed.

(*ii*) Absence of any operation or more than one operation does not change the order of BODMAS Rule.

Remember
- Divide and Multiply rank equally (and go left to right).

Operations on Numbers

- Add and Subtract rank equally (and go left to right)

So, we can simply state it as: After you have done "B" and "O", just go from left to right doing any "D" or "M" as you find them. Then go from left to right doing any "A" or "S" as you find them.

Some Examples

1. How do you work out $3 + 6 \times 4$?
   Multiplication before Addition :
   So, $6 \times 4 = 24$, then $3 + 24 = 27$
2. How do you work out $(3 + 6) \times 4$?
   Brackets first :
   First $(3 + 6) = 9$, then $9 \times 4 = 36$
3. How do you work out $12 / 6 \times 4 / 2$?
   Multiplication and Division rank equally, so just go left to right :
   First $12 / 6 = 2$, then $2 \times 4 = 8$, then $8/2 = 4$
4. How you will solve $8 + (6 \times 5^2 + 4)$?
   Start inside Brackets, and then use "Orders"(here power) first :
   $$8 + (6 \times 25 + 4)$$
   Then Multiply : $8 + (150 + 4)$
   Then Add : $8 + (154)$
   Brackets completed, last operation is Add:
   $$8 + 154 = 162$$

- Order of the letters which is used in BODMAS is always fixed.
- Absence of any operation or more than one operation does not change the order of BODMAS Rule.
- Divide and Multiply rank equally (and go left to right).
- Add and Subtract rank equally (and go left to right)

MULTIPLE CHOICE QUESTIONS

1. Simplify 7896540 + 2104276 – 5035688.
   (a) 10000816 (b) 10000800
   (c) 1000806 (d) none of these
2. Find 26012453 – 6767678 – 15439326.
   (a) 3805449 (b) 38054009
   (c) 980544 (d) None of these
3. Add 456456 + 367890
   (a) 844344 (b) 824346
   (c) 824306 (d) None of these
4. Arrange in columns and add
   1212121, 2303232 and 3434346
   (a) 6949609 (b) 6949699
   (c) 6949899 (d) 6949598
5. Replace * by the correct digit in
   $$\begin{array}{r} 6767678 \\ + 154{*}9326 \\ \hline 22207004 \end{array}$$
   (a) 2 (b) 3
   (c) 4 (d) 1
6. Subtract 780605 – 391236
   (a) 389369 (b) 389396
   (c) 389399 (d) 389393
7. Subtract seven lakh, fifty four thousand and seventy from one crore.
   (a) 1245940 (b) 1245931
   (c) 245631 (d) 9245930
8. Replace * by the correct digit in
   $$\begin{array}{r} 66452 \\ - 18{*}07 \\ \hline 47645 \end{array}$$
   (a) 1 (b) 2
   (c) 3 (d) 8
9. Simplify 656666 + 432141 – 765642
   (a) 323165 (b) 323105
   (c) 323195 (d) 323175
10. Simplify
    52345678 – 43216789 + 56565656
    (a) 65694545 (b) 65692255
    (c) 6569450 (d) 0
11. The difference of two numbers is 136452 and the smaller number is 910658. Find the larger number.
    (a) 1047199 (b) 1047110
    (c) 1047201 (d) 104700
12. Multiply 4132 × 27.
    (a) 115464 (b) 111564
    (c) 111574 (d) 1111584
13. Multiply 81.009 × 8989
    (a) 728189.901 (b) 728188.901
    (c) 728189.911 (d) 7281.89901
14. Find the quotient 618974 ÷ 56
    (a) 11053 (b) 11052
    (c) 11051 (d) 11000
15. Find the remainder 806873 ÷ 637
    (a) 431 (b) 298
    (c) 196 (d) 493
16. Simplify (15 × 3) ÷ 5 × 8 – 2 + 6 × (8 – 2)
    (a) 96 (b) 106
    (c) 86 (d) 56
17. Simplify the following and check
    (i) 12 × 6 ÷ 3 and; (ii) 12 × (6 ÷ 3)
    (a) (i) > (ii) (b) (i) < (ii)
    (c) (i) = (ii) (d) None of these
18. A factory produces 13780 bulbs everyday. How many bulbs will be produced in 278 days?
    (a) 3830824 (b) 3830840
    (c) 3830480 (d) 3830400
19. Divide the greatest number of 9 digits by the greatest number of 3 digits.
    (a) 1001001 (b) 1001101
    (c) 1001011 (d) 1000001
20. The product of two numbers is 127008. One of them is 882. Find the other number.
    (a) 144 (b) 124
    (c) 444 (d) 134

Operations on Numbers

21. Find the dividend when the divisor = 241, quotient = 135 and the remainder = 30.
    (a) 32563 (b) 32565
    (c) 32165 (d) 32265
22. The total no. of students in classes I to V in a state is 7325718. Of these 3367269 are girls. How many are boys?
    (a) 3958449 (b) 3958339
    (c) 3958149 (d) 395811
23. A poultry farm produced 1270080 eggs. It packs 144 eggs in a box. How many boxes are required to pack all the eggs ?
    (a) 77720 (b) 8820
    (c) 9820 (d) 7820
24. A building has 24 flats. Each flat has 4 rooms. Each room requires 132 floor tiles. How many tiles would be required for the building?
    (a) 12672 (b) 12472
    (c) 114772 (d) 11072
25. What is the value of 70 – 6 (4 – 2) + 12 =?
    (a) 94 (b) 70
    (c) 140 (d) 46
26. Evaluate: 378 – (14+39) × 6.
    (a) 125 (b) 25
    (c) 60 (d) 45
27. What is the value of 5 × 4 – 2 × 3 + 16 ÷ 4 ?
    (a) 10 (b) 11½
    (c) 18 (d) 34
28. What is the value of 30 – (5 × 2^3 – 15)?
    (a) –25 (b) 5
    (c) 15 (d) –15
29. What is the value of $(3 + 2)^2$ – 5 × 3 + 2^3?
    (a) 2 (b) 6
    (c) 18 (d) 38
30. What is the value of (15 ÷ 3 + 4) – (3^2 – 7 × 2)?
    (a) – 1.86 (b) 4
    (c) 5 (d) 14
31. What is the value of (4^2 – 6 + 5) / (3^2 + 8 – 7 × 2)?
    (a) 5 (b) 11
    (c) 6 (d) 7
32. What is the value of (3^3 – 2 × 7) + (5 × 3 – 2^2)?
    (a) 8 (b) 24
    (c) 186 (d) 536
33. Evaluate –24 – 45 ÷ 5 + 3
    (a) – 30 (b) – 10
    (c) 10 (d) – 12
34. Evaluate -4^3 + (8 × 11) ÷ 4.
    (a) -6 (b) 154
    (c) -42 (d) 6
35. Evaluate (6^3 ÷ 4) – 4 × 5 + 3(7 – 2).
    (a) 49 (b) 19
    (c) 15 (d) 53
36. Evaluate (3 + 9) × 2 – 8(6 – 3).
    (a) – 30 (b) – 3
    (c) 0 (d) – 21
37. Evaluate 10 – 3^3 + 5 – 2(4 – 8).
    (a) – 20 (b) 14
    (c) – 4 (d) – 12
38. What is the correct verbal phrase for the following expression?
    9 – 8 × 2
    (a) the difference of 9 and 8, multiplied by 2
    (b) the product of 8 and 2, subtracted from 9
    (c) the quotient of 8 and 2, subtracted from 9
    (d) the difference of 9 and 8, divided by 2
39. Which of the following expressions evaluates to 23?
    (a) 6 + 6 x 5 – 4 (b) 6 + 5 x 4 – 6
    (c) 4 + 6 x 6 – 5 (d) 5 + 4 x 6 – 6
40. Determine which step you would do first in the following problem :
    32 ÷ 4 + (3 × 7) × 18 + 5
    (a) 18 + 5 (b) 4 + 3
    (c) (3 × 7) (d) 32 ÷ 4

41. Determine which step you would do first in the following problem:
    $12 \div 3 \times (15 - 6) + 3$.
    (a) $6 + 3$ (b) $(15 - 6)$
    (c) $12 \div 3$ (d) 3×15

42. Determine which step you would do first in the following problem:
    $5 \times 4 + (16 + 7) - 15 \div 3$
    (a) $(16 + 7)$ (b) $15 \div 3$
    (c) 5×4 (d) $7 - 15$

43. Determine which step you would do first in the following problem:
    $(15 \div 5) + 9 + (14 - 5) \times 3$.
    (a) 5×3 (b) $(15 \div 5)$
    (c) $5 + 9$ (d) $9 + 14$

44. In what order should you perform the operations to correctly evaluate the expression $27 - 18 \div 3^2$
    (a) Evaluate the power, subtract, and then divide.
    (b) Subtract, evaluate the power, and then divide.
    (c) Divide, evaluate the power, and then subtract.
    (d) Evaluate the power, divide, and then subtract.

45. Which of the following expressions evaluates to 13?
    (a) $3 + 3 \times 5 - 5$ (b) $3 + 5 \times 5 - 3$
    (c) $5 + 5 \times 3 - 3$ (d) $5 + 3 \times 3 - 5$

HOTS

1. The population of a town is 93992. Out of which 49143 are men and 26161 are women and the remaining are children. Then the number of children is
   (a) 21883 (b) 18688
   (c) 18893 (d) 18783

2. A shop has 352 pens. Eighteen more pens were brought in. Then 58 of them were sold. The number of pens left was
   (a) $352 + 18 - 58$ (b) $352 - 18 - 58$
   (c) $352 + 18 + 58$ (d) $352 - 18 + 58$

3. Nagesh Mehra purchased a book for Rs. 218.45, a pair of shoes for Rs. 570.25 and a shirt for Rs. 655.75. How much money did Nagesh Mehra spend in all?
   (a) 1444.35 (b) 1454.45
   (c) 1454.53 (d) 1414.55

4. Divide 80 ones, 2 tenths and 4 hundredths by 4. The result is the same as _____.
   (a) $4280 \div 4$ (b) $824 \div 4$
   (c) $100.4 \div 4$ (d) $82.4 \div 4$

5. What is missing number here? $81472 = 80000 + 1000 + \underline{} + 70 + 2$
   (a) 4 (b) 400
   (c) 1400 (d) 4000

6. Which of the following step is wrong for the below given mathematical sentence?
   $37091 - 72 \div 3 \times 687 + 5973$
   Step I : $37091 - 24 \times 687 + 5973$ (Divide)
   Step II : $37091 - 16388 + 5973$ (Multiply)
   Step III : $43064 - 16488$
   Step IV : 26386
   (a) Step I only
   (b) Step III and IV
   (c) Step II only
   (d) Step II and IV

7. Find the value of P.

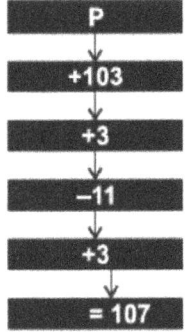

   (a) 3 (b) 7
   (c) -4 (d) 9

Operations on Numbers

8. In a box there are 99877 red marbles, 84457 blue marbles and 68155 green marbles. Find the total number of marbles.
   (a) 252489 (b) 264403
   (c) 245304 (d) 265344

9. Jay arranged 48 books in 4 equal piles to find the quotient of 48 ÷ 4. How can Jay use this method to find the quotient of 189 ÷ 9?
   (a) Put 189 books in 4 equal piles.
   (b) Put 189 books in 9 equal piles.
   (c) Add 189 to 48 books. Put them in 4 piles.
   (d) Add 189 to 48 books. Put them in 9 piles.

10. 17522.16 in word form is
    (a) seventeen thousand, five hundred, two, two and one tenths and six hundredths
    (b) seventeen, five hundreds, twenty-two and sixteen hundredths
    (c) seventeen thousand, five hundred, twenty-two and sixteen hundredths
    (d) seventeen thousand, five hundred, twenty-two and sixteen tenths

SUBJECTIVE QUESTIONS

1. Each digit 1, 2, 3, 4, 5, 6, 7, 8 and 9 is represented by a different letter A, B, C, D, E, F, G, H and I but not necessarily in that order. Further each of A + B + C, C + D + E, E + F + G and G + H + I is equal to 13. What is the sum of C, E and G?

   Solution
   A + B + C = 13 C + D + E = 13
   E + F + G = 13 G + H + I = 13
   Adding these equations and separating the one that are repeated
   (A + B + C + D + E + F + G + H + I)
   + (C + G + E) = 52
   Now putting the values as we know each letter represents a number even if it is not in same order.
   (1 + 2 + 3 + 4 + 5 + +6 + 7 + 8 + 9)
   + (C + G + E)
   = 52 + (C+ G + E)
   = 52 – 45 = 7
   Hence, C + G + E = 7

2. Look at these numbers:
   (a) 0.4 (b) 0.5
   (c) 0.8 (d) 0.6
   Which two numbers have a difference of 0.3?
   Solution:
   Look for the numbers in the box that are greater than 0.3.
   Try 0.4. What number can you subtract from 0.4 to get 0.3? 0.4 – 0.1 = 0.3 but 0.1 is not available.
   Try 0.5. What number can you subtract from 0.5 to get 0.3? 0.5 – 0.2 = 0.3 but 0.2 is not available.
   Try 0.8. What number can you subtract from 0.8 to get 0.3? 0.8 – 0.5 = 0.3 and 0.5 is available. Hence, 0.8 and 0.5 have a difference of 0.3.

3. What are different properties for Addition?
   Solution:
   (a) Commutative: It states that changing the order of the addends will not affect the sum.

Hence, a + b = b + a

(b) **Associative:** It states that changing the groupings of the addends will not affect the sum.

Hence, a + (b + c) = (a + b) + c

(c) **Identity property:** It states that when you add 0 to any number, the sum will be number itself.

Hence, a + 0 = 0 + a = a

4. Simplify 20 + 10 × 5 – 25 + 56 ÷ 8 + 27 ÷ 9

Solution:
20 + 10 × 5 – 25 + 56 ÷ 8 + 27 ÷ 9
Perform the division operation
20 + 10 × 5 – 25 + 7 + 3
Then, perform the multiplication
20 + 50 – 25 + 7 + 3
Arrange the '+' numbers and '–' numbers separately.
20 + 50 + 7 + 3 – 25

Then, perform the addition
80 – 25
Finally, perform the subtraction
80–25 = 55
So, the answer is 55.

5. Find two whole numbers that make this BODMAS rule work:
? × (3+?) = 10

Solution:
? × (3 +?) = 10.
The numbers should be 2 and 2. Let us figure out how these numbers are derived.
10 can be obtained by multiplying 2 and 5. Thus to make the numbers in bracket equal to 5, we should add 2 to 3. And then multiply the sum of 5 with 2, to obtain 10. Hence, both the numbers will be 2.

Decimals and Fractions   4

Learning Objectives : In this chapter, students will learn about:
- ✓ Decimal Point
- ✓ Adding and Subtracting Decimals
- ✓ Equivalent Fractions
- ✓ Comparing Fractions

CHAPTER SUMMARY

Whether it's about measuring ingredients for cooking or for splitting a bill at any restaurant or for any calculation of money we use fractions and decimals. Scientists and many other professionals use decimal numbers all the time in specific calculations.

Decimal Point

It is used to separate the whole number part from the fractional part. Decimal numbers are widely used in everyday life.

For example

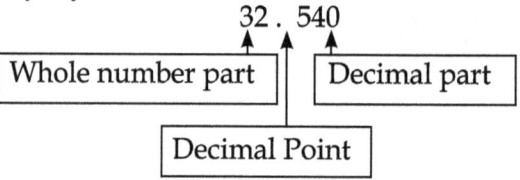

Below we have expressed the mixed number $57 \frac{49}{100}$ in expanded form and in decimal form.

Mixed Number	Expanded Form		Decimal Form
$57 \frac{49}{100}$	$= (5 \times 10) + (7 \times 1)$	$+ (4 \times \frac{1}{10}) + (9 \times \frac{1}{100})$	$= 57.49$

As you can see, it is easier to write in decimal form. Let's look at this decimal number in a decimal place-values chart to better understand how decimals work.

DECIMAL PLACE VALUES

(1000000) millions	(100,000) hundred thousands	(10,000) ten thousands	(1000) thousands	(100) hundreds	(10) tens	(1) ones	and	(1/10) tenths	(1/100) hundredths	(1/1000) thousandths	(1/10,000) Ten-thousandths	(1/100,000) hundred-thousandths	(1/1000000) millionths
					5	7	.	4	9				

As we move to the right in the place value chart, each number place is divided by 10. For example, thousands divided by 10 gives you hundreds. This is also true for digits to the right of the decimal point. For example, tenths divided by 10 gives you hundredths. When reading decimals, the decimal point should be read as "and." Thus, we read the decimal 57.49 as "fifty-seven and forty-nine hundredths." Note that in daily life it is common to read the decimal point as "point" instead of "and." Thus, 57.49 would be read as "fifty-seven point four nine." This usage is not considered mathematically correct.

Following example shows you place value of each digit in the number 17.591.

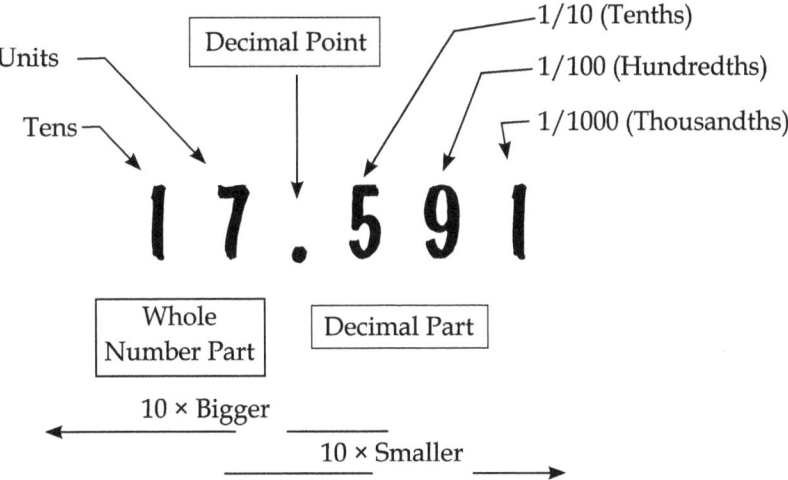

Example : Write each phrase as a fraction and as a decimal.

Phrase	Fraction	Decimal
Six tenths	$\frac{6}{10}$	.6
Five hundredths	$\frac{5}{100}$	.05

Decimals and Fractions

Thirty-two hundredths	$\frac{32}{100}$	.32
Two hundred sixty-seven thousandths	$\frac{267}{1000}$	.267

Note : 0.123 has the same value as .123. Let's look at some more examples of decimals.
Example : Write each phrase as a decimal.

Phrase	Decimal
Fifty-six hundredths	0.560
Twenty-five and nine tenths	25.900
Thirteen and five hundredths	13.050
nineteen and thirty-six thousandths	19.036

Example : Write each decimal using word.

Decimal	Phrase
0.0040	Four thousandths
200.9000	Two hundred and nine tenths
2.2500	Two and twenty-five hundredths
3.0582	Three and five hundred eighty-two ten-thousandths

It should be noted that four thousandths can also be written as zero and four thousandths.

Expanded Form
We can write the whole number 123 in expanded form as follows :

$123 = (1 \times 100) + (2 \times 10) + (3 \times 1)$. Decimals can also be written in expanded form. Expanded form is a way to write numbers by showing the value of each digit.

Example : Write each decimal number in expanded form.

Decimal	Expanded form
4.2400	$(4 \times 1) + (2 \times \frac{1}{10}) + (4 \times \frac{1}{100})$
0.5000	$(0 \times 1) + (5 \times \frac{1}{10})$
9.123	$(9 \times 1) + (1 \times \frac{1}{10}) + (2 \times \frac{1}{100}) + (3 \times \frac{1}{1000})$

TRIVIA

Different countries use different notations for the decimal point. For example, in Singapore the point is placed is placed mid-line, so 35·89 rather than 35.89. Also, in many European countries, a comma is used instead: 35,89

Comparing Two Numbers in Decimal Point

(a) Start at the left and compare corresponding digits. If the digits are the same, move one place to the right.

(b) When two digits are different, the larger number is the one with the larger digit.

Let us understand it with help of an example:

Example : Dominos caters to children's parties with square-shaped pizza. Each pizza is exactly the same size and is divided into equal parts called slices. At Shraddha's party, each child had 2 out of 10 slices from a single pizza. At Shubhra's party, each child had 15 out of 100 slices from a single pizza. At which party did each child have more pizza?

We can write a fraction to represent each party:

Party	Fraction
Shraddha's	$\frac{2}{10}$
Shubhra's	$\frac{15}{100}$

Writing it in decimal form :

Party	Fraction	Decimal
Shraddha's	$\frac{2}{10}$	0.20
Shubhra's	$\frac{15}{100}$	0.15

In the above example we compared two decimal numbers and found that 0.2 is greater than 0.15. So, we can see each child got more pizza at Shraddha's Party.

Decimal numbers are compared in the same way as other numbers : by comparing the different place values from left to right. We use the symbols <, > and = to compare decimals as shown below.

Comparison	Meaning
0.2 > 0.15	0.2 is greater than 0.15
0.15 < 0.2	0.15 is less than 0.2
0.2 = 0.2	0.2 is equal to 0.2
0.15 = 0.15	0.15 is equal to 0.15

Adding and Subtracting Decimals

To add decimals, follow these steps :

- Write down the numbers vertically and line up the decimal point.
- Put in zeros so the numbers have the same length
- Add all the digits with the same place value starting with the right column and moving to the left.

Example :

Add 2.456 to 1.3

Line up the decimals :			2.456
		+	1.3
"Pad" with zeros :			2.456
		+	1.300
Add :			2.456
		+	1.300
			3.756

Decimals and Fractions

Example:
Add 3.25, 0.025 and 7

Line up the decimals:			3.25
			0.025
		+	7.
"Pad" with zeros:			3.250
			0.025
		+	7.000
Add:			3.250
			0.025
		+	7.000
			10.275

Subtracting
To subtract, follow the same method: line up the decimals, then subtract.

Example:
Subtract 1.25 from 5.358

Line up the decimals:			5.358
		−	1.25
"Pad" with zeros:			5.358
		−	1.250
Subtract:			5.358
		−	1.250
			4.108

You can always check by adding the answer to the number subtracted.

Multiplication of Decimals: (*a*) Multiply the numbers just as you would multiply whole numbers. (*b*) Find the sum of the decimal point in the two factons. (*c*) Place the decimal point in the product so that the product has the same number of decimal places as the sum in step b.

Example: Multiply 0.04 × 0.5.

$$\begin{array}{rl} 0.04 & - \text{2 decimal places} \\ \times\, 0.5 & - \text{1 decimal place} \\ \hline 0.020 & - \text{3 decimal places in product} \\ & (2 + 1 = 3) \end{array}$$

Division of Decimals: Change the divisor and dividend into whole numbers respectively.

Now divide the new dividend by new divisor.

Example: $1.352 \div 0.026$

$$\begin{array}{r} 52 \\ 0.026 \overline{)1.352} \\ \underline{1.30} \\ 52 \\ \underline{52} \end{array}$$
Move each decimal point three places to the right and mark the new position by a caret.

Fraction
We often hear terms like half, one-fourth and three fourth. For example (*i*) My father gave me half a plate of rice (*ii*) I can drink only three fourths of a glass of milk. These parts show that they are parts of a whole.

A fraction is a part of a whole.

Example: Slice your favourite Domino's pizza and you will have fractions:

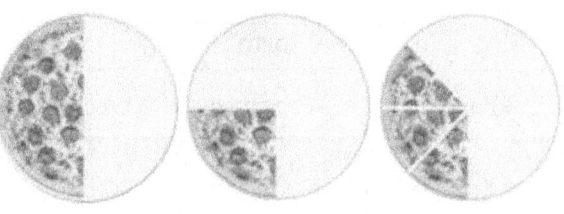

1/2 (One-Half), 1/4 (One-Quarter), 3/8 (Three-Eighths) all represent fractions. The top number tells how many slices you have and the bottom value tells how many slices the pizza was cut into.

Numerator / Denominator

We call the top number the Numerator, it is the number of parts you have. We call the bottom number the Denominator; it is the number of parts the whole is divided into.

$$\text{Fraction} = \frac{\text{Numerator}}{\text{Denominator}}$$

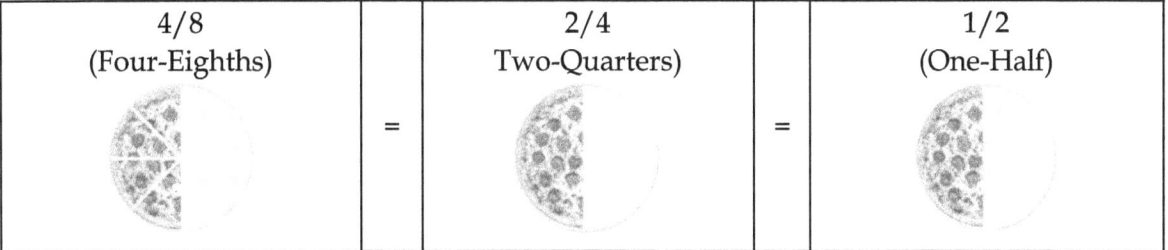

Example : These fractions are really the same:

$$\frac{1}{2} = 2/4 = 4/8$$

Why are they the same? Because when you multiply or divide both the top and bottom by the same number, the fraction keeps its value.

The rule to remember is :

"Change the bottom using multiply or divide, and the same to the top must be applied"

So, here is why those fractions are really the same :

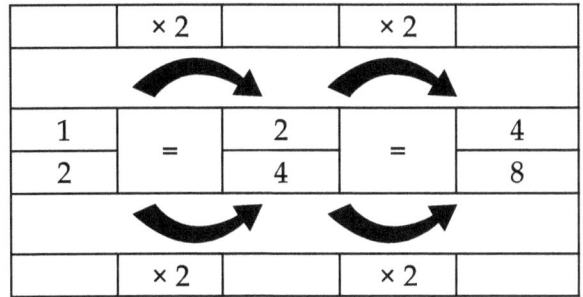

Note : Only divide when the top and bottom would still be whole numbers.

Convert Fractions into Decimals

To convert a Fraction to a Decimal, follow

It is usually best to show an answer using the simplest fraction. It is called Simplifying, or Reducing the Fraction.

Equivalent Fractions

Some fractions may look different but are really the same. For example :

these steps :

Step 1 : Find a number you can multiply to the bottom of the fraction to make it 10 or 100 or 1000 or any multiple of 10.

Step 2 : Multiply both top and bottom by that number.

Step 3 : Then write down just the top number, putting the decimal point in the correct spot (one space from the right hand side for every zero in the bottom number).

Example : Express 3/4 as a Decimal.

Step 1 : We can multiply 4 by 25 to make it 100

Step 2 : Multiply top and bottom by 25. Therefore:

$3 \times 25 = 75$ and

$4 \times 25 = 100$

So, $3/4 = 75/100$

Step 3 : Write down 75 with the decimal point 2 spaces from the right (because 100 has 2 zeros);

Answer : 0.75

Example : Express 3/16 as a Decimal.

Step 1 : We have to multiply 16 by 625 to make it 10,000

Step 2 : Multiply top and bottom by 625. Therefore:
3 × 625 = 1875 and
16 × 625 = 10000

Step 3 : Write down 1875 with the decimal point 4 spaces from the right (because 10,000 has 4 zeros);

Answer : 0.1875

Example : Express 1/3 as a Decimal.

Step 1 : There is no way to multiply 3 to make it 10 or 100 or any "1 followed by 0s", but we can calculate an approximate decimal by choosing to multiply by, say, 333.

Step 2 : Multiply top and bottom by 333. Therefore,
1 × 333 = 333 and
3 × 333 = 999

Step 3 : Now, 999 is nearly 1,000, so let us write down 333 with the decimal point 3 spaces from the right (because 1,000 has 3 zeros):

Answer : 0.333 (accurate to only 3 decimal places!!)

Convert Decimals into Fractions

Tip: Multiply top and bottom by 10 until you get a whole number, then simplify.

To convert a Decimal into a Fraction follows these steps :

Step 1 : Write down the decimal divided by 1, like this: decimal/1

Step 2 : Multiply both top and bottom by 10 for every number after the decimal point. (For example, if there are two numbers after the decimal point, then use 100, if there are three then use 1000, etc.)

Step 3 : Simplify (or reduce) the fraction.

Example : Express 0.75 as a fraction.

Step 1 : Write down 0.75 divided by 1 :
0.75/ 1

Step 2 : Multiply both top and bottom by 100 (there were 2 digits after the decimal point so that is 10×10=100) :

0.75 × 100 and 1 × 100 will become 75 and 100. Therefore, it will become 75/100.

Step 3 : Simplify the fraction :

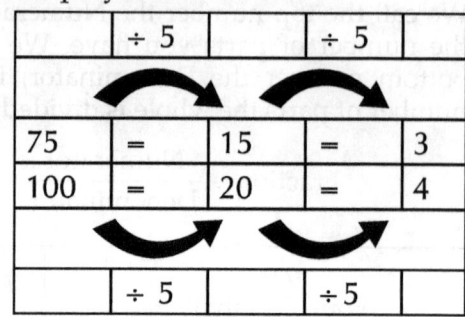

Answer : 3/4

Example : Express 0.625 as a fraction.

Step 1 : Write down :0.625/1

Step 2 : Multiply both top and bottom by 1,000 (there were 3 digits after the decimal point so that is 10 × 10 × 10 = 1,000) Therefore, it will become 625/1000.

Step 3 : Simplify the fraction :

	÷ 25		÷ 5	
625	=	25	=	5
1,000	=	40	=	8
	÷ 25		÷ 5	

Answer : 5/8

Example : Express 0.333 as a fraction.

Step 1 : Write down :
0.333/1

Step 2 : Multiply both top and bottom by 1,000 (there were 3 digits after the decimal point so that is 10 × 10 × 10 = 1,000)

Therefore, it will be 333/1000.

Step 3 : Simplify Fraction:
We can't get any simpler in this.

Answer : 333/1000

Comparing Fractions

Sometimes we need to compare two fractions to identify which is larger or smaller. There are two easy ways to compare fractions: using decimals or using the same denominator.

The Decimal Method of Comparing Fractions

Just convert each fraction into decimals, and then compare the decimals.

Example: Which is bigger: 3/8 or 5/12 ?
You can do this using the method of conversion.
These are the answers:
3/8 = 0.375, and 5/12 = 0.4166...
So, 5/12 is bigger.

The Same Denominator Method

The denominator is the bottom number in a fraction. It shows how many equal parts the item is divided into:

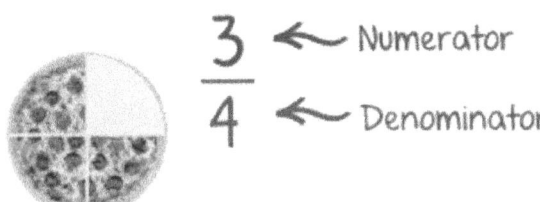

If two fractions have the same denominator then they are easy to compare:

Example: 4/9 is less than 5/9 (because 4 is less than 5)

But if the denominators are not the same you need to make them the same (using Equivalent Fractions).

Example: Which is larger: 3/8 or 5/12 ?
If you multiply 8 × 3 you get 24, and if you multiply 12 × 2 also you get 24, so let's do that. It is now easy to see that 9/24 is smaller than 10/24, (because 9 is smaller than 10).
So 5/12 is the larger fraction.

Estimating the degree of closeness of a fraction

With decimals, percents and fractions you have to think what the number means. Think: is it close to 1? Close to half? Close to zero?

Example: 1.7 × 30.
1.7 is close to 1.5, which is 1 and a half.
So 1.7 × 30 is close to 30 plus half of 30, which is 30 + 15 = 45. Adjust a little higher for an estimate of 47.

Example: 0.106 × 50.
0.106 is close to one-tenth, so 0.106 × 50 is close to one-tenth of 50 or about 5. Adjust a little higher for an estimate of 5.5

Also, a fraction might be close to zero, close to half or close to one.

Example: What is 9/10 plus 7/8?
Both 9/10 and 7/8 are close to one, so the answer must be close to 2.

Example: What is 4/9 times 12?
4/9 is nearly half so the answer must be close to half of 12, ie close to 6.

Percent, Decimal and Fraction Link

Here is a table of commonly occurring values shown in Percent, Decimal and Fraction form:

Percent	Decimal	Fraction
1%	0.01	1/100
5%	0.05	1/20
10%	0.1	1/10
12½%	0.125	1/8
20%	0.2	1/5
25%	0.25	1/4
33⅓%	0.333...	1/3
50%	0.5	1/2
75%	0.75	3/4
80%	0.8	4/5
90%	0.9	9/10
99%	0.99	99/100
100%	1	1/1
125%	1.25	5/4
150%	1.5	3/2
200%	2	2/1

Decimals and Fractions

- Decimal numbers are compared in the same way as other numbers : by comparing the different place values from left to right.
- We call the top number the Numerator, it is the number of parts you have. We call the bottom number the Denominator; it is the number of parts the whole is divided into.

MULTIPLE CHOICE QUESTIONS

1. Which of the following is equal to 5/100?
   (a) 5.
   (b) 0.5
   (c) 0.05
   (d) 0.005

2. Which of the following is equal to 462/200000?
   (a) 0.0231
   (b) 0.231
   (c) 231,000.
   (d) 0.00231

3. Which decimal represents seven hundred sixty-two and three tenths?
   (a) 7,623.
   (b) 76.23
   (c) 762.3
   (d) 76.3

4. Which of the following is the expanded form of 0.546?
   (a) $(0 \times 1) + (5 \times 1/10) + (4 \times 1/100) + (6 \times 1/1000)$
   (b) $(0 \times 1) + (6 \times 1/10) + (5 \times 1/100) + (4 \times 1/1000)$
   (c) $(0 \times) + (5 \times 1/10) + (4 \times 1/100) + (6 \times 1/1000)$
   (d) None of the above.

5. For the decimal number 347.92 what is the digit in the tenths place?
   (a) 2
   (b) 3
   (c) 4
   (d) 9

6. Which of the following is equal to twenty-five and sixty-nine thousandths?
   (a) 25.069
   (b) 25.0690
   (c) 25.06900
   (d) All of the above

7. The number 32747 written to 4 significant figures is
   (a) 32740
   (b) 32750
   (c) 3274
   (d) 32752

8. Which of the following is equal to seven hundred and five thousand and eighty-nine ten-thousandths?
   (a) 700.005.089
   (b) 705,000.089
   (c) 705,000.0089
   (d) 705,000.00089

9. Which of the following is equal to 9,842.1039?
   (a) Nine thousand, eight hundred, forty two and one thousand, thirty-nine millionths
   (b) Nine thousand, eight hundred, forty-two and one thousand, thirty-nine ten-thousandths
   (c) Nine thousand, eight hundred, forty-two and one thousand, thirty-nine thousandths
   (d) None of the above

10. Which of the following is equal to five hundred-thousandths?
    (a) 500,000
    (b) 0.500
    (c) 0.0005
    (d) 0.00005

11. Which of the following is the smallest decimal number?
    (a) 0.4981
    (b) 0.52
    (c) 0.4891
    (d) 0.6

12. What is the hundredths digit in the number 356.812?
    (a) 1
    (b) 2
    (c) 3
    (d) 8

13. For the decimal number 83.72 what is the digit in the hundredths place?
    (a) 2
    (b) 3
    (c) 7
    (d) 8

14. Which of the following choices lists these decimals in order from least to greatest : 0.910, 0.091, 0.9?
    (a) 0.9, 0.091, 0.910
    (b) 0.910, 0.9, 0.091
    (c) 0.091, 0.9, 0.910
    (d) None of the Above

15. Which of the following choices lists these decimals in order from least to greatest : 3.45, 3.0459, 3.5, 3.4059?
    (a) 3.0459, 3.4059, 3.45, 3.5
    (b) 3.4059, 3.5, 3.0459, 3.45
    (c) 3.5, 3.45, 3.4059, 3.0459
    (d) None of the above

Decimals and Fractions

16. (0.1 + 0.01) (0.1 − 0.01) =
    (a) 0.0001 (b) 0.001
    (c) 0.009 (d) 0.0099
17. For the number 489.6327, where do you find the smallest digit?
    (a) In the hundreds place
    (b) In the hundredths place
    (c) In the thousandths place
    (d) In the ten-thousandths place
18. Which of the following choices lists these decimals in order from least to greatest : 7.102, 7.0102, 7.012, 7.00102, 7.102021?
    (a) 7.102021, 7.00102, 7.012, 7.0102, 7.102
    (b) 7.00102, 7.0102, 7.012, 7.102, 7.102021
    (c) 7.102021, 7.102, 7.012, 7.0102, 7.00102
    (d) None of the above
19. What is the number obtained when 2.0837 is rounded to 2 decimal places?
    (a) 2.09 (b) 2.08
    (c) 2.1 (d) 2.10
20. For the number 36.2495, what is the place value of the digit 9?
    (a) 9 tenths
    (b) 9 hundredths
    (c) 9 thousandths
    (d) 9 ten-thousandths
21. What is the tenths digit in the number 43.765?
    (a) 7 (b) 6
    (c) 5 (d) 4
22. Add 20.15, 0.083 and 6.9
    (a) 27.133 (b) 27.033
    (c) 27.88 (d) 9.133
23. Add 3.032, 7.89 and 103.2
    (a) 114.41 (b) 114.122
    (c) 113.609 (d) 24.122
24. For the number 25.639, what is the place value of the digit 6?
    (a) 6 tens (b) 6 units
    (c) 6 tenths (d) 6 hundredths
25. For the number 2,367.981, where do you find the largest digit?
    (a) In the thousands place
    (b) In the units place
    (c) In the tenths place
    (d) In the hundredths place
26. How much pizza is left on the plate?

    (a) $\dfrac{8}{7}$ (b) $\dfrac{5}{8}$
    (c) $\dfrac{3}{4}$ (d) $\dfrac{7}{8}$
27. For the fraction of pizza shown in the diagram, what is the numerator?

    (a) 3 (b) 4
    (c) 5 (d) 8
28. What fraction has denominator 12 and equivalent to 2/3.
    (a) $\dfrac{8}{12}$ (b) $\dfrac{9}{12}$
    (c) $\dfrac{11}{12}$ (d) $\dfrac{7}{2} = \dfrac{49}{14}$
29. Which one of the following fractions is NOT equivalent to all the others?
    (a) $\dfrac{4}{10}$ (b) $\dfrac{6}{15}$
    (c) $\dfrac{9}{20}$ (d) $\dfrac{32}{80}$

30. Which of the following can be written in the box $\frac{7}{2} = \frac{49}{\square}$
    (a) 16
    (b) 14
    (c) 28
    (d) 35

31. Which of the following can be written in the box $\frac{\square}{5} = \frac{72}{20}$
    (a) 18
    (b) 12
    (c) 60
    (d) 15

32. The equivalent fraction of $\frac{3}{5}$ with denominator 20 is
    (a) $\frac{12}{20}$
    (b) $\frac{20}{12}$
    (c) $\frac{10}{20}$
    (d) $\frac{15}{20}$

33. Express 8/25 as a decimal
    (a) 0.16
    (b) 0.32
    (c) 0.33
    (d) 0.4

34. The equivalent fraction of $\frac{3}{5}$ with numerator 9 is
    (a) $\frac{15}{9}$
    (b) $\frac{9}{11}$
    (c) $\frac{9}{15}$
    (d) $\frac{9}{5}$

35. The simplest form of $\frac{48}{60}$ is
    (a) $\frac{5}{4}$
    (b) $\frac{4}{5}$
    (c) $\frac{8}{10}$
    (d) $\frac{12}{15}$

36. Express 4/9 as a decimal correct to 3 decimal places.
    (a) 0.400
    (b) 0.414
    (c) 0.444
    (d) 0.490

37. The next equivalent fraction of the given fraction $\frac{1}{2}, \frac{2}{4}, \frac{3}{6}, \frac{4}{8}$ ......, is
    (a) $\frac{7}{14}$
    (b) $\frac{6}{12}$
    (c) $\frac{15}{5}$
    (d) $\frac{5}{10}$

38. Which of the following pair of fractions are equivalent?
    (a) $\frac{5}{9}, \frac{30}{54}$
    (b) $\frac{7}{13}, \frac{5}{11}$
    (c) $\frac{3}{10}, \frac{12}{50}$
    (d) $\frac{8}{7}, \frac{16}{21}$

39. Which of the following fraction is close to fraction of $\frac{1}{15}$?
    (a) $\frac{2}{15}$
    (b) $\frac{15}{2}$
    (c) $\frac{3}{7}$
    (d) $\frac{5}{7}$

40. Express 0.85 as a fraction in its lowest terms.
    (a) $\frac{17}{20}$
    (b) $\frac{17}{25}$
    (c) $\frac{19}{20}$
    (d) $\frac{19}{25}$

41. Which of the following is the largest fraction?
    (a) $\frac{1}{9}$
    (b) $\frac{4}{9}$
    (c) $\frac{5}{9}$
    (d) $\frac{7}{9}$

42. Which of the following is the smallest fraction?
    (a) $\frac{7}{8}$
    (b) $\frac{5}{8}$
    (c) $\frac{3}{8}$
    (d) $\frac{1}{8}$

43. Which of the following is the greaterst fraction?
    (a) $\frac{4}{5}$
    (b) $\frac{5}{6}$
    (c) $\frac{5}{3}$
    (d) $\frac{5}{2}$

Decimals and Fractions

44. Express $1\frac{5}{9}$ as a decimal to 1 decimal place.
    (a) 0.5 (b) 0.6
    (c) 1.5 (d) 1.6
45. Which of the following is the smallest fraction?
    (a) $\frac{5}{6}$ (b) $\frac{4}{5}$
    (c) $\frac{5}{2}$ (d) $\frac{5}{3}$

HOTS

1. Which of the following holds true or false?
   A. 0.2 = 0.2000
   B. $0.2 = \frac{2}{100}$
   C. $0.2 = 2 \times \frac{1}{1000}$
   D. 0.2 = 2.0
   (a) FTFF (b) TFFF
   (c) FFTF (d) FFFT

2. A cook buys 4 kg of wheat and 3.5 kg of pulses for making the dinner for his customers and uses 2.5 kg of wheat and 1.5 kg of pulses in the dinner. What is the amount of wheat and pulses left with him?
   (a) 1.5 kg, 2.75 kg (b) 2.5 kg, 2 kg
   (c) 2.25 kg, 1.75 kg (d) 1.5 kg, 2 kg

3. The sum 0.5 + 0.75 = 1.25 can be expressed using fractions as:
   (a) 1/2 + 3/5 = 4/3
   (b) 1/2 + 3/4 = 5/4
   (c) 1/2 + 3/7 = 5/8
   (d) 1/2 + 7/3 = 2/7

4. Electricity bill of Mr. Bunny Mehra shows the following details:
   Monthly Rent = 500/-

Unit	Consumed Rate
1-100	3.50
101-150	4.25
151-200	4.50
greater than 201	4.75

   Calculate amount payable by Bunny to UPPCL if he consumes 124 units.
   (a) 935 (b) 952
   (c) 953 (d) 630

5. Find the value of 624.7 + 39.29.
   (a) 101.76 (b) 663.99
   (c) 66.399 (d) 660.79

SUBJECTIVE QUESTIONS

1. The product of the (sum of third multiple of 18 and the sixth multiple of 12) and sum of factors of 24 is _____.
   Solution:
   Third multiple of 18 = 54
   Sixth multiple of 12 = 72
   Sum of both, 54 + 72 = 126
   Factors of 24 = 1, 24, 2, 12, 3, 8, 4, 6
   Sum of factors
   = 1 + 24 + 2 + 12 + 3 + 8 + 4 + 6 = 60
   So, their product = 126 × 60 = 7560

2. Which one of the following digits should be placed in the middle of the digits of the number 529970 so that 3 becomes factor of it?
   Solution:
   Sum of digits of the number 529970
   = 5 + 2 + 9 + 9 + 7 + 0 = 32.
   Therefore, 1 should be placed in the middle of the digits such that sum of the digits will become divisible by 3

3. Convert 4.7, 2.79, 7.701 to like decimals.
   Solution:
   4.7 has 1 decimal place.
   2.79 has 2 decimal places.
   7.701 has 3 decimal places.
   The highest number of decimal place among above numbers is 3.
   Hence, we need to put two 0 in 4.7 to make it 3 decimal places. And one 0 in 2.79 to make it three decimal places. Now, the numbers are 4.700, 2.790, and 7.701 and these 3 are like decimals.

4. What fraction of the large square is Red (R), Blue (B), Orange (O), Green (G), White (W), Yellow (Y) and Grey shaded?

		R	G
	G/R	O	
W	R	Y	Y
O	B/O		G

   Solution:
   Grey shaded = $\dfrac{5}{16}$

   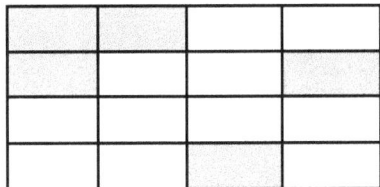

   Red (R) = $\dfrac{5}{32}$

		R	
	G/R		
	R		

   Green (G) = $\dfrac{5}{32}$

			G
	G/R		
			G

   Yellow (Y) = $\dfrac{2}{16}$

		Y	Y

   Orange (O) = $\dfrac{5}{32}$

   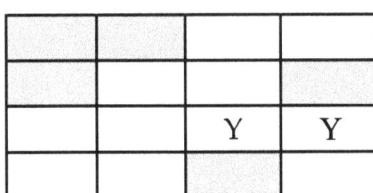

   Blue (B) = $\dfrac{1}{32}$

Decimals and Fractions

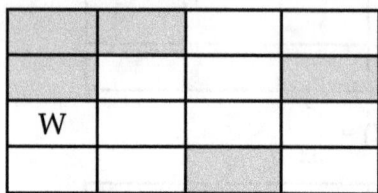

White (W) = $\frac{1}{16}$

W

5. Consider the following statements.
   Statement A: $\frac{1}{5}$ of ₹ 10 is 200 paisa.
   Statement B: There are 50 cm in $\frac{1}{6}$ th part of 3 meters.
   Which of them is correct?
   Solution:
   Both the statements are correct.
   ₹ 1 = 100 paisa;
   ₹ 10 = 10 × 100 = 1000 paisa.
   $\frac{1}{5}$ th of ₹ 10 = $\frac{1}{5}$ × 1000 paisa
   = 200 paisa.
   And 1 meter = 100 cm;
   3 meter = 300 cm.
   $\frac{1}{6}$ th of 3 meter = $\frac{1}{6}$ × 300 = 50 cm

Algebra

Learning Objectives: In this chapter, students will learn about:
- ✓ Basic concepts of Algebra

Algebra uses variables to find unknown numbers. Having a basic understanding of algebra concepts is useful for the students. The basic algebra operations are:
- Addition: $x + y$
- Subtraction: $x - y$
- Multiplication: xy
- Division: x/y or $x \div y$

Here, x and y are variables. These operations follows BODMAS rule only.

A few conditions and rules below give better clarity:

Condition	Rule
$x + (y + z) \Rightarrow x + y + z$	Open the bracket and add the terms normally.
$x - (y + z) \Rightarrow x - y - z$	Multiply the negative sign with each term inside the bracket and then open and add the terms as applicable. (All positive terms present in a bracket will become negative and vice-versa if there is a minus sign before bracket)
$x(y + z) \Rightarrow xy + xz$	Multiply the outside term (here x) with each term inside the bracket

TRIVIA

In 16th century, algebra had been defined in mathematical meaning. At first, it was defined as the surgical procedure, which fixed the dislocated or broken bones.

Some common algebraic formulas:
- $a^2 - b^2 = (a - b)(a + b)$
- $a^2 + b^2 = (a - b)^2 + 2ab$
- $(a + b)^2 = a^2 + 2ab + b^2$
- $(a - b)^2 = a^2 - 2ab + b^2$
- $(a + b + c)^2 = a^2 + b^2 + c^2 + 2ab + 2ac + 2bc$
- $(a - b - c)^2 = a^2 + b^2 + c^2 - 2ab - 2ac + 2bc$
- $(a + b)^3 = a^3 + 3a^2b + 3ab^2 + b^3$
- $(a - b)^3 = a^3 - 3a^2b + 3ab^2 - b^3$

Example 1: What is seven more than x?
(a) $(x + 7)$ (b) $x7$
(c) $7x$

Answer: $(x + 7)$

Example 2: What is the product of 5 and x?
(a) $5x$ (b) $5 + x$
(c) $x - 5$

Answer: $5x$

Example 3: Sum of a and b divided by 8 will be _____
(a) $(a+b)/8$ (b) $a/8+b$
(c) None of these
Answer: $(a+b)/5$

Example 4: n is divided by thrice of m =
(a) $n/3m$ (b) $3n/m$
(c) $3m/n$
Answer: $m/3n$

MUST REMEMBER

➡ Algebra is the branch of mathematics that helps in the representation of problems or situations in the form of mathematical expressions.
➡ It involves variables like x, y, z, and mathematical operations like addition, subtraction, multiplication, and division to form a meaningful mathematical expression.
➡ Algebra deals with symbols and these symbols are related to each other with the help of operators.
➡ The complexity of algebra is simplified by the use of numerous algebraic expressions.
➡ Elementary algebra deals with solving the algebraic expressions for a viable answer. In elementary algebra, simple variables like x, y, are represented in the form of an equation.
➡ Abstract algebra deals with the use of abstract concepts like groups, rings, vectors rather than simple mathematical number systems.
➡ An algebraic expression in algebra is formed using integer constants, variables, and basic arithmetic operations of addition(+), subtraction(-), multiplication(×), and division(/).

MULTIPLE CHOICE QUESTIONS

1. Two times b – six times a =
   - (a) $2b - 6a$
   - (b) $6b - 2a$
   - (c) $b - 2a$
   - (d) $b^2 - a6$
2. Sum of twice of x and 6 =
   - (a) $6x + 2$
   - (b) $2x + 6$
   - (c) $x + 8$
   - (d) $2(x + 6)$
3. Sum of n and 20 =
   - (a) $n + 20$
   - (b) $20 - n$
   - (c) $20n$
   - (d) $6 + 14n$
4. Three times x minus five times x =
   - (a) $3x - 5y$
   - (b) $5x - 3x$
   - (c) $x - 3y$
   - (d) $3x - 5x$
5. Twice the sum of d and e
   - (a) $d + 2e$
   - (b) $2d + e$
   - (c) $2(d + e)$
   - (d) $2de$
6. The quotient when twice x is divided by thrice y
   - (a) $2x/y$
   - (b) $2x/3y$
   - (c) $2x/4y$
   - (d) $3x/2y$
7. If $x = 2, y = 5$ then $x + y = ?$
   - (a) 12
   - (b) 10
   - (c) 3
   - (d) 7
8. If $x = 6, y = 2$ then $x - y = ?$
   - (a) 4
   - (b) 3
   - (c) 5
   - (d) 12
9. If $m = 5, n = 4$ then $mn = ?$
   - (a) 12
   - (b) 15
   - (c) 20
   - (d) 24
10. If $p = 1/6, q = 20$ then $p \times q = ?$
    - (a) 5/3
    - (b) 5/6
    - (c) 10/3
    - (d) None of these
11. If $p = 28, q = 7$ then $p/q = ?$
    - (a) 3
    - (b) 12
    - (c) 6
    - (d) 4
12. If $x = 50, y = 5$ then $x/y = ?$
    - (a) 5
    - (b) 10
    - (c) 12
    - (d) 8
13. If $a = 10, b = 3$, then $a - b = ?$
    - (a) 13
    - (b) 7
    - (c) 4
    - (d) 45
14. If $x + 5 = 10$, then x represents _____.
    - (a) known number
    - (b) unknown number
    - (c) none of these
15. In $x + 3$, x is known as
    - (a) variable
    - (b) none of these
    - (c) constant
    - (d) alphabet

HOTS

1. If $a = 9, b = 3$ then $a^2 \div b - a = ?$
   - (a) 3
   - (b) 9
   - (c) 18
   - (d) 15
2. If $a = 5, b = 2$ then $a^2 + b^2 - ab^3 = ?$
   - (a) –11
   - (b) –9
   - (c) –12
   - (d) –15
3. If $a = 2, b = 3, c = 4$ then $a^2 b - c = ?$
   - (a) 3
   - (b) 8
   - (c) 10
   - (d) 5
4. If $a = 5, b = 4$ then $a^2 \div (b + 1) = ?$
   - (a) 2
   - (b) 18
   - (c) 5
   - (d) 20
5. If $a = 30, b = 20, c = 40$ then $b^2 - a + c = ?$
   - (a) 300
   - (b) 410
   - (c) 180
   - (d) 250

Algebra

SUBJECTIVE QUESTIONS

1. Find four pairs of numbers, one for each of addition, subtraction, multiplication and division that make the number 15.
   Solution:
   Addition, (10 + 5) = 15
   Subtraction, (20 – 5) = 15
   Multiplication, (5 × 3) = 15
   Division, (30÷2) = 15

2. Fill in the blanks with the right symbol from <, > or =.
   (a) (50 ÷ 5) _____ (14 – 4)
   (b) (6 + 2) _____ (3×2)
   (c) (6 × 2) _____ (50 + 1)
   Solution:
   (a) (50 ÷ 5) = 10 and (14 – 4) = 10
   As they have equal results, the answer will be (50 ÷ 5) = (14 – 4)
   (b) (6 + 2) > (3×2)
   (6+2) = 8 and (3×2) = 6, as 8 is bigger than 6 so the answer will be (6+2) > (3×2).
   (c) (6 × 2) < (50 + 1)
   (6 × 2) = 12 and (50 + 1) = 51
   As 51 is bigger than 12, so the answer will be (6 × 2) < (50 + 1)

3. Fill in the blanks in the expressions with the proper numbers.
   (a) (1 × 8) = (? × 1)
   (b) (5 × 4) > (7 × ?)
   (c) (24 ÷ 3) < (? × 5)
   (a) In the right side (1×8) = 8, so find a number that after multiplying with 1 gives 8, and that number is 8
   (b) In the left side (5×4) = 20, as the '>' suggests that 20 should be bigger than the number on the right side. So, multiples of 7 that is smaller than 20 are 7, 14
   So, we can write (5 × 4) > (7 ×1) or (5 × 4) > (7 × 2)
   (c) In the left side (24÷3) = 8, as the '<' suggests that 8 should be smaller than the number on the right side.
   So, multiples of 5 that is larger than 8 can be (5×2) = 10
   So, the answer is (24 ÷ 3) < (2 × 5)

4. Soldiers are marching in a parade. There are 10 soldiers in a row. What is the rule which gives the number of soldiers, given the number of rows?
   Solution:
   Let n be the number of rows
   Number of soldiers in a row = 10
   Total number of soldiers = number of soldiers in a row × number of rows = $10n$

5. If a is the side-length of the equilateral triangle, then the perimeter of the triangle will be?
   Solution:
   Side of equilateral triangle = a
   The perimeter of triangle = sum of all its three sides
   Since we know that an equilateral triangle has all its sides equal.
   Therefore, Perimeter of equilateral triangle = $a + a + a = 3a$

LCM and HCF

Learning Objectives : In this chapter, students will learn about:
- ✓ Factors
- ✓ Common Factors
- ✓ Multiples

CHAPTER SUMMARY

We are surrounded by numbers in each and every sphere of our life. Factors and multiples are also commonly used in our everyday lives. We use factors when we want to arrange things in different ways. For example, arranging books in rows & columns, making groups of children in different ways etc.

Factors

Suppose your teacher has told you to put all the pencils in pencil box in a single line.

1 2 3 4 5 6 7 8 9 10 11 12

But all pencils are not coming in the frame. So you decide to make 2 lines of 6 pencils each.

1 2 3 4 5 6

7 8 9 10 11 12

This way also all the pencils are not fitting in the box. Then you make 4 lines of 3 each.

1 2 3 4

5 6 7 8

LCM and HCF

9 10 11 12

Now all the pencils fit in pencil box.
So here we saw three different ways to set 12 pencils in a pencil box.
First way is 1 × 12
Second way is 6 × 2
Third way is 4 × 3
Therefore, we can say that 1, 12, 2, 3, 4 and 6 are the factors of 12.
A natural number is said to be a factor if the number has the multiple part of some other number.
e.g., 3 × 2 = 6
Here 3 and 2 are the factors of 6.
Thus factors of a number divide the number completely.

Did you know?
- 1 is a factor of every number.
- Every number is the greatest factor of itself.
- Every number except 1 has at least 2 factors, that is 1 and the number itself.

Finding all the factors
A number can have many factors.
Example : Find all the factors of 20.
Start at 1 : 1 × 20 = 20, so put 1 at the start, and put its "partner" 20 at the other end :

1					20

Then go to 2 : 2×10=20, so put 2 and 10:

1	2			10	20

Then go to 3. 3 doesn't work
(3 × 6 = 18, 3 × 7 = 21).

Then go to 4 : 4 × 5 = 20, so put them in :

1	2	4		5	10	20

There is no whole number between 4 and 5 so you are done! (Don't forget the negative ones).

1	2	4	5	10	20
−1	−2	−4	−5	−10	−20

Example : The product 12 has several factors.
- 3 and 4 are factors of 12, because 3×4=12
- Also 2 × 6 = 12 so 2 and 6 are also factors of 12,
- And 1 × 12 = 12 so 1 and 12 are factors of 12 as well.
- And because multiplying negatives makes a positive, −1, −2, −3, −4, −6 and −12 are also factors of 12 like this : (−1) × (−12) = 12, (−2) × (−6) = 12, (−3) × (−4) = 12.

So all the factors of 12 are 1, 2, 3, 4, 6 and 12 AND − 1, − 2, − 3, − 4, − 6 and − 12.
But unless specified we generally consider the positive integers only.

Example : The product 24 has several factors.
$$24 = 1 \times 24$$
$$24 = 2 \times 12$$
$$24 = 3 \times 8$$
$$24 = 4 \times 6$$
So, the factors are 1, 2, 3, 4, 6, 8, 12, 24.

Common Factors
If the factors are same for two or more than two different numbers i.e., factors that two numbers have in common are called the common factors of those numbers.

Example : Find the common factors of 12 and 30.

Sol. Factors of 12 are 1, 2, 3, 4, 6 and 12
Factors of 30 are 1, 2, 3, 5, 6, 10, 15 and 30
Then the common factors are those that are found in both lists. Notice that 1, 2, 3 and 6 appear in both lists. So, the common factors of 12 and 30 are 1, 2, 3 and 6.

Here is another example with three numbers:

Example : Find the common factors of 15, 30 and 105.

Sol. Factors of 15 are 1, 3, 5, and 15
Factors of 30 are 1, 2, 3, 5, 6, 10, 15 and 30
Factors of 105 are 1, 3, 5, 7, 15, 21, 35 and 105
Thus, the common factors of 15, 30 and 105 are 1, 3, 5 and 15.

Example : What are the common factors of 20 and 25?

Sol. The factors of 20 are 1, 2, 4, 5, 10 and 20. and the factors of 25 are 1, 5, and 25.
So, the common factors of 20 and 25 are 1 and 5.

Example : What are the common factors of 15 and 30?

Sol. The factors of 15 are 1, 3, 5, and 15.
and the factors of 30 are 1, 2, 3, 5, 6, 10, 15, and 30.
So, the common factors of 15 and 30 are 1, 3, 5, and 15.

Example : What are the common factors of 9 and 20?

Sol. The factors of 9 are 1, 3 and 9.
and the factors of 20 are 1, 2, 4, 5, 10 and 20.
So, the only common factor of 9 and 20 is 1.

Highest Common Factor (HCF) or Greatest Common Factor (GCF)

The largest common factor of two or more numbers is called their greatest common factor or highest common factor. The "Greatest Common Factor" is often abbreviated to "GCF", and is also known as the "Greatest Common Divisor (GCD)", or the "Highest Common Factor (HCF).

Finding the Greatest Common Factor

(i) By Listing Factors
- find all factors of both numbers
- then select the ones that are common to both, and
- then choose the greatest.

Find HCF of 24, 40 and 80.

Sol. Prime factors of 24 = 2 × 2 × 2 × 3
Prime factors of 40 = 2 × 2 × 2 × 5
Prime factors of 80 = 2 × 2 × 2 × 2 × 5
The common prime factors are 2 × 2 × 2.
∴ HCF = 2 × 2 × 2 = 8

(ii) By Division Method

Divide the greater number by the smaller one, the divisor by the remainder then the second divisor by the second remainder and so on, until there is no remainder. The last divisor is the required HCF.

Example : Find the HCF of 48 and 168.

Sol.
$$48\overline{)168}(3$$
$$\quad\ \ 144$$
$$\overline{24\overline{)48}(2}$$
$$\quad\ \ 48$$
$$\quad\ \ \overline{\ \times\ }$$

∴ 24 is the required HCF.

Example : Greatest Common Factor of 12 and 16
1. Find all the Factors of each number,
2. Circle/Select the Common factors
3. Choose the Greatest of those

This is shown in figure below :

Factors of 12 : ①, ②, ③, ④, ⑥, ⑫
Factors of 16 : ①, ②, ④, ⑧, ⑯

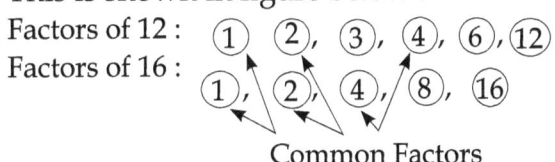

Common Factors

④ is the Greatest Common Factor.

TRIVIA

You know 111, 111, 111 × 111, 111, 111
= 12,345,678,987,654,321

LCM and HCF

Multiples

A multiple is a number that is the product of a given number and some other number. A multiple is formed by multiplying a given number by the counting numbers. The counting numbers are 1, 2, 3, 4, 5, 6, etc. It is the result of multiplying a number by an integer (not a fraction).

For example if $a \times b = c$, then c is multiple of both a and b.

Examples : Multiples of 3 :
12 is a multiple of 3, because $3 \times 4 = 12$
-3 is a multiple of 3, because $3 \times -1 = -3$
This is shown in the following diagram:

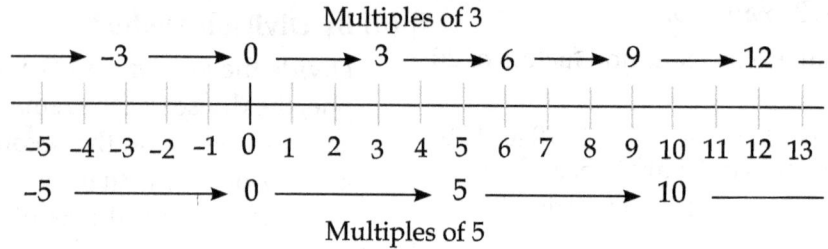

Also you can see multiples of 5 :
10 is a multiple of 5, because $5 \times 2 = 10$
But 11 is NOT a multiple of 5

So you must multiply by an integer, but the number that is being multiplied can be anything.

Example : Multiples of π
..., -2π, $-\pi$, 0, π, 2π, 3π, 4π, ...

Common Multiple

When you list the multiples of two (or more) numbers, and find the same value in both lists, then that is a common multiple of those numbers. For example, when you write down the multiples of 4 and 5, the common multiples are those that are found in both lists:

Least Common Multiple (LCM)

The smallest (non-zero) number that is a multiple of two or more numbers is known as their least common multiple (LCM). Least Common Multiple is made up of the words Least, Common and Multiple:
It is the smallest number which can be divided without remainder by two or more numbers. It is simply the smallest of the common multiples. In our above example, the smallest of the common multiples is 20 so the Least Common Multiple of 4 and 5 is 20.

The multiples of 4 are : 4, 8, 12, 16, 20, 24, 28, 32, 36, 40, 44,...
The multiples of 5 are : 5, 10, 15, 20, 25, 30, 35, 40, 45, 50, ...

Note that 20 and 40 appear in both lists. So, the common multiples of 4 and 5 are: 20, 40, (and 60, 80, etc ..., too). But 20 is the smallest common multiple.

Finding the Least Common Multiple

It is a really easy thing to do. Just start listing the multiples of the numbers until you get a match.

Example : Find the least common multiple for 3 and 5 :

The multiples of 3 are 3, 6, 9, 12, 15, ...,
and the multiples of 5 are 5, 10, 15, 20, ..., like this :

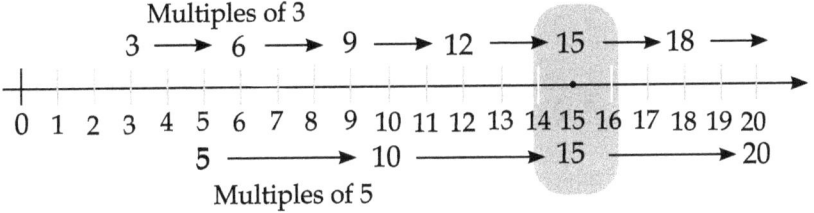

As you can see on this number line, the first time the multiples matchup is 15, so LCM is 15.

More than 2 Numbers

We can also find the least common multiple of 3 (or more) numbers easily.

Example : Find the least common multiple for 4, 6, and 8.

Sol. Multiples of 4 are: 4, 8, 12, 16, 20, 24, 28, 32, 36, ...

Multiples of 6 are: 6, 12, 18, 24, 30, 36, ...

Multiples of 8 are: 8, 16, 24, 32, 40, ...

So, 24 is the least common multiple (LCM).

Table of Factors and Multiples

Here are the factors (not including negatives) and some multiples for 1 to 100:

Factors	Multiples								
1	1	2	3	4	5	6	7	8	9	10
1, 2	2	4	6	8	10	12	14	16	18	20
1, 3	3	6	9	12	15	18	21	24	27	30
1, 2, 4	4	8	12	16	20	24	28	32	36	40
1, 5	5	10	15	20	25	30	35	40	45	50
1, 2, 3, 6	6	12	18	24	30	36	42	48	54	60
1, 7	7	14	21	28	35	42	49	56	63	70
1, 2, 4, 8	8	16	24	32	40	48	56	64	72	80
1, 3, 9	9	18	27	36	45	54	63	72	81	90
1, 2, 5, 10	10	20	30	40	50	60	70	80	90	100
Factors	Multiples								
1, 11	11	22	33	44	55	66	77	88	99	110
1, 2, 3, 4, 6, 12	12	24	36	48	60	72	84	96	108	120
1, 13	13	26	39	52	65	78	91	104	117	130
1, 2, 7, 14	14	28	42	56	70	84	98	112	126	140
1, 3, 5, 15	15	30	45	60	75	90	105	120	135	150
1, 2, 4, 8, 16	16	32	48	64	80	96	112	128	144	160
1, 17	17	34	51	68	85	102	119	136	153	170
1, 2, 3, 6, 9, 18	18	36	54	72	90	108	126	144	162	180
1, 19	19	38	57	76	95	114	133	152	171	190
1, 2, 4, 5, 10, 20	20	40	60	80	100	120	140	160	180	200

LCM and HCF

Factors	Multiples								
1, 3, 7, 21	21	42	63	84	105	126	147	168	189	210
1, 2, 11, 22	22	44	66	88	110	132	154	176	198	220
1, 23	23	46	69	92	115	138	161	184	207	230
1, 2, 3, 4, 6, 8, 12, 24	24	48	72	96	120	144	168	192	216	240
1, 5, 25	25	50	75	100	125	150	175	200	225	250
1, 2, 13, 26	26	52	78	104	130	156	182	208	234	260
1, 3, 9, 27	27	54	81	108	135	162	189	216	243	270
1, 2, 4, 7, 14, 28	28	56	84	112	140	168	196	224	252	280
1, 29	29	58	87	116	145	174	203	232	261	290
1, 2, 3, 5, 6, 10, 15, 30	30	60	90	120	150	180	210	240	270	300
1, 31	31	62	93	124	155	186	217	248	279	310
1, 2, 4, 8, 16, 32	32	64	96	128	160	192	224	256	288	320
1, 3, 11, 33	33	66	99	132	165	198	231	264	297	330
1, 2, 17, 34	34	68	102	136	170	204	238	272	306	340
1, 5, 7, 35	35	70	105	140	175	210	245	280	315	350
1, 2, 3, 4, 6, 9, 12, 18, 36	36	72	108	144	180	216	252	288	324	360
1, 37	37	74	111	148	185	222	259	296	333	370
1, 2, 19, 38	38	76	114	152	190	228	266	304	342	380
1, 3, 13, 39	39	78	117	156	195	234	273	312	351	390
1, 2, 4, 5, 8, 10, 20, 40	40	80	120	160	200	240	280	320	360	400
1, 41	41	82	123	164	205	246	287	328	369	410
1, 2, 3, 6, 7, 14, 21, 42	42	84	126	168	210	252	294	336	378	420
1, 43	43	86	129	172	215	258	301	344	387	430
1, 2, 4, 11, 22, 44	44	88	132	176	220	264	308	352	396	440
1, 3, 5, 9, 15, 45	45	90	135	180	225	270	315	360	405	450
1, 2, 23, 46	46	92	138	184	230	276	322	368	414	460
1, 47,	47	94	141	188	235	282	329	376	423	470
1, 2, 3, 4, 6, 8, 12, 16, 24,	48	96	144	192	240	288	336	384	432	480
1, 7, 49	49	98	147	196	245	294	343	392	441	490
1, 2, 5, 10, 25, 50	50	100	150	200	250	300	350	400	450	500
1, 3, 17, 51	51	102	153	204	255	306	357	408	459	510
1, 2, 4, 13, 26, 52	52	104	156	208	260	312	364	416	468	520
1, 53	53	106	159	212	265	318	371	424	477	530
1, 2, 3, 6, 9, 18, 27, 54	54	108	162	216	270	324	378	432	486	540
1, 5, 11, 55	55	110	165	220	275	330	385	440	495	550

Factors	\multicolumn{9}{c}{Multiples}
1, 2, 4, 7, 8, 14, 28, 56	56	112	168	224	280	336	392	448	504	560
1, 3, 19, 57	57	114	171	228	285	342	399	456	513	570
1, 2, 29, 58	58	116	174	232	290	348	406	464	522	580
1, 59	59	118	177	236	295	354	413	472	531	590
1, 2, 3, 4, 5, 6, 10, 12, 15, 20, 30, 60	60	120	180	240	300	360	420	480	540	600
1, 61	61	122	183	244	305	366	427	488	549	610
1, 2, 31, 62	62	124	186	248	310	372	434	496	558	620
1, 3, 7, 9, 21, 63	63	126	189	252	315	378	441	504	567	630
1, 2, 4, 8, 16, 32, 64	64	128	192	256	320	384	448	512	576	640
1, 5, 13, 65	65	130	195	260	325	390	455	520	585	650
1, 2, 3, 6, 11, 22, 33, 66	66	132	198	264	330	396	462	528	594	660
1, 67	67	134	201	268	335	402	469	536	603	670
1, 2, 4, 17, 34, 68	68	136	204	272	340	408	476	544	612	680
1, 3, 23, 69	69	138	207	276	345	414	483	552	621	690
1, 2, 5, 7, 10, 14, 35, 70	70	140	210	280	350	420	490	560	630	700
1, 71	71	142	213	284	355	426	497	568	639	710
1, 2, 3, 4, 6, 8, 9, 12, 18, 24, 36, 72	72	144	216	288	360	432	504	576	648	720
1, 73	73	146	219	292	365	438	511	584	657	730
1, 2, 37, 74	74	148	222	296	370	444	518	592	666	740
1, 3, 5, 15, 25, 75	75	150	225	300	375	450	525	600	675	750
1, 2, 4, 19, 38, 76	76	152	228	304	380	456	532	608	684	760
1, 7, 11, 77	77	154	231	308	385	462	539	616	693	770
1, 2, 3, 6, 13, 26, 39, 78	78	156	234	312	390	468	546	624	702	780
1, 79	79	158	237	316	395	474	553	632	711	790
1, 2, 4, 5, 8, 10, 16, 20, 40, 80	80	160	240	320	400	480	560	640	720	800
1, 3, 9, 27, 81	81	162	243	324	405	486	567	648	729	810
1, 2, 41, 82	82	164	246	328	410	492	574	656	738	820
1, 83	83	166	249	332	415	498	581	664	747	830
1, 2, 3, 4, 6, 7, 12, 14, 21, 28, 42, 84	84	168	252	336	420	504	588	672	756	840
1, 5, 17, 85	85	170	255	340	425	510	595	680	765	850
1, 2, 43, 86	86	172	258	344	430	516	602	688	774	860
1, 3, 29, 87	87	174	261	348	435	522	609	696	783	870

LCM and HCF

1, 2, 4, 8, 11, 22, 44, 88	88	176	264	352	440	528	616	704	792	880
1, 89	89	178	267	356	445	534	623	712	801	890
1, 2, 3, 5, 6, 9, 10, 15, 18, 30, 45, 90	90	180	270	360	450	540	630	720	810	900
1, 7, 13, 91	91	182	273	364	455	546	637	728	819	910
1, 2, 4, 23, 46, 92	92	184	276	368	460	552	644	736	828	920
1, 3, 31, 93	93	186	279	372	465	558	651	744	837	930
1, 2, 47, 94	94	188	282	376	470	564	658	752	846	940
1, 5, 19, 95	95	190	285	380	475	570	665	760	855	950
1, 2, 3, 4, 6, 8, 12, 16, 24, 32, 48, 96	96	192	288	384	480	576	672	768	864	960
1, 97	97	194	291	388	485	582	679	776	873	970
1, 2, 7, 14, 49, 98	98	196	294	392	490	588	686	784	882	980
1, 3, 9, 11, 33, 99	99	198	297	396	495	594	693	792	891	990
1, 2, 4, 5, 10, 20, 25, 50, 100	100	200	300	400	500	600	700	800	900	1000

Note
Relationship between L.C.M and H.C.F of two numbers.
L.C.M × H.C.F = Products of the two numbers.

MUST REMEMBER

- If the factors are same for two or more than two different numbers i.e., factors that two numbers have in common are called the common factors of those numbers.
- The largest common factor of two or more numbers is called their greatest common factor or highest common factor. The "Greatest Common Factor" is often abbreviated to "GCF", and is also known as the "Greatest Common Divisor (GCD)", or the "Highest Common Factor (HCF).
- When you list the multiples of two (or more) numbers, and find the same value in both lists, then that is a common multiple of those numbers.
- The smallest (non-zero) number that is a multiple of two or more numbers is known as their least common multiple (LCM).
- Relationship between L.C.M and H.C.F of two numbers.
- L.C.M × H.C.F = Products of the two numbers

MULTIPLE CHOICE QUESTIONS

1. Find the greatest number that will divide 43, 91 and 183 so as to leave the same remainder in each case.
   (a) 4 (b) 77
   (c) 9 (d) 13

2. What is a factor?
   (a) A number that divides exactly into another number.
   (b) A number that can be halved.
   (c) A number that can be multiplied by itself.
   (d) A number that can be divided only by two.

3. The H.C.F. of two numbers is 23 and the other two factors of their L.C.M. are 13 and 14. The larger of the two numbers is :
   (a) 276 (b) 299
   (c) 322 (d) 345

4. Which numbers are all factors of 10?
   (a) 2, 3, 5 (b) 1, 2, 4
   (c) 2, 5, 10 (d) All of these

5. Which numbers are all factors of 16?
   (a) 4, 6, 8. (b) 2, 8, 4.
   (c) 1, 2, 9. (d) All of these

6. Which number is a multiple of 2?
   (a) 1321 (b) 2543
   (c) 5620 (d) 1211

7. Let N be the greatest number that will divide 1305, 4665 and 6905, leaving the same remainder in each case. Then sum of the digits in N is :
   (a) 4 (b) 5
   (c) 6 (d) 8

8. Which number is a multiple of 5?
   (a) 2876 (b) 1985
   (c) 1423 (d) 1202

9. Which pair of factors makes 20?
   (a) 2 and 18 (b) 15 and 5
   (c) 4 and 5 (d) 2 and 7

10. What is the least common multiple of 6 and 8?
    (a) 12 (b) 16
    (c) 24 (d) 48

11. What is the least common multiple of 6, 8 and 9?
    (a) 48 (b) 60
    (c) 63 (d) 72

12. What is the least common multiple of 8, 12 and 15?
    (a) 60 (b) 120
    (c) 240 (d) 300

13. What is the least common multiple of 4, 6 and 7?
    (a) 42 (b) 48
    (c) 56 (d) 84

14. What is the least common multiple of 12, 15 and 18?
    (a) 108 (b) 144
    (c) 180 (d) 216

15. What is the least common multiple of 9, 12 and 24?
    (a) 48 (b) 54
    (c) 72 (d) 84

16. What is the least common multiple of 16, 24 and 30?
    (a) 120 (b) 180
    (c) 192 (d) 240

17. What is the least common multiple of 8, 9, 12 and 16?
    (a) 144 (b) 136
    (c) 128 (d) 120

18. The greatest number of four digits which is divisible by 15, 25, 40 and 75 is :
    (a) 9000 (b) 9400
    (c) 9600 (d) 9800

19. The product of two numbers is 4107. If the H.C.F. of these numbers is 37, then the greater number is :
    (a) 101 (b) 107
    (c) 111 (d) 185

LCM and HCF

20. What is the greatest common factor of 27 and 126?
    (a) 6   (b) 9
    (c) 18   (d) 27
21. What is the greatest common factor of 81 and 180?
    (a) 9   (b) 18
    (c) 27   (d) 36
22. Three numbers are in the ratio of 3: 4: 5 and their L.C.M. is 2400. Their H.C.F. is :
    (a) 40   (b) 80
    (c) 120   (d) 200
23. What is the greatest common factor of 126 and 196?
    (a) 28   (b) 21
    (c) 18   (d) 14
24. What is the greatest common factor of 180, 225 and 270?
    (a) 15   (b) 30
    (c) 45   (d) 60
25. What is the greatest common factor of 72 and 252?
    (a) 12   (b) 18
    (c) 45   (d) 36
26. What is the greatest common factor of 196 and 462?
    (a) 4   (b) 14
    (c) 22   (d) 28
27. The G.C.D. of 1.08, 0.36 and 0.9 is :
    (a) 0.03   (b) 0.9
    (c) 0.18   (d) 0.108
28. The product of two numbers is 2028 and their H.C.F. is 13. The number of such pairs is :
    (a) 1   (b) 2
    (c) 3   (d) 4
29. The least multiple of 7, which leaves a remainder of 4, when divided by 6, 9, 15 and 18 is :
    (a) 74   (b) 94
    (c) 184   (d) 364
30. The least number which should be added to 2497 so that the sum is exactly divisible by 5, 6, 4 and 3 is :
    (a) 3   (b) 13
    (c) 23   (d) 33
31. The least number which when divided by 5, 6, 7 and 8 leaves a remainder 3, but when divided by 9 leaves no remainder, is :
    (a) 1677   (b) 1683
    (c) 2523   (d) 3363
32. A, B and C start at the same time in the same direction to run around a circular stadium. A completes a round in 252 seconds, B in 308 seconds and C in 198 seconds, all starting at the same point. After what time will they meet at the starting point next?
    (a) 26 minutes and 18 seconds
    (b) 42 minutes and 36 seconds
    (c) 45 minutes
    (d) 46 minutes and 12 seconds
33. The ratio of two numbers is 3 : 4 and their H.C.F. is 4. Their L.C.M. is :
    (a) 12   (b) 16
    (c) 24   (d) 48
34. The greatest possible length which can be used to measure exactly the lengths 7 m, 3 m 85 cm, 12 m 95 cm is :
    (a) 15 cm   (b) 25 cm
    (c) 35 cm   (d) 42 cm
35. The least number, which when divided by 12, 15, 20 and 54 leaves in each case a remainder of 8 is :
    (a) 504   (b) 536
    (c) 544   (d) 548

HOTS

1. **Statement A:** If one of the two given numbers is a multiple of the other, the greater number is the L.C.M. of the given numbers.
   Statement B: The Highest Common Factor of two or more given numbers is the greatest among all their common factors.
   (a) Statement A is correct.
   (b) Statement B is correct.
   (c) Both are correct.
   (d) Both are incorrect.

2. **Statement A:** The multiples of 4 are 8, 12, 16, 20, 24....
   Statement B: The common multiples of 8 & 6 are 24 & 48.
   (a) Statement A is correct.
   (b) Statement B is correct.
   (c) Both are correct.
   (d) Both are incorrect.

3. **Statement A:** The L.C.M. of two or more numbers is the smallest number which is divisible by each one of the given numbers
   Statement B: The H.C.F. is the greatest number which divides two or more numbers without a remainder.
   (a) Statement A is correct.
   (b) Statement B is correct.
   (c) Both are correct.
   (d) Both are incorrect.

4. Beginning at 7:30 am, the Delhi Zoo starts tours of the tiger and elephant areas. Tours for the tiger area leave every 15 minutes. Tours of the elephant area leave every 20 minutes. How often do the tours leave at the same time?
   (a) Every 25 minutes
   (b) Every 30 minutes
   (c) Every 60 minutes
   (d) Every 45 minutes

5. If x is 6th multiple of 3 and y is 4th multiple of 3, then the LCM of x and y is _____.
   (a) 36
   (b) 72
   (c) 48
   (d) 54

LCM and HCF

SUBJECTIVE QUESTIONS

1. Find HCF of 64, 128 and 256.
   Solution:
   Factors of 64 are = 1, 2, 4, 8, 16, 32 and 64
   Factors of 128 = 1, 2, 4, 8, 16, 32, 64 and 128
   Factors of 256 = 1, 2, 4, 8, 16, 32, 64, 128 and 256
   Highest common factor of 64, 128 and 256 is 64.

2. The HCF of the two numbers is 29 & their sum is 174. What are the numbers?
   Solution:
   Let the two numbers be $29x$ and $29y$.
   Given, $29x + 29y = 174$
   $29(x + y) = 174$
   $x + y = 174/29 = 6$
   Since x and y are co-primes, therefore, possible combinations would be (1,5), (2,4), (3,3).
   The only combination that follows the co-prime part is (1,5)
   For (1,5): $29 x = 29 \times 1$ and $29 y = 29 (5)$
   = 145
   Therefore, the required numbers are 29 and 145.

3. What is the relation between L.C.M and H.C.F? Also, list some common rules of divisibility.
   Solution:
   Relationship between L.C.M. and H.C.F:
   L.C.M. × H.C.F. = Product of the two numbers
   Some common rules of Divisibility:
   (a) A number is divisible by 2 if it has 0 or an even number in its one's place.
   (b) A number is divisible by 3 if the sum of its digits is divisible by 3.
   (c) A number is divisible by 4 if the number formed by the tens and one's digits is divisible by 4.
   (d) A number is divisible by 5 if it has 0 or 5 in its one's place.
   (e) A number is divisible by 10 if it has 0 in its one's place.
   (f) If a number is divisible by another number, it is also divisible by each factor of that number.

4. Determine the LCM of 4 and 12 using the prime factorisation method.
   Solution:
   To find the LCM of 4 and 12 using the prime factorisation method, follow the below steps.
   Step 1: Find the prime factorization of given numbers:
   The prime factorisation of 4 is 2×2
   The prime factorisation of 12 is $2 \times 2 \times 3$.
   Step 2: The LCM of given numbers is found by multiplying the product of all factors. (Note: The common factor is included only once)
   Hence, the product of prime factors
   $= 2 \times 2 \times 3 = 12$.
   Therefore, the LCM of 4 and 12 is 12.

5. What is the LCM of 54 and 60?
   Solution:
   The prime factorisation of 54 is $2 \times 3 \times 3 \times 3$.
   The prime factorisation of 60 is $2 \times 2 \times 3 \times 5$.
   Thus, the product of prime factors
   $= 2 \times 2 \times 3 \times 3 \times 3 \times 5 = 540$
   Hence, the LCM of 54 and 60 is 540.

Ratio and Proportion

Learning Objectives : In this chapter, students will learn about:
- Relation between Ratio and Proportion
- Comparison of Ratio
- Checking Proportionality

CHAPTER SUMMARY

We use ratios to make comparisons between two or more similar things. For example we may use the concept of ratio in cooking. Your mother uses ingredients in a certain fixed ratio like ratio of flour to sugar There are three ways to write a ratio.

Ratio
Ratio defines the relationship between the quantities of two or more objects. It is used to compare the quantities of the same kind. If two or more ratios are equal, then it is said to be in proportion.
- In words : a is to b. Example, 3 is to 1.
- In odd notation: $a : b$. Example, 3 : 1.
- In fractional notation: a/b. Example, 3/1.

All three mean the one and the same thing. But, you should recognize all three notations.

Example : The ratio of dog with bone: dog without bone is 2 : 1.

The ratio of total number of dogs: dogs without bone is 6 : 3 = 2 : 1.

Note :
The order is very important, and must be followed. Let us understand with an example. Suppose there are 40 people, out of which 25 are men and 15 are women. So, if we say "the ratio of men to women", it will be "25 to 15" but if we say "the ratio of women to men", then it would be "15 to 25".

Example : There are 25 ducks and 9 birds in a certain park. Express the ratio of ducks to birds in all three formats.

Answer : The ratio of ducks to birds in all three formats are 25 : 9, 25 / 9, 25 to 9.

Example : Consider the above park. Express the ratio of birds to ducks in all three formats.

Answer : The ratio of birds to ducks in all three formats are 9 : 25, 9 / 25, 9 to 25

Did you know?
The ratio of length to breadth of Indian flag is 3 : 2 and breadth to length is 2 : 3.

Ratio
Ratio is generally expressed in its simplest form. If a and b are two numbers, then ratio of a to b is a/b or $a \div b$ and the ratio of b to a is b/a or $b \div a$. It is denoted by $a : b$ or $b : a$. The two quantities that are being compared are called terms. The first term is called antecedent and the second term is called consequent.

Relation between Ratio and Percentage
Ratio can be expressed in percentage. To express the value of a ratio in percentage, we multiply the ratio by 100.

Thus, $3/4 = (3/4) \times 100 = 75\%$.

Important properties
(i) If we multiply or divide the numerator and denominator of a ratio with the same number, the ratio remains same.
   Example : Consider 3/4, then $3/4 = (3 \times 5)/(4 \times 5)$ and $3/4 = [(3/2)/(4/2)]$.
(ii) If the ratio between two corresponding sides of two figures is $a : b$ then ratio of their areas will be $a^2 : b^2$.
   Example : Ratio between two diagonal of two squares is 2 : 1. What is the ratio of their areas?
   Answer : Ratio of their areas = $2^2 : 1^2 = 4 : 1$.
(iii) If the ratio between two corresponding sides of two figures (a three dimensional figure) is $a : b$ then ratio of their volumes is $a^3 : b^3$.

Example : If two full time employees accomplish 10 tasks in a week, how many such tasks will 10 employees accomplish in a week?

Answer : Let x is required no. of tasks then
$2 : 10 = 10 : x$
$\Rightarrow 2 \times x = 10 \times 10$
$\Rightarrow x = 50$ tasks

Comparison of Ratio
We can find greater or lesser ratio in a pair of two or more ratios. To understand the comparison of ratio, let us take an example.

Example : Which one of the two ratios is greater?
  4 : 5 or 5 : 6.

Answer :
1st ratio = 4/5 and 2nd ratio = 5/6
To compare, denominator of both should be made equal.
So, 4/5 or 5/6 are same as $(4 \times 6)/(5 \times 6)$ and $(5 \times 5)/(6 \times 5)$
Or, 24/30 and 25/30
∵ 25/30 is greater than 24/30
Hence, 5/6 > 4/5.

> **TRIVIA**
> Gender Ratio in the World in 2021 is 101.68 males per 100 females. There were more females than males until 1957.

Proportion
A proportion is a statement of the equality of two ratios. Proportion says that two ratios (or fractions) are equal.

It is denoted by $a : b :: c : d$. Here, a, b, c and d are the 1st 2nd, 3rd and 4th terms of the proportions. The first and fourth terms are called extremes and second and third terms are called the means. The product of the extremes is equal to the product of the means.

Hence $\boxed{a \times d = b \times c}$

Example : The ratio of dog with bone: dog without bone is 2 : 4 = 1 : 2 or 2 / 4= 1 / 2 are ways to write the proportion expressed as : 2 is to 4 as 1 is to 2.

The ratios are the same, so they are in proportion.

Note : When things are "in proportion" then their relative sizes are the same.

Here you can see that the ratios of head length to body length are the same in both drawings.

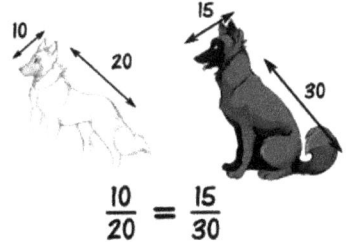

$$\frac{10}{20} = \frac{15}{30}$$

Find missing term

If any three terms in a proportion are given, the fourth may be found. If a, b, c and d are in proportion then

$a : b = c : d$ or $a/b = c/d$.

So, using the principals of manipulating equations, we see that

| $a = (b \times c) / d$ |
| $c = (a \times d) / b$ |
| $b = (a \times d) / c$ |
| $d = (b \times c) / a$ |

To remember this, assume there is proportion: $a / b = c / d$. For this, always $a \times d = b \times c$. Here "a" and "d" are extremes and "b" and "c" are means.

Example : You want to draw the dog's head, and would like to know how long it should be :

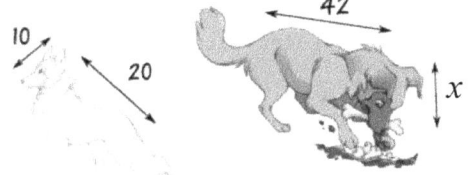

Let us write the proportion with the help of the 10/20 ratio from above:

Now we solve it using a special method :

Multiply across the known corners, then divide by the third number

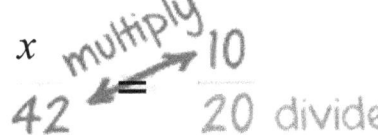

And you get this :

$x = (42 \times 10) / 20 = 420 / 20 = 21$

So you should draw the head 21 long.

Example : Find the value of x in $16 : 8 = x : 5$.

Answer : Given

$\Rightarrow \quad 16 : 8 = x : 5$

$\Rightarrow \quad 16/8 = x/5$

$\Rightarrow \quad x \times 8 = 16 \times 5$

$\quad x = 10$

Example : Find the value of x in $25 : 15 = 10 : x$.

Answer : We have

$25 : 15 = 10 : x$

$\Rightarrow \quad x \times 25 = 15 \times 10$

$\Rightarrow \quad x = 6$

Example : A pipe transfers 234 gallons of fuel to the tank of a ship in 4 hours. How long will it take to fill the tank of the ship that holds 4554 gallons?

Answer : Let x be the required time then
$$234 : 4 = 4554 : x$$
$$\Rightarrow x \times 234 = 4 \times 4554$$
$$\Rightarrow x = 77.8 \text{ hours}$$

Example : An iron pole 10 feet long weighs 20 kg. How much does an iron pole of the same width weigh if it is 18 feet long?

Answer : If x is required weight then
$$10 : 20 = 18 : x$$
$$\Rightarrow x \times 10 = 20 \times 18$$
$$\Rightarrow x = 36 \text{ kg}$$

Checking Proportionality

You may have to find if the two given ratios are in proportion or not. Understand it with an example.

Example : Is 20/150 proportional to 50/250?

Answer : For these ratios to be proportional we have to show that the product of the means is equal to the product of the extremes. So let us check:

Here, $250 \times 20 = 5000$
and $50 \times 150 = 7500$

You can see, they are not equal, so the answer is that they are not proportional.

Some More Examples

Example : The salaries of A, B and C are in the ratio 1 : 3 : 4. If the salaries are increased by 5%, 10% and 15% respectively, then what will be the increased salaries in the ratio?

Answer :
Let A's Salary = ₹ 100
Then, B's Salary = ₹ 300
And, C's Salary = ₹ 400

Salary given in 1 : 3 : 4 ratios.
Now,
A's Salary increases 5%, then
A's new Salary = (100 + 5% of 100)
= ₹ 105.
B's Salary increases 10%, then,
B's new Salary = (300 + 10% of 300)
= ₹ 330.
C's Salary increases 15%, then,
C's new Salary = (400 + 15% of 400)
= ₹ 460.
Then, ratio of increased salaries,
A : B : C = 105 : 330 : 460 = 21 : 66 : 92.

Alternative Method

100(A's Salary) = = = 5% ↑ = = =>
105 (A's increased Salary);
300 (B's Salary)= = = 10%
↑= = = > 330 (B's increased Salary);
400 (C's salary) = = =15% ↑ = = = > 460 (C's increased Salary).
Ratio of their increased Salary= 105 : 330 : 480 = 21 : 66 : 92

Example : In a class, the number of girls is 20% more than that of the boys. The strength of the class is 66. If 4 more girls are admitted to the class, what is the ratio of the number of boys to that of the girls?

Answer : According to question,
Girls: boys= 6 : 5;
Hence, No. of girls= 6 × 66/11= 36;
and No. of Boys = 66 – 36 = 30;
∴ Required ratio = 30 : (36+4) = 30 : 40 = 3 : 4.

Example : If two times A is equal to three times of B and also equal to four times of C, then find the value of A : B : C.

Answer : We have
2A = 3B;
Or, B= (2/3)A; And, 2A= 4C;
Or, C=(1/2)A;
Hence, A : B : C= A : 2A/3 : A/2= 1 : 2/3 : 1/2= 6 : 4 : 3

Example : If 30 oxen can plough 1/7th of a field in 2 days, how many days will 18 oxen take to do the remaining work?

Answer :

Using work equivalence method,
$30/18 = (1/7)/(6/7) \times x/2;$
$\Rightarrow \quad 5/3 = (1/6) \times x/2;$
$\Rightarrow \quad x = 60/3 = 20$ days.

Example : A box has 210 coins of denominations of one-rupee and fifty paise only. The ratio of their respective values is 13:11. Find the number of one-rupee coins.

Answer : Respective ratio of the number of coins;

$= 13 : (11 \times 2) = 13 : 22$

Hence, Number of 1 rupee coins;

$= 13 \times 210/(13+22) = \dfrac{13 \times 210}{35} = 78.$

MUST REMEMBER

- If a and b are two numbers, then ratio of a to b is a/b or $a \div b$ and the ratio of b to a is b/a or $b \div a$.
- Ratio can be expressed in percentage. To express the value of a ratio in percentage, we multiply the ratio by 100.
- If we multiply or divide the numerator and denominator of a ratio with the same number, the ratio remains same.
- If the ratio between two corresponding sides of two figures is $a : b$ then ratio of their areas will be $a^2 : b^2$.

MULTIPLE CHOICE QUESTIONS

1. The ratio of 90 cm to 1.5 m is.
   (a) 3 : 5   (b) 5 : 3
   (c) 60 : 1   (d) 4 : 3
2. 6 : 4 is equivalent to.
   (a) 2 : 3   (b) 3 : 2
   (c) 1 : 2   (d) 1 : 4
3. Find the ratio of 81 to 108.
   (a) 3 : 4   (b) 5 : 9
   (c) 4 : 3   (d) 9 : 20
4. Fill in the blank : 15 /18 = __/6
   (a) 5   (b) 4
   (c) 3   (d) 7
5. Find the value of × in 4 : 3 = x : 12.
   (a) 4   (b) 12
   (c) 16   (d) 3
6. In proportion first and the last terms are called _____.
   (a) Mean terms
   (b) Extreme terms
   (c) Middle terms
   (d) None of these
7. The ratio is said to be in simplest form if common factor is _____.
   (a) 1
   (b) 0
   (c) -1
   (d) None of these
8. Three terms a, b, c are said to be in proportion if _____.
   (a) $a : b = b : c$ (b) $a : b = c : b$
   (c) $b : a = c : a$ (d) $c : a = a : b$
9. Four terms a, b, c, d are said to be in proportion if.
   (a) $a : b = c : d$ (b) $a : c = d : b$
   (c) $a : d = b : c$ (d) None of these
10. If the cost of 6 cans of juice is ₹ 210, then what is the cost of 4 cans of juice?
    (a) ₹ 120   (b) ₹ 140
    (c) ₹ 100   (d) ₹ 80
11. Fill in the blank : 32 m : 64 m = 6 sec : _____.
    (a) 13 sec   (b) 12 sec
    (c) 8 sec   (d) 24 sec
12. Which of the following is correct :
    (a) 3 : 4 = 15 : 25
    (b) 12 : 24 = 6 : 12
    (c) 7 : 3 = 14 : 3
    (d) 5 : 10 = 9 : 20
13. 7 : 42 is equivalent ratio of.
    (a) 7 : 6   (b) 6 : 1
    (c) 1 : 6   (d) 6 : 7
14. Fill in the blank : 35 /42 = ___/6
    (a) 5   (b) 4
    (c) 3   (d) 7
15. Find the value of x in 3 : 4 = x : 16.
    (a) 4   (b) 16
    (c) 12   (d) 3
16. Two quantities can be compared only if they are in the same ____.
    (a) Ratio   (b) Units
    (c) Proportion (d) None of these
17. The ratio is said to be not in simplest form if common factor is _____.
    (a) 1   (b) Other than 1
    (c) 0   (d) None of these
18. In Proportion the Symbol :: is used for _____.
    (a) To show greater ratio
    (b) To equate the two ratios
    (c) To show smaller ratio
    (d) None of these.
19. The ratio 35 : 84 in simplest form is :
    (a) 5 : 7   (b) 7 : 12
    (c) 5 : 12   (d) None of these
20. In a class there are 20 boys and 15 girls. The ratio of boys to girls is :
    (a) 4 : 3   (b) 3 : 4
    (c) 4 : 5   (d) None of these

21. Two numbers are in the ratio 7: 9. If the sum of the numbers is 112, then the larger number is :
    (a) 49 (b) 72
    (c) 63 (d) 42
22. The ratio of 1.5 m to 10 cm is :
    (a) 1 : 15 (b) 15 : 10
    (c) 10 : 15 (d) 15 : 1
23. The ratio of 1 hour to 300 seconds is :
    (a) 1 : 12 (b) 12 : 1
    (c) 1 : 5 (d) 5 : 1
24. In 4 : 7 : : 16 : 28, 7 and 16 are called
    (a) Extreme terms
    (b) Means
    (c) 7 middle and 16 extreme term
    (d) None of these
25. The first, second and fourth terms of a proportion are 16, 24 and 54 respectively. Then the third term is :
    (a) 36 (b) 28
    (c) 48 (d) 32
26. If 12, 21, 72, 126 are in proportion, then:
    (a) 12 × 21 = 72 × 126
    (b) 12 × 72 = 21 × 126
    (c) 12 × 126 = 21 × 72
    (d) none of these
27. If x, y and z are in proportion, then :
    (a) $x : y :: z : x$ (b) $x : y :: y : z$
    (c) $x : y :: z : y$ (d) $x : z :: y : z$
28. The length and breadth of a rectangle are in the ratio 3 : 1. If the breadth is 7 cm, then the length of the rectangle is:
    (a) 14 cm (b) 16 cm
    (c) 18 cm (d) 21 cm
29. The value of m, if 3, 18, m, 42 are in proportion is :
    (a) 6 (b) 54
    (c) 7 (d) None of these
30. Length and width of a field are in the ratio 5 : 3. If the width of the field is 42 m then its length is :
    (a) 100 m (b) 80 m
    (c) 50 m (d) 70 m
31. If a:b:c=3:4:7, then the ratio (a+b+c):c is equal to
    (a) 2:1 (b) 14:3
    (c) 7:2 (d) 1:2
32. The number of students in 3 classes is in the ratio 2:3:4. If 12 students are increased in each class this ratio changes to 8:11:14. The total number of students in the three classes in the beginning was
    (a) 162 (b) 108
    (c) 96 (d) 54
33. If 2/3 of A=75% of B=0.6 of C, then A:B:C is
    (a) 2:3:3 (b) 3:4:5
    (c) 4:5:6 (d) 9:8:10
34. If A and B are in the ratio 3:4, and B and C in the ratio 12:13, then A and C will be in the ratio
    (a) 3:13 (b) 9:13
    (c) 36:13 (d) 13:9
35. In a school having roll strength 286, the ratio of boys and girls is 8 : 5. If 22 more girls get admitted into the school, the ratio of boys and girls becomes
    (a) 12 : 7 (b) 10 : 7
    (c) 8 : 7 (d) 4 : 3
36. Two numbers are in ratio 4 : 5 and their LCM is 180. The smaller number is
    (a) 9 (b) 15
    (c) 36 (d) 45
37. If A : B = 2 : 3, B : C = 4 : 5 and C : D = 5 : 9 then A : D is equal to
    (a) 11 : 17 (b) 8 : 27
    (c) 5 : 9 (d) 2 : 9
38. What must be added to each term of the ratio 7 : 11, so as to make it equal to 3 : 4?
    (a) 8 (b) 7.5
    (c) 6.5 (d) 5
39. Two numbers are in ratio 7 : 11. If 7 is added to each of the numbers, the ratio becomes 2 : 3. The smaller number is
    (a) 39 (b) 49
    (c) 66 (d) 77

40. The ratio of water and milk in a 30 litre mixture is 7 : 3. Find the quantity of water to be added to the mixture in order to make this ratio 6 : 1.
    (a) 30 litre   (b) 32 litre
    (c) 33 litre   (d) 35 litre

41. The difference between two positive numbers is 10 and the ratio between them is 5 : 3. Find the product of the two numbers.
    (a) 375   (b) 175
    (c) 275   (d) 125

42. A cat can do 5 leaps for every 4 leaps of a dog, but 3 leaps of the dog are equal to 4 leaps of the cat. What is the ratio of the speed of the cat to that of the dog?
    (a) 11 : 15   (b) 15 : 11
    (c) 16 : 15   (d) 15 : 16

43. The present ratio of ages of A and B is 4 : 5. 18 years ago, this ratio was 11 : 16. Find the sum of their present ages.
    (a) 90 years   (b) 105 years
    (c) 110 years   (d) 80 years

44. A dishonest milk man mixed 1 litre of water for every 3 litres of milk and thus made up 36 litres of milk. If he now adds 15 litres of milk to mixture, find the ratio of milk and water in the new mixture.
    (a) 12 : 5   (b) 14 : 3
    (c) 7 : 2   (d) 9 : 4

45. If the ratio of the ages of Maya and Chhaya is 6 : 5 at present, and fifteen years from now the ratio will get changed to 9 : 8, then find Maya's present age.
    (a) 24 years   (b) 30 years
    (c) 18 years   (d) 33 years

HOTS

1. What is the ratio of (● − ■) to ● ?

   (a) 4/11   (b) 5/11
   (c) 4/15   (d) 5/15

2. Ankita stitches a curtain that is 5 feet long and 3 feet wide. She stitches another curtain of with same ratio. If the breadth of the curtain is 9 feet, what is the length of the curtain.
   (a) 15 feet   (b) 12 feet
   (c) 14 feet   (d) 13 feet

3. This ratio in the simplest form $1\frac{1}{6} : 2\frac{5}{6}$
   (a) 17 : 6   (b) 7 : 17
   (c) 17 : 7   (d) 15 : 7

4. Hari can walk 12 km in 3 hours. How much can he walk in 8 hours, if he maintains the same speed all the time?
   (a) 29 km   (b) 34 km
   (c) 32 km   (d) 38 km

5. If the two numbers are in the ratio 4 : 3 and the sum of the two numbers is 56. Find the two numbers?
   (a) First number = 28, Second number = 20
   (b) First number = 24, Second number = 32
   (c) First number = 32, Second number = 24
   (d) First number = 32, Second number = 24

SUBJECTIVE QUESTIONS

1. Which of the following is a better buy?
   (a) 6 pens for ₹ 60
   (b) 4 pens for ₹ 36
   (c) 5 pens for ₹ 35
   (d) 8 pens for ₹ 48
   Solution:
   (a) Cost of 1 pen = $\dfrac{60}{6}$ = ₹ 10
   (b) Cost of 1 pen = $\dfrac{36}{4}$ = ₹ 9
   (c) Cost of 1 pen = $\dfrac{35}{5}$ = ₹ 7
   (d) Cost of 1 pen = $\dfrac{48}{8}$ = ₹ 8

   Hence, 4 pens for 36 is a better buy.

2. Navneet needs to fence the field shown is the figure below. How much wire will be needed?

   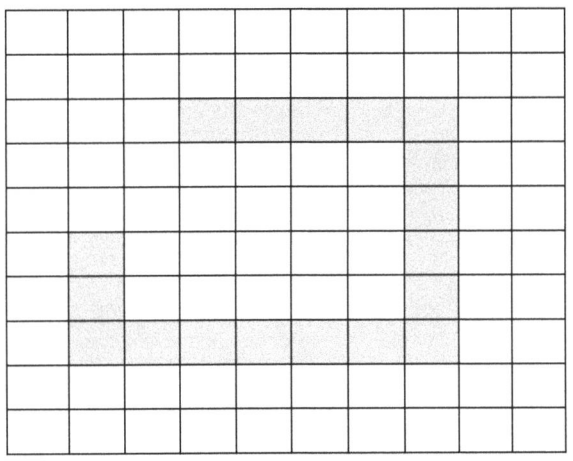

   1 unit/box = 3 meter
   Solution:
   As 1 unit/box is equivalent to 3 meters, we have marked the number using lines to indicate the numbers.

   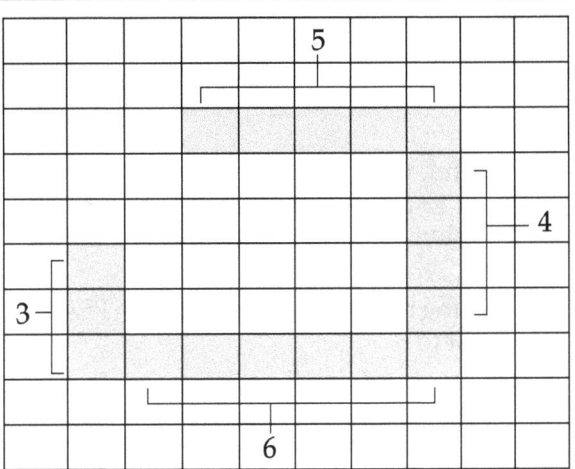

   Units around the field = 5 + 4 + 3 + 6 = 18
   Length of wire that will be needed
   = 18 × 3 = 54 meters

3. Match the following:

	List I		List II
A	5m to 200 cm	1	1:2
B	28 days to 5 weeks	2	5:2
C	240 seconds to 8 minutes	3	9:10
D	1800 ml to 2 litre	4	4:5

   Solution:
   5 m to 200 cm = 500 cm to 200 cm
   = $\dfrac{500}{200} = \dfrac{5}{2}$

   28 days to 5 weeks = 28 days to 35 days
   = $\dfrac{28}{35} = \dfrac{4}{5}$

   240 seconds to 8 minutes = 4 minutes to 8 minutes = $\dfrac{4}{8} = \dfrac{1}{2}$

   1800 ml to 2 litre = 1800 ml to 2000 ml
   = $\dfrac{1800}{2000} = \dfrac{9}{10}$

Ratio and Proportion

4. Compare the ratios 3 : 2 and 1 : 3?
   Solution:
   We can write
   $3:2 = \dfrac{3}{2}$ and $1:3 = \dfrac{1}{3}$

   To find, which Ratio is greater, we would need to convert the two Ratios into Like Fractions. LCM of Denominator 2 and 3 is 6.

   Making the Denominator of each Fraction equal to 6

   In case of Like Fractions, the Fraction whose numerator is greater is larger.

   Hence, we can say $\dfrac{9}{6} > \dfrac{2}{6}$

   That is $\dfrac{3}{2} > \dfrac{1}{3}$

   Hence, 3 : 2 > 1 : 3

5. Divide ₹ 1200 between A and B in the ratio 3 : 5?
   Solution:
   Total Sum of money = ₹ 1200
   Given ratio = 3 : 5
   Sum of ratio terms = (3 + 5) = 8
   A would receive $\dfrac{3}{8}$ part of ₹ 1200
   B would receive $\dfrac{5}{8}$ part of ₹ 1200

   That is,
   A's share = ₹ $\left(1200 \times \dfrac{3}{8}\right)$ = ₹ 450
   B's share = ₹ $\left(1200 \times \dfrac{5}{8}\right)$ = ₹ 750

Measurement

Learning Objectives : In this chapter, students will learn about:
- ✓ Length
- ✓ Weight
- ✓ Time
- ✓ Volume
- ✓ Clock
- ✓ Calendar

CHAPTER SUMMARY

Measurement is the action of measuring something. One can measure time, weight, temperature, length and more. If we didn't have measurement, it would be very hard to know when to go to school, how much is weight of 5 apples or is one suffering from fever or not. Life is so much easier when you know how to measure things, and that is why measurement is so important.

Length

The standard unit for measuring length is metre.

One meter equals roughly one long step of an adult man.

Length of cloth, the height of a wall, the height of tree, the distance between two objects are all measured in metres. Carpenters use measuring tape for measuring furniture. Cloth merchant uses a meter rod for measuring length of clothes.

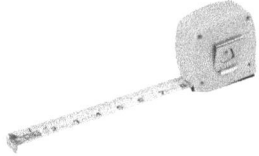

Measuring tape is also used by tailors for measuring length.

The metric system has prefix modifiers that are multiples of 10.
- A kilometre = 1000 metres
- A hectometre = 100 metres
- A decametre = 10 metres
- A decimetre = 1/10 metres
- A centimetre = 1/100 metres
- A millimetre = 1/1000 metres

As we move down the units, the next unit is one tenth as long. As we move upward, each unit is 10 times as long. One hundred millimetres, which is 1/10 metre (100/1000=1/10) are larger than one centimetre (1/100th metre).

Shortcut to Problem Solving for Length
- Always start from '0' while using measuring instruments.
  - Millimetre (mm) and centimetre (cm) are used to measure small objects.
  - Meter(m) is used to measure large objects.

- Meter (m) and kilometre (km) are used to measure large distances.
- Always convert the length of given objects into same unit of length before solving them.

Weight
The standard unit for measuring mass or weight is kilogram. We weigh things in kilograms. Lighter objects and smaller quantities of things are weighed in grams. We write Kilogram as kg and gram as gm.

 A paperclip weighs about 1 gram.

We commonly see cast iron weights in vegetable shops used to measure weight of vegetables.

Kilograms
Once you have 1,000 grams, you have 1 kilogram.

$\qquad$ 1 kilogram = 1,000 grams

Tonne
Tonnes (also called Metric Tons) are used to measure things that are very heavy.
Once you have 1,000 kilograms, you will have 1 tonne.

$\qquad$ 1 tonne = 1,000 kilograms

Things like cars, trucks and large cargo boxes are weighed using the tonne.

Shortcut to Problem Solving for Weight
- Always start from '0' while using weighing balance.
- Gram (gm) is used to weigh lighter objects.
- Kilogram (kg) is used to measure heavier objects.
- Always convert the weight of given objects into same unit of weight before adding or subtracting them.

Adding Feet and Inches
- Add the inches together.
- If the number of inches is greater than 12, divide the inches by 12.
- The quotient is the number of feet that need to be added to the other feet.
- The remainder is the number of extra inches.
- Add the original feet plus the whole feet resulting from the addition of the inches.

TRIVIA
A giraffe can clean its ears with its 21 inch tongue.

Example : Add 5 feet 8 inches plus 3 feet 10 inches.
- Add 8 inches to 10 inches : 8 + 10 = 18 inches
- The number of inches is greater than 12 so divide by 12 : 18 ÷ 12 = 1 foot 6 inches
- Add the Feet : 5 + 3 + 1 = 9 feet

Answer : 9 feet 6 inches

Subtract Feet and Inches
- If the number of inches being subtracted is greater than the number of inches in the length that is being subtracted from, decrease the number of feet by one and increase the number of inches by 12 in the length from which you are subtracting.
- Subtract the inches.

- Subtract the feet.

Example : Subtract 3 feet 10 inches from 6 feet 8 inches.

Sol. The number of inches being subtracted is larger so adjust the number of inches:

  6 feet 8 inches = 5 feet 20 inches
- Subtract the inches : 20 – 10 = 10 inches
- Subtract the feet : 5 – 3 = 2 feet

Answer : 2 feet 10 inches

Volume

The capacity of a container is the maximum amount of liquid it can hold. The standard unit for measuring capacity is litre.

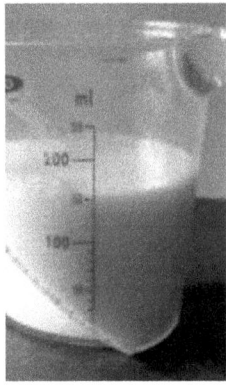

Milliliters are often written as ml (for short), so "100 ml" means "100 milliliters".

Here we have 150 ml of milk in a measuring cup.

It doesn't say "150" ... it says "50" ... but it is half-way between 100 and 200 so you can figure out it is 150 ml. A litre is the basic unit of volume

The metric system has prefix modifiers that are multiples of 10.
- A kilolitre = 1000 litres
- A hectolitre = 100 litres
- A decalitre = 10 litres
- A decilitre = 1/10 litre
- A centilitre = 1/100 litre
- A millilitre = 1/1000 litre

As we move down the units, the next unit is one tenth as large. As we move upward, each unit is 10 times as large. One hundred millilitres, which is 1/10 litre (100/1000=1/10) are larger than one centilitre (1/100th litre).

Shortcut to Problem Solving for Volume
- Always use a container of capacity 1 litre to find the capacity of other containers
- To find the volume of a liquid, just pour it in a container with a measuring scale marked on it.
- Millilitre is used to measure smaller quantity of liquids.
- Litre is used to measure greater quantity of liquids.
- Always convert the volume of given liquids into same unit of volume before adding or subtracting them.

Time

The time between one midnight and the next midnight is called one day. The hour hand goes twice round the clock face in one day.

∴ 1 day = 24 hours

We divide a day as follows :

(*i*) Morning (*ii*) Noon (*iii*) Evening.

The time between mid night and noon is called ante meridien (a m or am), that is before Noon.

The time between noon and mid night is called post-meridien (PM or p.m.), that is after noon.

Relationship between Hours, Minutes and Seconds

  1 hour = 60 minutes
  1 minute = 60 seconds

Clock

Look at the clock-face given below. It has three hands. Shorter hand (hour hand), longer hand (minute-hand) and the longest hand (second hand). The face of the clock is divide into 12 equal big divisions marked as 1, 2, 3, 4, 5, 6, 7, 8, 9, 10, 11 and 12 or i, ii, iii, iv, v, vi, vii, viii, ix, x, xi, xii.

There are five small divisions between two

successive numbers. So, there are 60 small divisions in all. Each big division represents an hour ard each small division represents a minute.

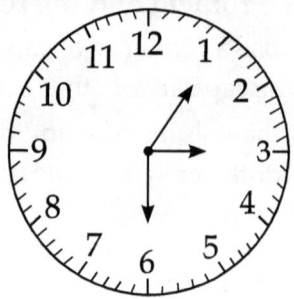

Calendar
A week has seven days. The days of a week are Sunday, Monday, Tuesday, Wednesday Thursday, Friday and Saturday.
A Year has 12 months called calender months

Month		Days
January	–	31
February	–	28 or 29
March	–	31
April	–	30
May	–	31
June	–	30
July	–	31
August	–	31
September	–	30
October	–	31
November	–	30
December	–	31

Note: If the name of the month is not mentioned, then take the number of days in it to be 30 days.

Leap Year
There are 365 days in a year. A leap year has 366 days. An year which is exactly divisible by 4 is a leap year. e.g., 1996, 2000 etc.

Note: The years divisible by 100 but not by 400 are not leap years.

Conversions
1 hour = 60 minutes
1 minute = 60 seconds
1 day = 24 hours
1 week = 7 days
1 year = 12 months
1 year = 365 days
1 leap year = 366 days
1 month = 30 or 31 days

Various Operations on Time
With the help of above relations we can convert years into months, and weeks into days and days into hours, minutes and seconds.

Example : Convert:
(a) 5 months into days
(b) 6 weeks and 2 days into days
(c) 3 hours 30 minutes into minutes
(d) 4 minutes 20 seconds into seconds

Answer :
(a) ∵ 1 month = 30 days
∴ 5 months = 5 × 30 = 150 days
(b) 1 week = 7 days
6 weeks = 6 × 7 = 42 days
∴ 6 weeks and 2 days = 42 + 2 = 44 days
(c) ∵ 1 hour = 60 minutes
∴ 3 hours = 3 × 60 = 180 minutes
∴ 3 hours 30 minutes = 180 + 30 = 210 minutes
(d) ∵ 1 minute = 60 seconds
∴ 4 minutes = 4 × 60 = 240 seconds
∴ 4 minutes 20 seconds = 240 + 20 = 260 seconds

MUST REMEMBER

- The standard unit for measuring mass or weight is kilogram.
- The capacity of a container is the maximum amount of liquid it can hold. The standard unit for measuring capacity is litre.
- Temperature tells how hot or cold a thing is. It is measured by an instrument, called thermometer.
- Water freezes at 0° Celsius and boils at 100° Celsius. Water freezes at 32° Fahrenheit and boils at 212°
- The time between one midnight and the next midnight is called one day. The hour hand goes twice round the clock face in one day.
- The time between midnight and noon is called ante meridien (a m or a m), that is before Noon. The time between noon and mid night is called post-meridien (PM or p.m.), that is after noon.

MULTIPLE CHOICE QUESTIONS

1. Shraddha has written following statements about the metric unit she would use to measure some objects. Find the incorrect sentence among them :
   (a) Centimetre is used to measure the length of a pencil.
   (b) Kilometre is used to measure distance from any city to another.
   (c) Metre is used to measure depth of a bucket.
   (d) Metre is used to measure height of a tree.

2. A carpenter was putting up a shelf. Shelf has to be 86 cm long but piece of wood he had was 1 m and 26 cm long. His saw was 33 cm long. How much wood did he have to cut off to make it fit?
   (a) 40 cm   (b) 43 cm
   (c) 50 cm   (d) 53 cm

3. If 1 metre : 100 centimetre : : then 1 kilometre : ?
   (a) 100 metre
   (b) 100 centimetre
   (c) 1000 metre
   (d) 1000 centimetre

Direction (4–6) : Add the following capacities:

4. 25 l 850 ml and 19 l 390 ml.
   (a) 45 l 240 ml
   (b) 46 l 245 ml
   (c) 40 l 240 ml
   (d) 45 l 290 ml

5. 17 l 708 ml and 13 l 993 ml
   (a) 30 l 700 ml
   (b) 31 l 701 ml
   (c) 31 l 700 ml
   (d) 32 l 750 ml

6. 75 l 955 ml and 12 l 938 ml
   (a) 80 l 30 ml
   (b) 85 l 35 ml
   (c) 88 l 893 ml
   (d) 84 l 345 ml

7. A container has 2550 ml of water. How many litres and millilitres of water is there in the container?
   (a) 2 l 500 ml
   (b) 2 l 525 ml
   (c) 2 l 505 ml
   (d) 2 l 550 ml

8. Rohan bought a 50 l container of oil. He used 44 litres 300 ml of it. How much oil is left?
   (a) 5 l 700 ml
   (b) 6 l 700 ml
   (c) 5 l 300 ml
   (d) 6 l 300 ml

9. A jar can hold 4 l 250 ml honey. How much honey will be needed to fill 4 jars?
   (a) 16 litres
   (b) 15 litres
   (c) 17 litres
   (d) 17 l 250 ml

10. Shraddha needs 6 containers which can hold 15 l 600 ml oil. Find the capacity of each container.
    (a) 2 l 500 ml
    (b) 2 l 600 ml
    (c) 3 l 200 ml
    (d) 2 l 100 ml

11. If the cost of 1 litre of cough syrup is ₹ 480. 40, find the cost of 500 ml.
    (a) ₹ 200.40
    (b) ₹ 220.40
    (c) ₹ 260.40
    (d) ₹ 240.20

12. Three large containers of water, each holding 15 l 500 ml, are poured into a water tank. How much water is there in the tank now?
    (a) 46 l 500 ml
    (b) 45 l 500 ml
    (c) 45 l 200 ml
    (d) 46 l 200 ml

Direction (13–17): Read the table given below and answer the questions:

Giraffes	Height of Giraffes
1.	438 cm
2.	620 cm
3.	286 cm
4.	526 cm

13. Which is the tallest Giraffe?
    (a) 4   (b) 3
    (c) 2   (d) 1
14. How much taller is Giraffe 2 than 1?
    (a) 180 cm   (b) 181 cm
    (c) 182 cm   (d) 183 cm
15. How much shorter is Giraffe 3 than 4?
    (a) 210 cm   (b) 220 cm
    (c) 230 cm   (d) 240 cm
16. Which is the shortest Giraffe?
    (a) 4   (b) 3
    (c) 2   (d) 1
17. How much taller is the tallest Giraffe than the shortest Giraffe?
    (a) 331 cm   (b) 332 cm
    (c) 333 cm   (d) 334 cm
18. The length of your little finger is about
    (a) 1.5 mm   (b) 1.5 cm
    (c) 1.5 m   (d) 1.5 km
19. The distance from New York (US) to Southampton (UK) is about
    (a) 5,500 mm   (b) 5,500 cm
    (c) 5,500 m   (d) 5,500 km
20. The height of a male basketball player is about
    (a) 2 mm   (b) 2 cm
    (c) 2 m   (d) 2 km
21. To convert minutes into seconds we multiply the number of minutes by
    (a) 70   (b) 60
    (c) 30   (d) 50
22. The time from 12'O clock noon to 12'O clock mid-night is called.
    (a) am
    (b) pm
    (c) both (a) and (b)
    (d) none of these
23. The number of seconds in 7 minutes is
    (a) 400 sec
    (b) 320 sec
    (c) 420 sec
    (d) 460 sec
24. The time from 12'O clock midnight to 12'O clock-noon is
    (a) am
    (b) pm
    (c) both (a) and (b)
    (d) None of these
25. The number of seconds in 5 minutes is
    (a) 400 sec   (b) 500 sec
    (c) 100 sec   (d) 300 sec
26. To convert hours into seconds, we multiply the number of hours by
    (a) 60   (b) 1200
    (c) 3600   (d) 300'

Measurement

27. To convert hours into minutes, we multiply the number of hours by
    (a) 60　　　　　　(b) 120
    (c) 360　　　　　 (d) 120

28. To convert days into hours we multiply the no. of days by
    (a) 20　　　　　　(b) 30
    (c) 24　　　　　　(d) 31

29. The number of days in the month of February in a leap year is
    (a) 30　　　　　　(b) 29
    (c) 31　　　　　　(d) All of them

30. To convert seconds into minutes we divide the number of seconds by
    (a) 60　　　　　　(b) 120
    (c) 30　　　　　　(d) None of these

HOTS

1. Shubhra participated in a race. She took 1 hour 36 minutes and 14 seconds to complete the race. How many seconds did she take to complete the race?
   (a) 2220 seconds　　(b) 2234 seconds
   (c) 5760 seconds　　(d) 5774 seconds

2. Golu has holidays on every second and fourth Saturday of a month. On which dates does he have holidays in January 2015?

   2015 JANUARY

Sunday	Monday	Tuesday	Wednesday	Thursday	Friday	Saturday
				1	2	3
4	5	6	7	8	9	10
11	12	13	14	15	16	17
18	19	20	21	22	23	24
25	26	27	28	29	30	31

   (a) 3rd and 31st　　(b) 3th and 17th
   (c) 1st and 22nd　　(d) 10th and 24th

3. Look at the calendar. What best describes the dates that are on Saturdays?

Sunday	Monday	Tuesday	Wednesday	Thursday	Friday	Saturday
March 2015						
1	2	3	4	5	6	7
8	9	10	11	12	13	14
15	16	17	18	19	20	21
22	23	24	25	26	27	28
29	30	30	31	Note:		

   (a) Multiples of 2　　(b) Multiples of 3
   (c) Multiples of 4　　(d) Multiples of 7

4. Praveen bought 5 tins of orange juice each containing 0.75 litre of orange juice. He poured the orange juice into a 6-litre container. How many more tins must Praveen buy to fill up the container with orange juice?
   (a) 30　　　　　　(b) 2
   (c) 5　　　　　　 (d) 3

5. The ratio of Anita's mass to Mamata's mass is 4:7. If their total mass is 99 kg, what is Mamata's mass?
   (a) 63 kg　　　　　(b) 45 kg
   (c) 36 kg　　　　　(d) 54 kg

SUBJECTIVE QUESTIONS

1. Beena bought 3 kg 760 grams of wool to make a carpet. How much more wool does she need to make the weight 4 kg?
   Solution:
   Given the weight of wool = 3 kg 760 grams
   Let us convert this weight into grams.
   3 kg 760 grams = (3 × 1000 + 760) grams
   = (3000 + 760) grams
   = 3760 grams
   4 kg = (4 × 1000) grams = 4000 grams
   Difference
   = (4000 – 3760) grams = 240 grams
   Therefore, 240 grams of more wool will be required.

2. A furlong is a unit of length used in horse racing; it equals one-eighth of a mile. To the nearest tenth, how many metres are equal to a furlong if 1.609 km equals a mile?
   Solution:
   Given,
   1.609 km = 1 mile
   That means 1609 m = 1 mile
   Also, one furlong = one-eighth of a mile
   = (1/8) × 1.609 km
   = (1/8) × 1609 m
   = 201.125
   = 201.1 m (approx.)

3. The cost of 1 litre of syrup is Rs. 840.80. Find the cost of 600 ml of the syrup.
   Solution:
   Given,
   The cost of 1 litre of syrup = Rs. 840.80
   As we know,
   1 litre = 1000 ml
   The cost of 600 ml of the syrup = (600/1000) × Rs. 840.80 = Rs. 504.48

4. Vinu and Shan together weigh 72 kg 350 g. If Vinu weighs 39 kg 185 g, what is Shan's weight?
   Solution:
   Given,
   Vinu's weight = 39 kg 185 g
   Let x be Shan's weight.
   According to the given,
   39 kg 185 g + x = 72 kg 350 g
   x = 72 kg 350 g – 39 kg 185 g
   = (72 – 39) kg (350 – 185) g
   = 33 kg 165 g
   Therefore, Shan's weight is 33 kg 165 g.

5. A tabletop measures 2 m 25 cm by 1 m 50 cm. What is the perimeter of the tabletop?
   Solution:
   We know that,
   1 m = 100 cm
   1 cm = 0.01 m
   Length of tabletop = 2 m 25 cm = 2.25 m
   Breadth of tabletop = 1 m 50 cm = 1.50 m
   Perimeter of tabletop
   = 2 (Length + Breadth)
   = 2 (2.25 + 1.50)
   = 2 (3.75)
   = 2 × 3.75
   = 7.5 m
   Therefore, the perimeter of the tabletop is 7.5 m.

Temperature   9

Learning Objectives : In this chapter, students will learn about:
- ✓ Temperature
- ✓ Units of Measurement of Temperature
- ✓ Conversions
- ✓ Thermometer

CHAPTER SUMMARY

Temperature is how hot or cold something is. Our bodies can feel the difference between something which is hot and something which is cold. To measure temperature more accurately, a thermometer can be used.

In the early years of the eighteenth century, Gabriel Fahrenheit (1686-1736) created the Fahrenheit scale. The celsius scale is known as universal system unit. It is used throughout science and in most countries.

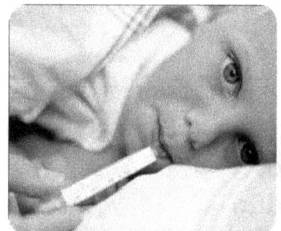 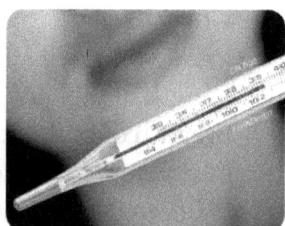

Temperature
It is the degree of hotness or coldness of a body or environment around us. It is measured in a unit which is called as degree.

Units of Measurement of Temperature
There are two main temperature scales :
- °F, the Fahrenheit Scale (used in the US), and
- °C, the Celsius Scale (used in most other countries)

You can see this being represented in the figure below:

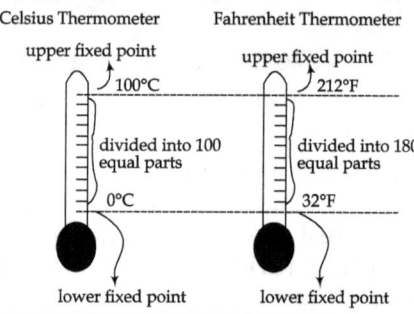

They both measure the same thing (temperature), but use different numbers.
- Boiling water (at normal pressure) measures 100° in Celsius, but 212° in Fahrenheit
- And as water freezes it measures 0° in Celsius, but 32° in Fahrenheit

The difference between freezing and boiling is 100° in Celsius, but 180° in Fahrenheit.
- The temperature of our body is about 37°C or 98.6°F.

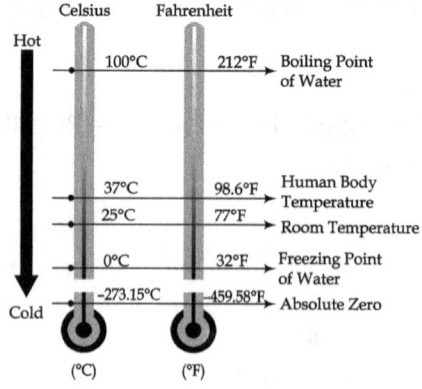

Conversions
Points to see here:
- The scales start at a different number (0 vs 32), so we will need to add or subtract 32.
- The scales rise is at a different rate (100 vs 180), so we will also need to multiply.

And this is how it works out:

- To convert from Celsius to Fahrenheit, first multiply by 180/100, then add 32
- To convert from Fahrenheit to Celsius, first subtract 32, then multiply by 100/180

Note : 180/100 can be simplified to 9/5, and likewise 100/180=5/9, so this is the easiest way:

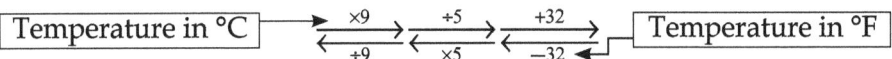

You can remember their formula as :

Celsius to Fahrenheit	(°C × 9/5) + 32 = °F or °C × 1.8 + 32 = °F
Fahrenheit to Celsius	(°F − 32) × 5/9 = °C or (°F − 32)/1.8 = °C

Note : For conversion
1. Celsius to Fahrenheit : (°C × 2) less 10% + 32 = °F
2. To remember 9/5 for °C to °F think "F is greater than C, so there are more °F than °C"

TRIVIA

Fahrenheit and Celsius are equal at −40 degrees.

Example : Convert 26° Celsius to Fahrenheit.
First : 26° × 9/5 = 234/5 = 46.8
Then : 46.8 + 32 = 78.8° F

Example : Convert 98.6° Fahrenheit to Celsius.
First : 98.6° − 32 = 66.6
Then : 66.6 × 5/9 = 333/9 = 37° C

Example : Convert 20° Celsius to Fahrenheit (we will use the above discussed tip)
- 20 × 2 = 40
- less 10% = 40 − $\frac{40 \times 10}{100}$ = 40 − 4 = 36
- 36+32 = 68° F

Since both scales cross at −40° (−40° C equals −40° F) you can:
- add 40,
- multiply by 5/9 (for °F to °C), or 9/5 (for °C to °F)
- subtract 40

Example : Convert 10° Celsius to Fahrenheit
- 10 + 40 = 50
- 50 × 9/5 = 90
- 90 − 40 = 50° F

Typical Temperatures

°C	°F	Description
100	212	Water boils
40	104	Hot Bath
37	98.6	Body temperature
30	86	Beach weather
21	70	Room temperature
10	50	Cool Day
0	32	Freezing point of water
−18	0	Very Cold Day
−40	−40	Extremely Cold Day (and the same number!)

Thermometer
It is used to measure the temperature. A small glass thermometer is designed with a narrowing above the bulb so that the mercury

column stays in position when the instrument is removed from the body.

Thermometer was made containing mercury, but today thermometers no longer contain mercury due to potential health risks; they are filled with a combination of mineral spirits or alcohol mixed with red dye. The problem with a mercury thermometer is that the device can break, spilling mercury and posing a risk to human or animal health.

Such thermometers can also be difficult to use, as they need to be held in place for several minutes, and they need to be swung to reset, as the thermometer is designed to hold the mercury in place once a maximum temperature has been reached so that the device can be taken out for an accurate reading.

In these thermometers, the red liquid rises and falls as it gets hotter or cooler. The hotter the temperature, the higher the liquid climbs upward in the thermometer. The lower the temperature, the lower it goes down the thermometer.

Did you know?

- The hottest temperature ever recorded on earth is 57.8°C (136 °F). It is recorded in Al' Aziziyah, Libya on September 13, 1922.
- The coldest temperature ever recorded on earth is –89.2°C (–128 °F). It is recorded in Vostak Station, Antarctica on July 21, 1983.
- Celsius and Fahrenheit are equal at point –40 degrees.
- Not all liquid boil at 100°C and freeze at 0°C. This is the melting and freezing point of water only. Each and every liquid has different properties and thus melt and freeze at different temperatures.

MUST REMEMBER

➡ There are two main temperature scales :
➡ °F, the Fahrenheit Scale (used in the US), and
➡ °C, the Celsius Scale (used in most other countries)
➡ In these thermometers, the red liquid rises and falls as it gets hotter or cooler. The hotter the temperature, the higher the liquid climbs upward in the thermometer. The lower the temperature, the lower it goes down the thermometer

MULTIPLE CHOICE QUESTIONS

1. Ten celsius equals _Fahrenhiet.
   (a) 20^0 (b) 30^0
   (c) 40^0 (d) 50^0
2. Convert 32° Celsius to Fahrenheit.
   (a) 100°F (b) 89.6°F
   (c) 57.6°F (d) 0°F
3. Eighty Fahrenheit is _ Celsius.
   (a) 17^0 (b) 27^0
   (c) 37^0 (d) 47^0
4. Which is the formula to convert Celsius to Fahrenheit?
   (a) $T_f = 1.8 \times T_c + 52$ (b) $T_f = 1.8 \times T_c + 42$
   (c) $T_f = 1.8 \times T_c + 32$ (d) None of these
5. Convert 11° Celsius to Fahrenheit.
   (a) 51.8°F (b) 19.8°F
   (c) 6.11°F (d) –11.67°F
6. Convert 68° Fahrenheit to Celsius.
   (a) 154.4°C (b) 64.8°C
   (c) 55.6°C (d) 20°C
7. Convert 18° Fahrenheit to Celsius.
   (a) –25.2°C (b) –7.8°C
   (c) 7.8°C (d) 64.4°C
8. The highest temperature ever recorded on Earth was 57.8°C, in Libya, Africa in 1922. How many degrees Fahrenheit was this, to the nearest degree?
   (a) 14°F (b) 104°F
   (c) 136°F (d) 140°F
9. The highest temperature ever recorded in the UK was 101.3°F, recorded in Kent in 2003. How many degrees Celsius was this?
   (a) 38.5°C (b) 39.5°C
   (c) 56.3°C (d) 214.3°C
10. Convert 41° Fahrenheit to Celsius:
    (a) 5 °C (b) – 25.2°C
    (c) – 5 °C (d) 7.8°C
11. The lowest temperature ever recorded on Earth was – 89.2°C, recorded in Antarctica in 1983. How many degrees Fahrenheit was that, to the nearest degree?
    (a) – 67°F (b) – 82°F
    (c) – 129°F (d) – 193°F
12. Convert 13° Fahrenheit to Celsius:
    (a) – 10.6 (b) 45.0°C
    (c) 88.2°C (d) – 20.4°C
13. The fastest temperature drop ever recorded was 49°F in 15 minutes, recorded in Rapid City, South Dakota, USA in 1911. How many degrees Celsius was this?
    (a) 9.4°C (b) 27.2°C
    (c) 45.0°C (d) 88.2°C
14. What is the formula to convert to fahrenheit to celsius?
    (a) $T_c = ((T_f - 32) / 9) \times 5$
    (b) $T_c = ((T_f - 32) / 9) \times 6$
    (c) $T_c = ((T_f - 32) / 9) \times 7$
    (d) None of the above
15. Convert 100° Celsius to Fahrenheit
    (a) 212°F (b) 51.8°F
    (c) 20.8°F (d) 29.11°F
16. Convert 19° Celsius to Fahrenheit
    (a) 15.8°F (b) 66.2° F
    (c) 49.11°F (d) 71.60°F
17. On the Fahrenheit scale, the freezing point of water is ____ degrees and the boiling point is ____ degrees.
    (a) 32, 212 (b) 30, 220
    (c) 25, 200 (d) 40, 100
18. The Celsius temperature scale is still sometimes referred to as the scale.
    (a) Kelvin scale (b) Absolute
    (c) Centigrade (d) None of these
19. Convert 14° Celsius to Fahrenheit.
    (a) 89.8°F (b) 9.8°F
    (c) 57.2°F (d) 64.11°F
20. Convert 73° Fahrenheit to Celsius.
    (a) 14.2°C (b) 22.8 °
    (c) 64.3°C (d) 55.1°C

Temperature

HOTS

1. Choose the correct option.
   (a) 95°C = 105°F
   (b) 60°C = 120°F
   (c) 33°C = 95°F
   (d) 75°C = 167°F

2. What temperature is shown on the thermometer?
   (a) 33 degree   (b) 38 degree
   (c) 39 degree   (d) 32 degree

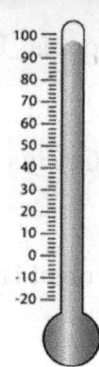

3. What temperature is shown on the thermometer?
   (a) 91 degree   (b) 99 degree
   (c) 94 degree   (d) 100 degree

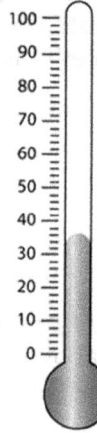

4. The temperature of water in a swimming pool is 51°F. As the freezing point of water is 32°F, how many degrees would the water temperature of the water have to drop to reach the freezing point?
   (a) 19°F   (b) 11°F
   (c) 20°F   (d) 15°F

5. Observe the given thermometer. Which temperature of human beings does the thermometer show?

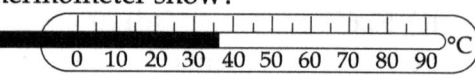

   (a) High fever
   (b) Low fever
   (c) Normal body temperature
   (d) Very high fever

SUBJECTIVE QUESTIONS

1. What temperature is shown in below figures:

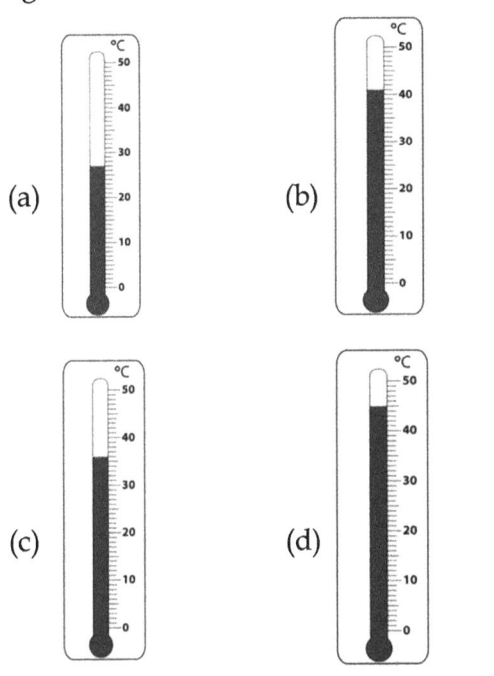

Solution:
(a) The tip of the fluid showing the temperature is at 27 degrees. Thus, the temperature that is shown by the thermometer is 27 degrees.
(b) The tip of the fluid showing the temperature is at 41 degrees. Thus, the temperature that is shown by the thermometer is 41 degrees.
(c) The tip of the fluid showing the temperature is at 36 degrees. Thus, the temperature that is shown by the thermometer is 36 degrees.
(d) The tip of the fluid showing the temperature is at 45 degrees. Thus, the temperature that is shown by the thermometer is 45 degrees.

2. Compare each pair of thermometers and choose the one which has low temperature

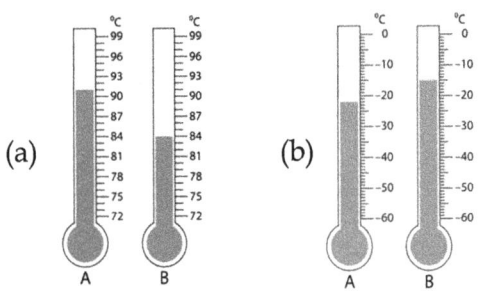

Solution:
(a) You can clearly see, Thermometer A reads 91 and Thermometer B reads 84. Hence, thermometer B has low temperature than A.
(b) You can clearly see, thermometer A reads –22 and Thermometer B reads –15. Hence, thermometer A has low temperature than B.

3. An industrial machine heats up to 161°F when it's being used. After being unused for an hour the temperature drops to 144°F. How much did the machine cool off?

Solution:
Temperature of machine when it is used = 161°F; temperature of machine when left unused for an hour = 144°F, Drop in temperature of the machine
= (161 – 144) = 17°F.

4. Convert the following given temperatures from degree Fahrenheit- to degree Celsius.
86°F=_____°C

Solution:
86 – 32 = 54;
54 × 5 = 270;
270 ÷ 9 = 300°C

5. The temperature in these cities were noted at 3 am on the same day. Look at the table and answer the questions.

Temperature

(a) Which place had the lowest temperature at 3 am? Imagine yourself being there and describe how it would feel.
(b) What is the difference between the temperatures at 3 pm and 3 am in Chennai? In Bhopal?

City	Temperature at 3 am
Chennai	21.1
Mumbai	19.0
Th'puram	21.6
Kolkata	13.1
Bhopal	9.8
Srinagar	1.3
Guwahati	12.8
Jaipur	10.2

Answer:
(a) Srinagar had the lowest temperature at 3 am 1.3°C temperature means it would be cold, and water would be frozen to ice. People living there should wear woollen clothes and sit near the fire to keep themselves warm.
(b) The difference in temperature in Chennai is given below.
Temperature at 3 pm = 29.9°C
Temperature at 3 am = 21.1°C
So, the difference = 29.9 – 21.1 = 8.8°C
The difference in temperature in Bhopal is given below.
Temperature at 3 pm = 25.9°C
Temperature at 3 am = 9.8°C
So, the difference = 25.9 – 9.8 = 16.1°C

Money 10

Learning Objectives : In this chapter, students will learn about:
- ✓ Unit of Currency in India
- ✓ Misconception/Fact

CHAPTER SUMMARY

"Money doesn't grow on trees". You all must have heard this from your parents when you wanted to buy your favorite toy? But do you know what is money? If you go to a shop and ask for your favourite chocolate, the shopkeeper ask you to give 20 rupees to get the chocolate, right? This is called money. Thus, money is what we give for buying food, toys, clothes, bikes, houses, etc. Money is something that everyone accepts in exchange for goods or services.

Unit of Currency in India

The unit of currency in India is Rupees and one Rupee = 100 paisa
- 10 coins of 10 paisa make one Rupee
- 2 coins of 50 paisa make one Rupee
- 4 coins of 25 paisa make one Rupee
- 1 coin of 50 paisa and 2 coins of 25 paisa make one Rupee

The paper based notes available in India are of ₹ 2000, ₹ 500, ₹ 200, ₹ 100, ₹ 50, ₹ 20, ₹ 10, ₹ 5 as shown below :

Till few years back there were paper notes for ₹ 2000, ₹ 2 and ₹ 1 as well but they are no longer in use. Their picture is as shown below :

The coins available in India for circulation are of ₹ 20, ₹ 10, ₹ 5, ₹ 2 and ₹ 1. Some of them are shown below :

Few important currencies of the world are United States – Dollars, UK – Pound and in most European countries it is Euro.

When one goes to market to purchase and gives more money than the price of material, then the shopkeeper will return the extra money. That returned money is known as change.

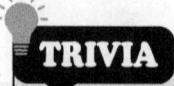

Paper money was first used in China over 1,000 years ago.

Misconception/Fact

Misconception : If a paper note is mutilated or torn, then you lose money as you feel that it cannot be used as no shopkeeper is ready to take it.

Fact : Mutilated notes can be tendered at all bank branches for exchange. Payment exchange value of mutilated notes is governed by the Reserve Bank of India (Note Refund) Rules and one can get full/half/no value depending on the condition of the note.

- Few important currencies of the world are United States – Dollars, UK – Pound and in most European countries it is Euro.
- When one goes to market to purchase and gives more money than the price of material, then the shopkeeper will return the extra money. That returned money is known as change.
- Mutilated notes can be tendered at all bank branches for exchange.

MULTIPLE CHOICE QUESTIONS

1. Golu went to purchase cricket kit and gave two coins of ₹ 5, four notes of ₹ 10, three notes of ₹ 50 and two notes of ₹ 500 to cashier. If the price of cricket kit was ₹ 1162, the change that he would have got back is _____.
   (a) ₹ 38 (b) ₹ 15
   (c) ₹ 30 (d) ₹ 32

2. Kapil bought 5 cookies all having equal price. If the total amount paid is ₹ 33, what was the price of one cookie?
   (a) ₹ 5 (b) ₹ 5.50
   (c) ₹ 6.00 (d) ₹ 6.60

Direction (3-7) : Consider the prices of these items below to answer questions.

   Apple _____ ₹ 180 per kg
   Pen _____ ₹ 8 per piece
   Eraser _____ ₹ 5 for 2 erasers
   Chocolates _____ ₹ 15 for 3 chocolates

3. Ankit wants to buy half kg apples and one chocolate. The total amount he needs to pay is :
   (a) ₹ 85 (b) ₹ 95
   (c) ₹ 90 (d) ₹ 105

4. If Bunny wants to buy one pen and 3 erasers, how much he needs to pay?
   (a) ₹ 13 (b) ₹ 15
   (c) ₹ 15.50 (d) ₹ 16.25

5. One kg apples can be bought for ₹ 180 and two chocolates can be bought for ₹ 7.50. This statement is _____.
   (a) True
   (b) False
   (c) Insufficient information
   (d) None of these

6. If Manpreet has ₹ 122 and he wants to buy as many chocolates he can with this amount, the number of chocolates that he can buy is:
   (a) 15 (b) 20
   (c) 24 (d) 30

7. Which of the following statement is false?
   (a) Cost of (one kg apples + 2 pens) > Cost of (half kg apples + 5 pens)
   (b) Cost of 5 erasers > Cost of 2 chocolates.
   (c) Cost of 6 erasers > Cost of 3 chocolates.
   (d) Cost of (half kg apples + 2 pen + 1 erasers) > Cost of 9 chocolates

8. Yuvraj is very fond of reading books. Once he bought books for ₹ 465 and he paid ₹ 500 to the bookstore, which expression shows the correct amount of change that he will get back?
   (a) ₹ 500 + ₹ 465
   (b) ₹ 500 – ₹ 465
   (c) ₹ 500 ÷ ₹ 465
   (d) ₹ 500 × ₹ 465

Direction (9-12) : Consider the following scenario to answer questions.

Shraddha and Shubhra are two friends and one day they decided to go for shopping together. Shraddha had ₹ 1500 and Shubhra had ₹ 2000 with them. Shraddha purchased shoes for ₹ 550, a skirt for ₹ 275 and movie DVD for ₹ 50. Shubhra purchased top for ₹ 250, a bag for ₹ 480, a book for ₹ 115 and a tennis racket for ₹ 500.

9. What is the total money spent by Shraddha and Shubhra together in shopping?
   (a) ₹ 2220 (b) ₹ 2170
   (c) ₹ 1720 (d) ₹ 880

10. The amount left with Shubhra after shopping is _____.
    (a) ₹ 540 (b) ₹ 550
    (c) ₹ 555 (d) ₹ 655

11. On the way back home, Shraddha purchased a toy for her little brother worth ₹ 99. Now how much money is left with her?
    (a) ₹ 426 (b) ₹ 476
    (c) ₹ 526 (d) ₹ 626

12. If the amount left with Shubhra is to be divided equally into 5 parts, what will be the amount of one part?
    (a) ₹ 108 (b) ₹ 110
    (c) ₹ 111 (d) ₹ 131

Direction (13-14) : Consider the following scenario to answer the questions.

The sum of money with Ankit and Golu is equal to the money with Sheetal. The total money with all three of them is ₹ 150.

13. How much money is present with Sheetal?
    (a) ₹ 35 (b) ₹ 50
    (c) ₹ 60 (d) ₹ 75

14. The amount of money present with Golu is _____.
    (a) ₹ 25
    (b) ₹ 40
    (c) ₹ 75
    (d) Data insufficient. Cannot be determined

15. Sohan's father has to pay ₹ 3000 for Sohan's quarterly school fees. He has the following amount with him. How much more money does his father require so that he can pay ₹ 3000 as quarterly fees?
    • 1 note of ₹ 1000
    • 2 notes of ₹ 500
    • 4 note of ₹ 100
    • 7 notes of ₹ 50
    • 3 notes of ₹ 20
    (a) ₹ 150 (b) ₹ 590
    (c) ₹ 250 (d) ₹ 190

16. Ashu's father returns from a foreign trip and he bought with him some currencies like 10 notes of US dollars, 5 notes of 10 UK pounds. If the price of 1 US Dollar = ₹ 50 and price of 1 UK pound = ₹ 80, then the total amount in ₹ that he has is _____.
    (a) ₹ 900 (b) ₹ 1000
    (c) ₹ 800 (d) ₹ 1200

Direction (17-18) : Consider the following scenario to answer questions.

A family of four i.e. father, mother and two children went to visit zoo and took ₹ 1000 with them. The cost of zoo ticket is ₹ 50 per adult and ₹ 20 per child. They spent ₹ 200 for food and ₹ 50 to purchase bananas for monkeys.

17. What is the total amount spent by the family during zoo visit?
    (a) ₹ 320 (b) ₹ 390
    (c) ₹ 400 (d) None of these

18. While returning back, father lost ₹ 110 from his purse. What is the amount left with father after the zoo visit?
    (a) ₹ 420 (b) ₹ 480
    (c) ₹ 500 (d) ₹ 650

19. Swati is very fond of collecting different kinds of currencies both coins and paper notes. She has coins of 10 p, 25 p, 50 p, Re 1, ₹ 5, ₹ 10, and notes of ₹ 5 ₹ 10, ₹ 20, ₹ 50, and ₹ 100. What is the total amount of money with her if she has only one of each type?
    (a) ₹ 195.75 (b) ₹ 201.85
    (c) ₹ 200.75 (d) ₹ 200.85

20. Rajesh needs to buy an ice-cream worth ₹ 10. He has same coins of 25p, 50 p and ₹ 1. Which of the following combination of coins will help him in buying the ice-cream?
    (a) 3 coins of 25 p, 6 coins of 50 p, and 6 coins of ₹ 1.
    (b) 2 coins of 25 p, 2 coins of 50 p and 4 coins of ₹ 1.
    (c) 8 coins of 25 p, 4 coins of 50 p and 5 coins of ₹ 1.
    (d) 4 coins of 25 p, 8 coins of 50 p and 5 coins of ₹ 1.

HOTS

1. Which shape looks the most expensive of all?

   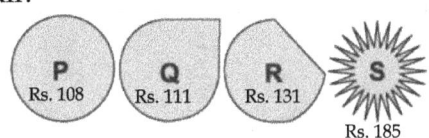

   (a) Q (b) P
   (c) R (d) S

2. The cost of 1 litre of milk is ₹ $16\frac{3}{5}$. What is cost of $12\frac{1}{2}$ litres of milk?
   (a) ₹ $207\frac{1}{2}$ (b) ₹ $205\frac{3}{2}$
   (c) ₹ 207 (d) ₹ $217\frac{1}{2}$

3. The price of a watch is ₹ 982.75. How much money will be needed to buy 46 such watches?
   (a) ₹ 45106.50 (b) ₹ 45206.50
   (c) ₹ 45000.50 (d) ₹ 45200.00

4. A typewriter costs Rs. 240. A calculator costs only $\frac{1}{20}$ as much as a typewriter and a staplercost only $\frac{1}{4}$ as much as the calculator. Find the total cost of 1 typewriter, 2 calculators and 3 staplers.
   (a) ₹ 249 (b) ₹ 234
   (c) ₹ 273 (d) ₹ 237

5. A total of 576 buttons and pins were shared equally among; some children. Each child received 4 buttons and 5 pins. How many children and buttons were there respectively?
   (a) 256 buttons, 64 children
   (b) 256 children, 64 buttons
   (c) 64 buttons, 64 children
   (d) 256 children, 256 buttons

SUBJECTIVE QUESTIONS

1. Answer the following:

Items	Price
Burger	70.25
Tea	20.15
Hot Chocolate	50.10
Pastry	85.50

   (i) How much Ankit will pay for a cup of tea and a pastry?
   (ii) How much money Golu has to pay for 2 pastries and 1 hot chocolate?
   (iii) How much Bunny has to pay for 1 burger and tea?
   (iv) How much Navneet has to pay for all item on the list?

   Solution:

Items	Price
Burger	70.25
Tea	20.15
Hot Chocolate	50.10
Pastry	85.50

   (i) (20.15 + 85.5) = Ankit will pay ₹ 105.65 for a cup of tea and pastry.
   (ii) (2×85.5 + 50.10) = ₹ 221.1 will be paid by Golu for two pastry and one hot chocolate.
   (iii) Bunny has to pay for 1 burger and tea is ₹ 90.4
   (iv) Navneet has to pay (70.25 + 20.15 + 50.10 + 85.50) = ₹ 226 for all the items

2. Thulasi and her husband work on Karunya's farm. The Government has said that farm workers should be paid at least ₹ 71 for one day's work. But he pays ₹ 55 to Thulasi and ₹ 58 to her husband.

   If Thulasi works for 49 days, how much money does she get?

   If her husband works for 42 days, how much money does he get?

   Find the money they earn together.

   Solution:
   Thulasi is paid ₹ 55 for one day's work.
   So, if she works for 49 days, she will get
   = ₹ 55 × 49

   ```
     5 5
   × 4 9
   ─────
     4 9 5   (55 × 9)
   2 2 0 0   (55 × 40)
   ─────
   2 6 9 5
   ```

   Thus, Thulasi will get ₹ 2,695 for working 49 days in the farm.

   Thulasi's husband is paid ₹ 58 for a day's work.

   So, if he works for 42 days, he will get
   = ₹ 58 × 42

   ```
     5 8
   × 4 2
   ─────
     1 1 6   (58 × 2)
   2 3 2 0   (58 × 40)
   ─────
   2 4 3 6
   ```

   Thus, Thulasi's husband will get ₹ 2,436 for working 42 days in the farm.

   Total money earned by both
   = ₹ 2,695 + ₹ 2,436 = ₹ 5,131

3. Satish is a 13 year old boy. His father had taken a loan for farming. But the crops failed. Now Satish's mother has to pay Rs 5000 every month for the loan. Satish started working — he looked after 17 goats of the village. He earns Rupee 1 every day for one goat.
   - How much will he earn in one month?
   - Does he earn enough to help pay the loan every month?

- How much will he earn in one year?

Answer:

Satish earns Rs 1 for one goat every day. He looked after 17 goats of his village.

So, Satish will earn = ₹ 1 × 17 = ₹ 17 for a day

Hence,

For a month Satish will earn = ₹ 17 × 30

```
    30
  × 17
  ────
   210  (30 × 7)
   300  (30 × 10)
  ────
   510
```

Thus, Satish will earn ₹ 510 in one month. Satish's mother has to pay ₹ 5,000 every month for the loan. But, the earnings of Satish will not help pay the loan every month.

We know, 1 year = 12 months

Satish's earning in one year = ₹ 510 × 12

```
    510
  ×  12
  ─────
   1020  (510 × 2)
   5100  (510 × 10)
  ─────
   6120
```

Therefore, Satish will earn ₹ 6,120 in one year for looking after 17 goats.

4. Sukhi works on a farm. He is paid Rs 98 for one day. If he works for 52 days, how much will he earn?

Answer:

Sukhi is paid ₹ 98 for working one day on a farm.

So, his earning if we works 52 days will be = ₹ 98 × 52

```
    52
  × 98
  ────
   416  (52 × 8)
  4680  (52 × 90)
  ────
  5096
```

Hence, Sukhi will earn ₹ 5,096 by working in the farm for 52 days.

5. Isha has ₹ 1000 with her. She wants to buy petrol. One litre of petrol costs ₹ 47. How many litres can she buy?

Money with Isha = ₹ 1000

Cost of 1 litre = ₹ 47

Litres of petrol she can buy

= ₹ 1000 ÷ ₹ 47 = ?

Isha can buy _____ litres of petrol.

Answer:

Dividing ₹ 1000 ÷ ₹ 47 we have,

```
      21
  47)1000
    - 94↓
    ────
      60
    - 47
    ────
      13
```

Remainder = 13

Hence, Isha can only buy 21 litres of petrol with ₹ 1,000.

Money

Area, Perimeter and Volume 11

Learning Objectives : In this chapter, students will learn about:
- Cube
- Cuboid
- Cone
- Cylinder
- Square
- Rectangle
- Circle

CHAPTER SUMMARY

In everyday life, area and perimeter terms are used constantly. This is applicable for any shape and size whether it is regular or irregular. For example, it can be used to describe the size of a house by talking about its floor area or can be used to find out how much wire is needed to fence off playground. The concept of area and perimeter is covered here.

Area
The area of a plane figure is the measure of the surface enclosed by its boundary. Area is measured in square units such as square centimeter and square meters written as cm^2 and m^2 respectively.

The area of the adjoining figure (rectangle) = 10 square units.

$\therefore$ A = 5 cm × 2 cm = 10 square cm

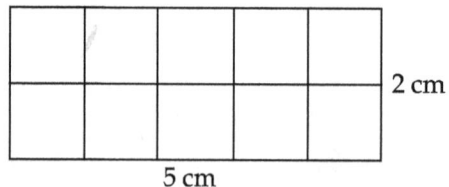

Perimeter
The perimeter of a plane figure is the length of its boundary. It is found by adding all the lengths of the figure. The unit of perimeter is same as the unit of length.

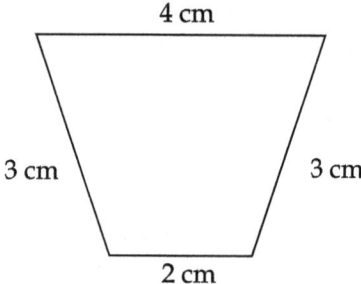

Here, perimeter of the given figure
= 4 cm + 3 cm + 2 cm + 3 cm = 12 cm
Hence, the perimeter of this figure is 12 cm.

Cube
A solid bounded by six square surfaces is called a cube.

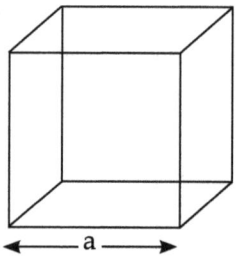

Volume of a cube = (side)^3 = a^3
Diagonal of a cube = $a\sqrt{3}$
Surface area of a cube = 6 × side^2 = $6a^2$

Cuboid
A solid bounded by six rectangular surfaces is called a cuboid.

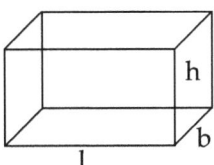

Volume of cuboid = $l \times b \times h$
Surface area of cuboid = $2(lb + bh + hl)$
Diagonal of cuboid
$= \sqrt{l^2 + b^2 + h^2}$

Cone
A figure which has a lateral surface and a circular base is called a circular cone.

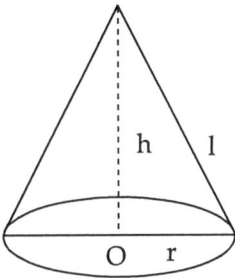

Volume of cone = $\frac{1}{3}\pi r^2 h$

Curved surface area of the cone = $\pi r l$
Total surface area of the cone = $\pi r l + \pi r^2$
where $l = \sqrt{h^2 + r^2}$

Cylinder
The solid which has two circular ends and a lateral face is called circular cylinder.
Volume of cylinder = $\pi r^2 h$

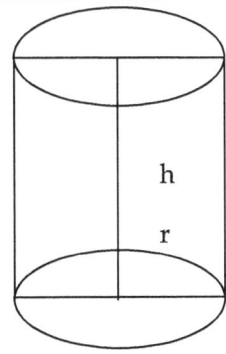

Curved surface area of cylinder = $2\pi rh$
Total surface area of cylinder = $2\pi rh + 2\pi r^2$

Perimeter of a Triangle
The perimeter of a triangle is the distance around all the sides of a triangle and can be determined by adding each length of all the sides of a triangle.
∴ Perimeter of $\triangle ABC = a + b + c$ = addition of all the sides of a triangle.

Area of a Triangle
The area of a triangle is simply defined as half base times height which can be represented as shown below. Area of a triangle = $\frac{1}{2} \times$ base $\times$ height

Here ABC is a triangle with sides a, b and c and altitude h.
then area of triangle
$= \sqrt{s(s-a)(s-b)(s-c)}$
where a, b, c are sides, $s = \frac{a+b+c}{2}$

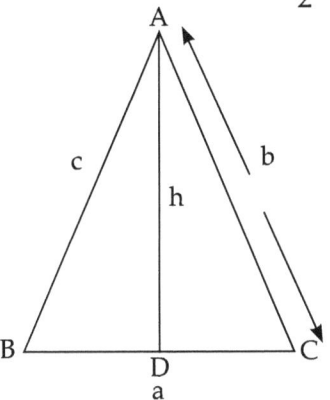

Area of a right angled triangle
= $\frac{1}{2} \times$ product of the sides containing the right angle

Area of an equilateral triangle
= $\frac{\sqrt{3}}{4} \times$ (side)^2

Area of an isosceles triangle
= $\frac{a}{4}\sqrt{4b^2 - a^2}$

Area, Perimeter and Volume

Volume

Volume is the number of cubic units needed to fill a container. It can be found by counting cubes. The volume can also be found by multiplying the length by the width by the height. This is shown by the formula:
$V = l \times w \times h$.

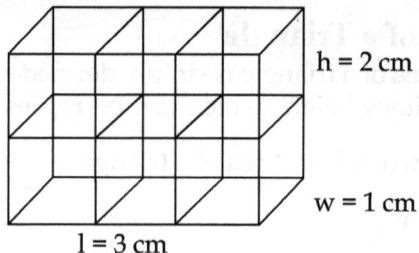

Here volume of rectangle = 3 cm × 1 cm × 2 cm = 6 cubic centimetres $\Rightarrow V = 6$ cm^3

Square

A four sided regular polygon with all sides equal and all internal angles 90°. From this it follows that the opposite sides are also parallel.

Here ABCD is a square of side a.
Then perimeter of a square = 4 × side = 4 × a
Diagonal of a square = $\sqrt{2}$ .side = $a\sqrt{2}$

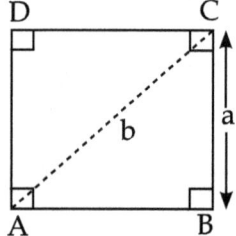

Area of a square = (sides)^2 = a^2 and side of a square = $\sqrt{\text{Area}}$ = $\dfrac{\text{Perimeter}}{4}$

Rectangle

A four sided polygon where all interior angles are 90° and opposite sides are equal. The rectangle, like the square is one of the most commonly known quadrilaterals.

Here ABCD is a rectangle with length a, breadth b and diagonal d then area of a rectangle = length × breadth = ab and perimeter of rectangle ABCD = 2 × [length + breadth) = 2 $(a + b)$

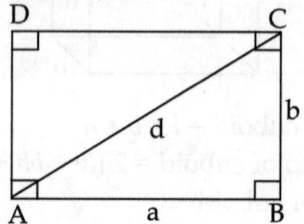

Diagonal of a rectangle = $\sqrt{\text{length}^2 + \text{breadth}^2} = \sqrt{a^2 + b^2}$

Circle

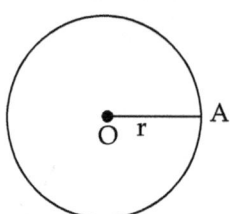

Diameter = 2 × radius
The perimeter of a circle is called circumference.
Circumference = $2\pi r = \pi d$
Where $d = 2r$
Area = πr^2

> **TRIVIA**
> Perimeter for squares and rectangles is always less than their area, whereas it can be more than the area in case of triangles.

Area and Perimeter of some common shapes

1. Trapezium

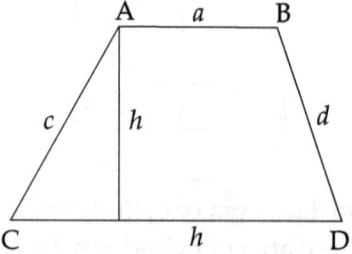

AB || CD
∠A+∠D=∠B+∠C =180°
$Area = \frac{(a+B)h}{2}$

Perimeter = Sum of all sides
= a + b + c + d

2. Parallelogram

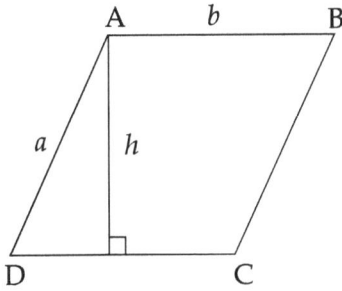

AB || CD and AD || CB
∠A = ∠C and ∠B = ∠D

Area = b × h
Perimeter = 2 (a + b)

3. Rhombus

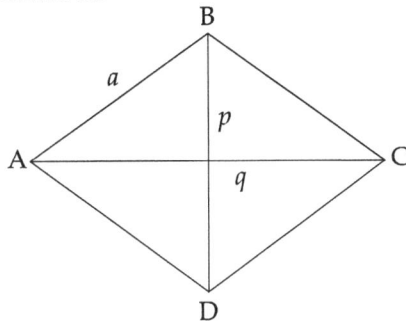

AB = BC = CD = DA
∠A = ∠C, ∠B = ∠D
$Area = \frac{p \times q}{2}$

Perimeter = 4a

MUST REMEMBER

- The area of a plane figure is the measure of the surface enclosed by its boundary.
- The perimeter of a plane figure is the length of its boundary. It is found by adding all the lengths of the figure.
- The perimeter of a triangle is the distance around all the sides of a triangle and can be determined by adding each length of all the sides of a triangle.
- The volume can also be found by multiplying the length by the width by the height.

Area, Perimeter and Volume

MULTIPLE CHOICE QUESTIONS

1. Find the area of the triangle shown.

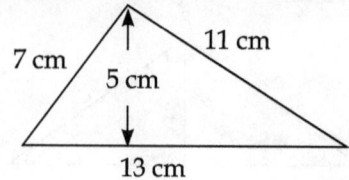

   (a) 2.5 cm² (b) 45.5 cm²
   (c) 65 cm² (d) 71.5 cm²

2. Find the perimeter of the triangle shown in the previous question.
   (a) 15.5 cm (b) 29 cm
   (c) 31 cm (d) 62 cm

3. Find the area of the parallelogram shown.

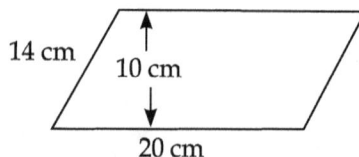

   (a) 140 cm² (b) 200 cm²
   (c) 240 cm² (d) 280 cm²

4. Find the perimeter of the parallelogram shown in the previous question.
   (a) 34 cm (b) 56 cm
   (c) 60 cm (d) 68 cm

5. Find the area of the trapezoid shown.

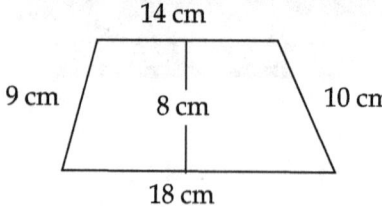

   (a) 128 cm² (b) 252 cm²
   (c) 256 cm² (d) 324 cm²

6. Find the perimeter of the trapezoid shown in the previous question.

   (a) 25.5 cm (b) 32 cm
   (c) 48 cm (d) 51 cm

7. Find the area of the circle shown.

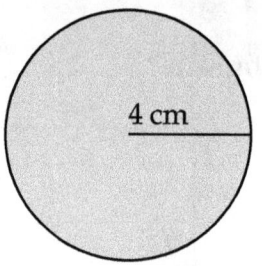

   (a) 16 cm² (b) 25 cm²
   (c) 50 cm² (d) 101 cm²

8. Find the perimeter of the circle shown in the previous question.
   (a) 12.5 cm (b) 25 cm
   (c) 50 cm (d) 101 cm

9. Find the area of the figure shown.

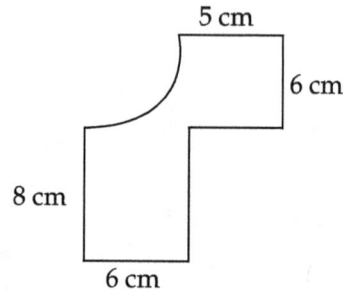

   (a) 154 cm² (b) 114 cm²
   (c) 85.7 cm² (d) 57.5 cm²

10. Find the perimeter of the figure shown in the previous question.
    (a) 47.4 cm (b) 56.8 cm
    (c) 75.7 cm (d) 94.8 cm

11. A square has an area of 64 cm². What is the length of each side?
    (a) 8 cm (b) 16 cm
    (c) 32 cm (d) 60 cm

12. The figure below is made up of 3 squares of sides 5 cm. What is the perimeter of the figure?

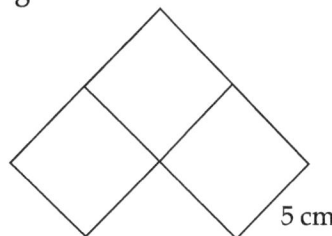

5 cm

(a) 15 cm (b) 30 cm
(c) 40 cm (d) 50 cm

13. The figure below is made up of three squares. Find the perimeter of the figure.

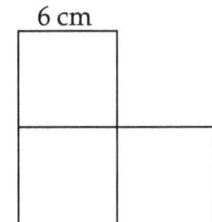

6 cm

(a) 48 cm (b) 60 cm
(c) 72 cm (d) 144 cm

14.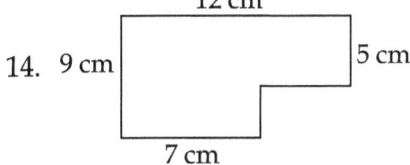

12 cm, 9 cm, 5 cm, 7 cm

The area of the figure above is _____ m².
(a) 42 (b) 88
(c) 108 (d) 123

15. The perimeter of a square is 20 cm. What is the length of each side of the square?
(a) 80 cm (b) 18 cm
(c) 5 cm (d) 4 cm

16. Which of the following figures have the same area?

P   Q   R   S

(a) P and Q (b) Q and R
(c) Q and S (d) R and S

17. Which one of the following rectangles had the biggest perimeter?

(a) 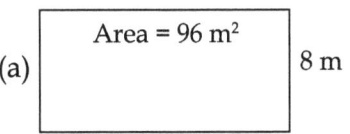 Area = 96 m², 8 m

(b) 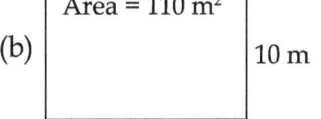 Area = 110 m², 10 m

(c) 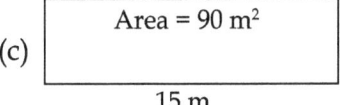 Area = 90 m², 15 m

(d) 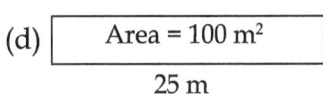 Area = 100 m², 25 m

18. The perimeter of the figure shown below is 36 m. What is the length of DE?

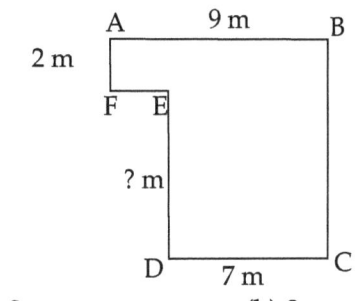

(a) 8 m (b) 9 m
(c) 16 m (d) 18 m

19. What is the area of the figure given below?

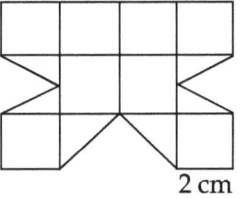

2 cm

(a) 48 cm² (b) 44 cm²
(c) 40 cm² (d) 20 cm²

20. A rectangular garden measures 25 m by 20 m. What is the cost of erecting a wooden fence around it if every 5 metres of wooden fencing cost ₹ 27?

(a) ₹ 486 (b) ₹ 500
(c) ₹ 2 430 (d) ₹ 2 700

HOTS

1. How many small cubes of side 2 cm can be put in a cubical box of side 6 cm?
   (a) 9 (b) 12
   (c) 27 (d) 611

2. A cuboid measures 24 m × 12 m × 16 m. How many cubes of side 8 m can fit in the box?
   (a) 9 (b) 16
   (c) 15 (d) 24

3. Find area of unshaded region if each box = 3 m².

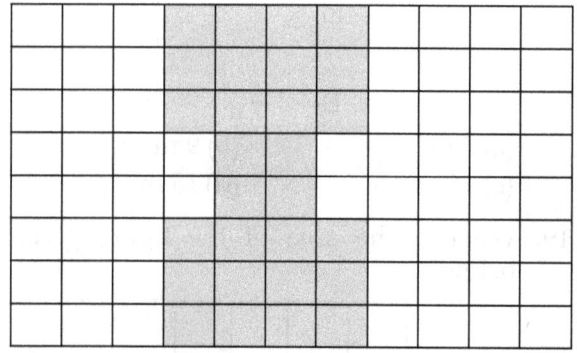

   (a) 88 m² (b) 60 m²
   (c) 84 m² (d) 180 m²

4. Identify the correct shape by seeing the following features:
   A. It's length and breadth are equal.
   B. Its area is side × side.
   C. Its perimeter is 4 times its side.
   D. It is a four-sided polygon.
   (a) Rectangle (b) Parallelogram
   (c) Square (d) Trapezium

5. How many of the following letters have only 2 lines of symmetry?

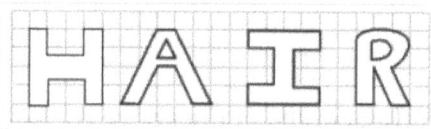

   (a) 0 (b) 1
   (c) 2 (d) 3

SUBJECTIVE QUESTIONS

1. The difference between the length and the breadth of a rectangle is 8 cm and the perimeter is 64 cm. Which of the following can be the length and breadth of this rectangle?
   Solution:
   Length of rectangle = x cm
   Breadth of rectangle = $(x - 8)$ cm
   Perimeter of rectangle
   = $2(x + x - 8) = 2(2x - 8)$
   Given $2(2x - 8) = 64$
   $\Rightarrow 2x = 40$
   $\Rightarrow x = 20$
   Hence, L = 20, B = 20 − 8 = 12

2. The area of a square is 100 sq. cm. If the sides this square are increased by 10% then what will be the area of new square?
   Solution:
   Given area of square = 100
   side × side = 100 = 10 × 10
   $\Rightarrow$ side = 10 cm

   Increased in side of square = 10% of 10 = 1
   ∴ New side = 10 + 1 = 11
   ∴ Area of new square = $(11)^2$ = 121 sq. cm.

3. Find the area and perimeter of the figure:

   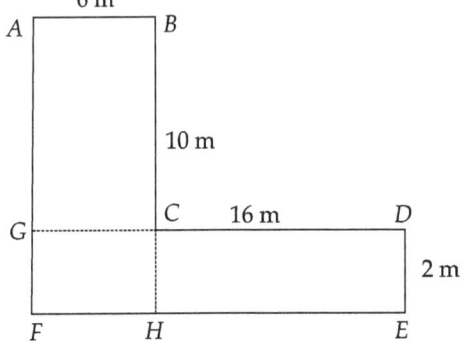

   Solution:
   Calculate the lengths of the sides which are not given:
   AB = 6 m,
   BC = 10 m,
   CD = 16 m,
   DE = 2 m
   Now, FE = CD + AB = 16 + 6 = 22 m
   AF = BC + DE = 10 + 2 = 12 m

   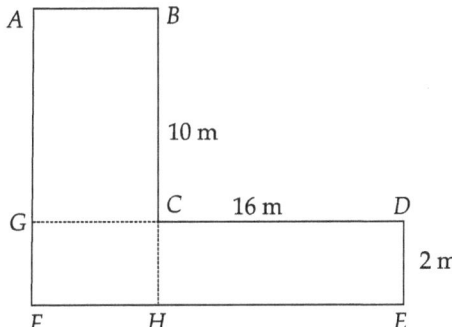

   Required area = Area of rectangle ABCG + area of rectangle GDEF = 6 × 10 + 2 × 22
   = 60 + 44 = 104 m²
   PERIMETER = Sum of all sides = 6 + 10 + 16 + 2 + 22 + 12 = 68 m.

4. The perimeter of an equilateral triangle and of a square measure the same. Which of the following can be the measures of the side of the equilateral triangle and of the square?
   (a) Equilateral triangle = 9 cm; square = 12 cm
   (b) Equilateral triangle = 12 cm; square = 9 cm
   (c) Equilateral triangle = 15 cm; square = 10 cm
   (d) Equilateral triangle = 6 cm; square = 4 cm
   Solution:
   (a) Perimeter of equilateral Triangle = 9 × 3 = 27
   Perimeter of square = 12 × 4 = 48.
   (b) Perimeter of equilateral Triangle = 12 × 3 = 36
   Perimeter of square = 9 × 4 = 36.

(c) Perimeter of equilateral Triangle
= 15 × 3 = 45
Perimeter of square = 40.
Hence, answer is b.

5. The perimeter of two squares is 12 cm and 24 cm. The area of the bigger square is how many times that of the smaller?
Solution:
Perimeter of smaller square with side a_1 = 12 cm
$\Rightarrow 4a_1 = 12$
$\Rightarrow a_1 = 3$ cm

Area of smaller square = $(a_1)^2 = (3)^2$
= 9 cm²
Perimeter of bigger square with side a_2 = 24 cm
$\Rightarrow 4a_2 = 24$
$\Rightarrow a_2 = 6$ cm
Area of bigger square = $(a_2)^2 = (6)^2$
= 36 cm².
The area of bigger square is 4 times that of smaller square.

Geometrical Shapes and Angles   12

Learning Objectives : In this chapter, students will learn about:
- ✓ Geometry
- ✓ Labeling Angles
- ✓ Parts of triangles
- ✓ Types of triangles
- ✓ Reflection Symmetry
- ✓ Rotational Symmetry

CHAPTER SUMMARY

Geometry is a kind of mathematics that deals with shapes and figures. It explains how to build or draw shapes, measure them, and compare them. We use geometry in many different types of work, from building malls and houses to planning travel to space. Let us understand some important concepts of Geometry.

Geometry

It is the study of angles, lines and their relationship with each other.

Point: Point is represented by a dot on which length, breadth and height cannot be measured.

Point

Line: The distance between two points is called a line. It is represented by $\overleftrightarrow{XY}$.

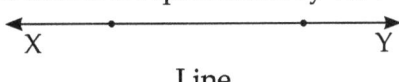
Line

Line Segment: A portion of a line having two end points is called a line segment $\overline{PQ}$.

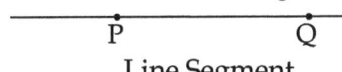
Line Segment

Angle: A figure consisting of two rays with common initial point is called an angle.

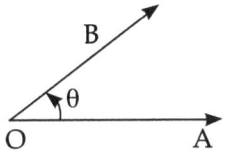

$\theta \rightarrow$ Angle = $\angle BOA$.

It is measured in degrees. *e.g.*, 30°, 45° etc.

Labeling Angles

There are two main ways to label angles:

(i) Give the angle a name, usually a lower-case letter like a or b, or sometimes a Greek letter like α (alpha) or θ (theta).

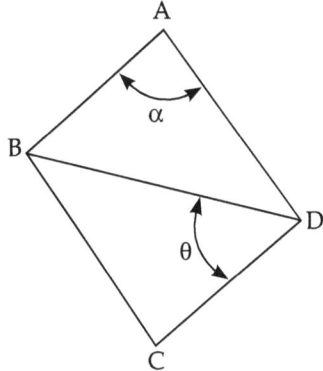

(ii) Or by the three letters on the shape that define the angle, with the middle letter being where the angle actually is (its vertex).

Geometrical Shapes and Angles   111

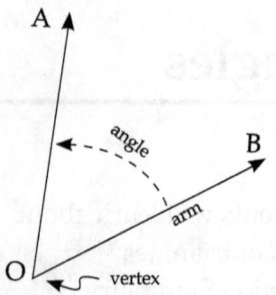

Positive and Negative Angles
When measuring from a line :
- A positive angle goes counterclockwise (opposite direction that clocks go)
- A negative angle goes clockwise

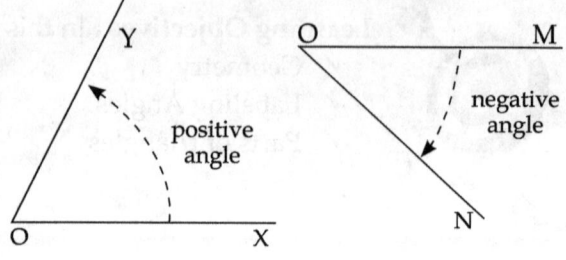

Parts of an Angle
The corner point of an angle is called the vertex and the two straight sides are called arms. The angle is the amount of turn between each arm. In the above figure, O is the vertex and , OA and OB are the arms.

Classification of Angles

Type of Angle	Description
Acute Angle	an angle measures less than 90°
Right Angle	an angle measures exactly 90°
Obtuse Angle	an angle measures more than 90° but less than 180°
Straight Angle	an angle measures exactly 180°
Reflex Angle	an angle measures more than 180° but less than 360°

Acute Angle
An Acute Angle measures less than 90°.

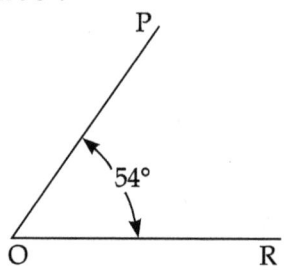

All the angles below are acute angles:

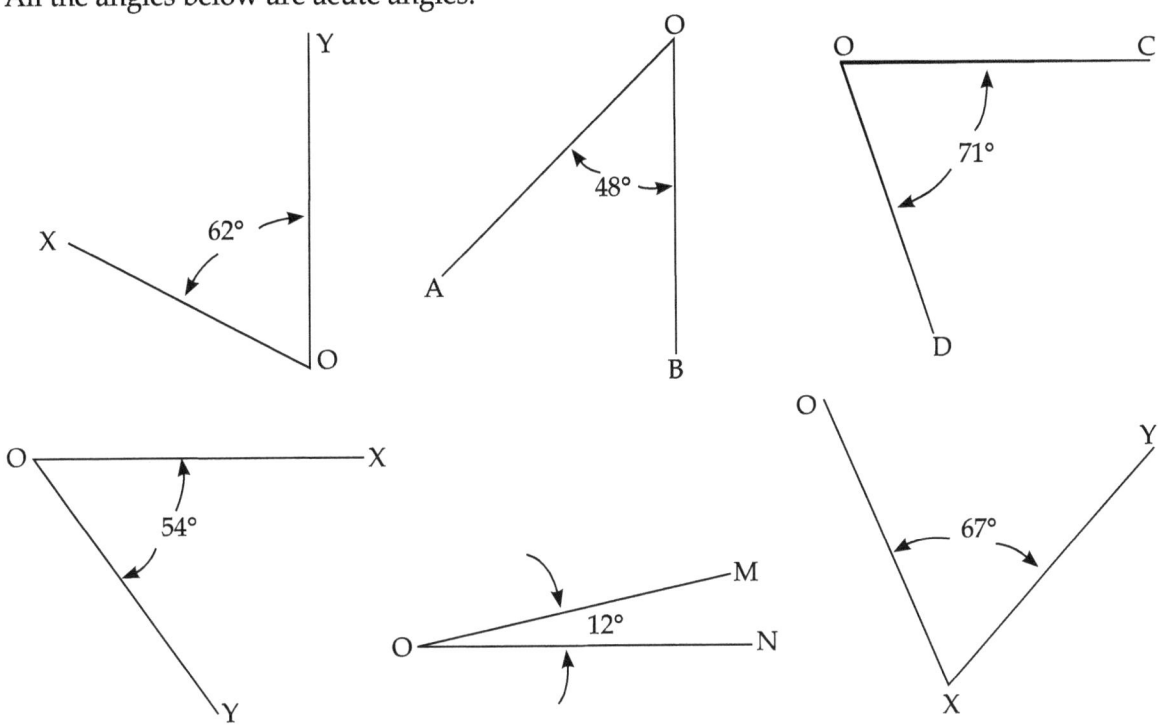

Right Angle
A right angle measures 90°

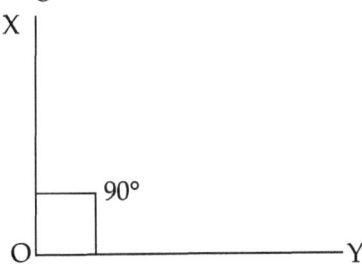

Here ∠XOY is a right angle.

Note : The special symbol like a box in the angle. If you see this, it is a right angle. The 90° is rarely written. If you see the box in the corner, you are being told it is a right angle.

TRIVIA

The word 'geometry' comes from the Greek words 'geo', meaning earth, and 'metria', meaning measure.

All the angles below are right angles:

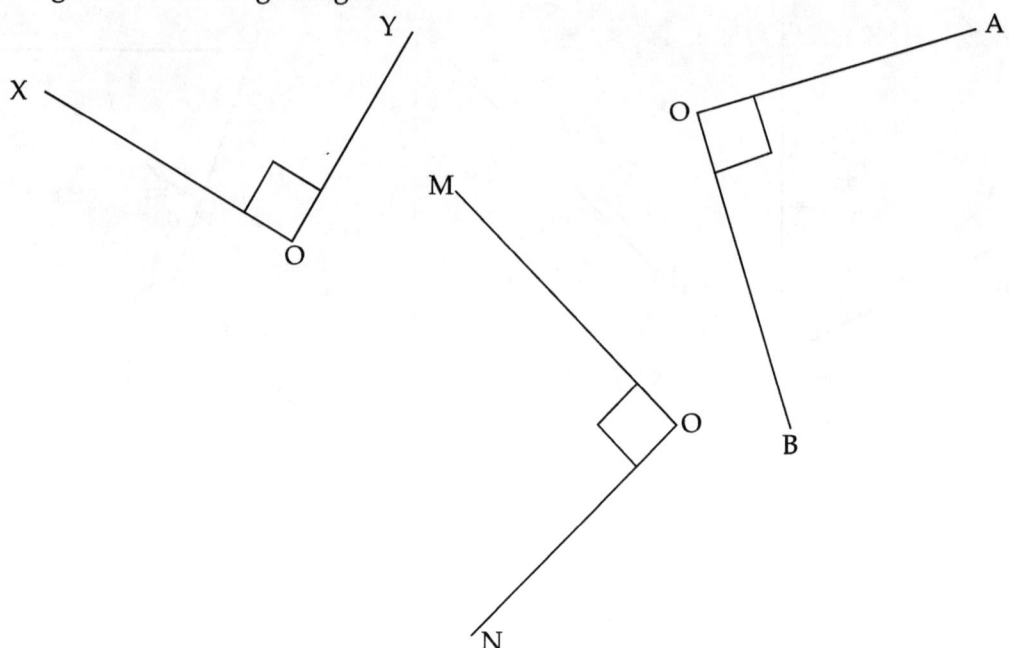

A right angle can be in any orientation or rotation as long as the internal angle is 90°.

Do you know?
The intersection of four roads on a traffic signal is an example of right angle.

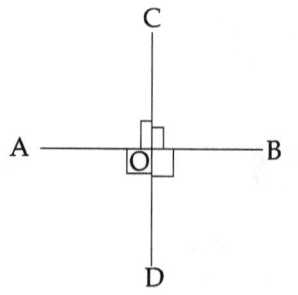

Obtuse Angle
An Obtuse Angle is more than 90° but less than 180°.

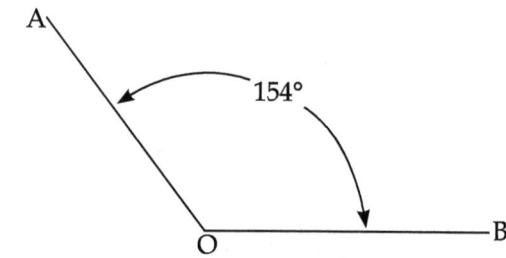

Here ∠AOB is an obtuse angle.
All the angles below are obtuse angles:

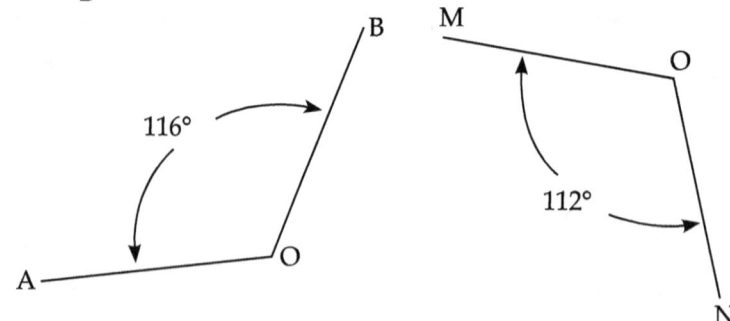

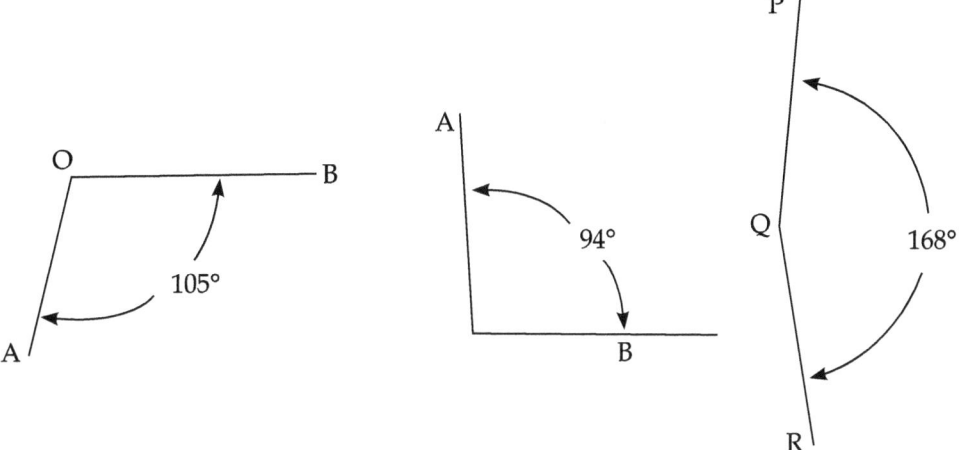

Straight Angle

A straight angle measures 180°.
Here ∠AOB is a straight angle.
A straight angle changes the direction to point the opposite way.
All the angles below are straight angles:

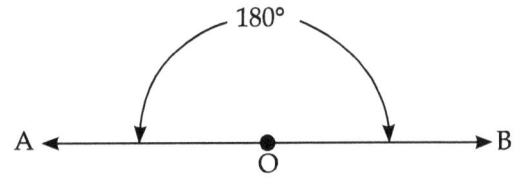

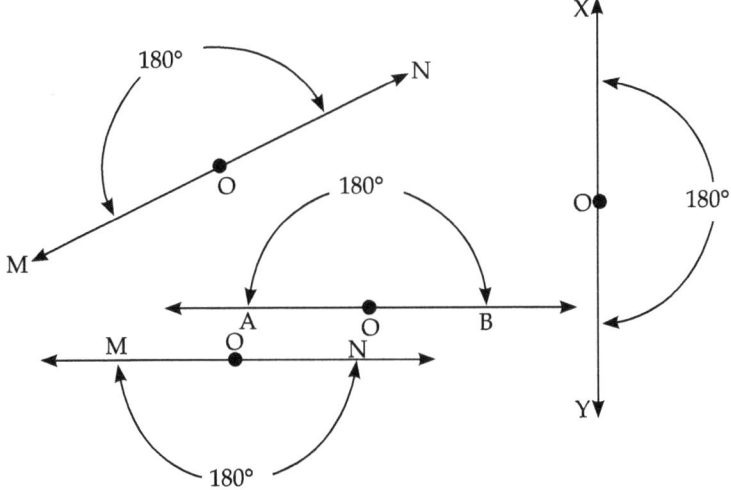

Reflex Angle

A reflex angle measures more than 180° but less than 360°.

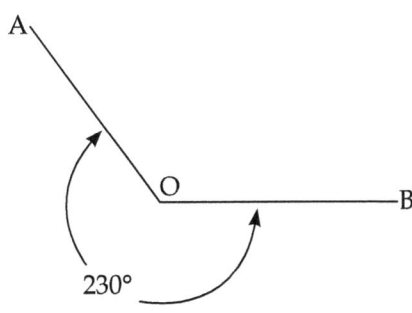

Geometrical Shapes and Angles

Here ∠AOB is a reflex angle.
All the angles below are reflex angles :

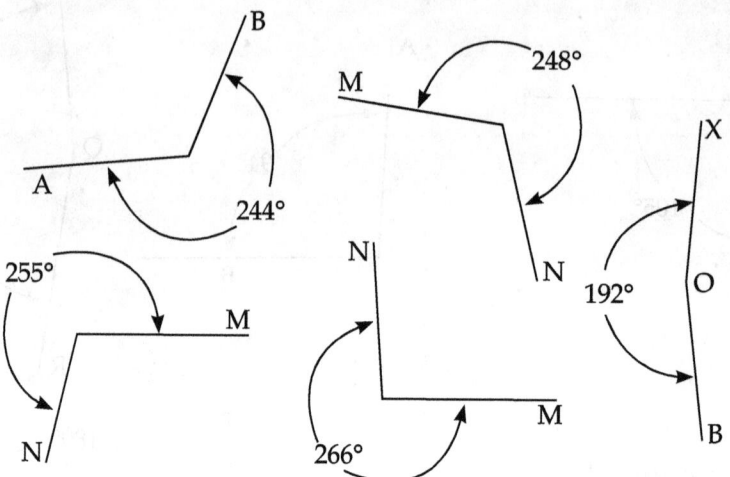

In One Diagram
This diagram might make it easier to remember :

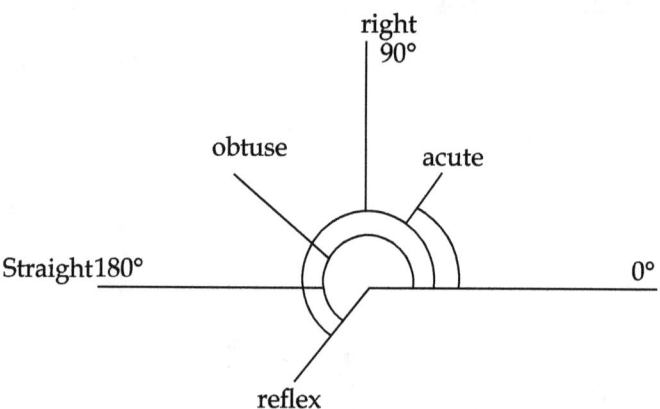

Note : Acute, Obtuse and Reflex are in alphabetical order.
Be Careful What You Measure

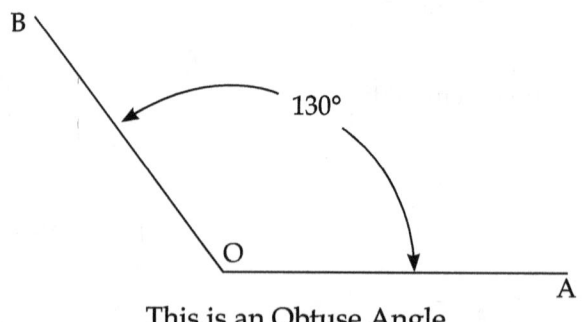

This is an Obtuse Angle

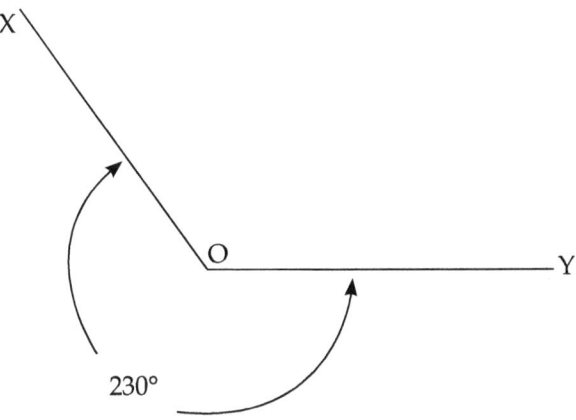

Above one is a Reflex Angle.

But the lines are the same, so when naming the angles make sure that you know which angle is being asked for!

Example : 67°

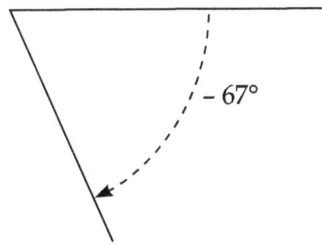

Triangle : A closed figure consisting of three line segments linked end to end.

Parts of a Triangle

(*i*) Vertex   (*ii*) Base
(*iii*) Altitude   (*iv*) Median

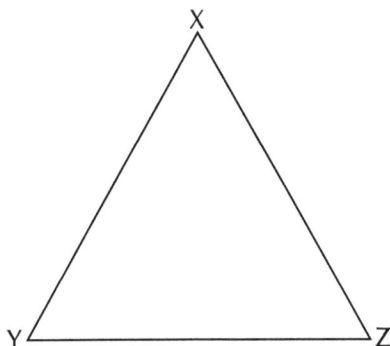

Types of Triangle

There are six types of triangles listed below:

Note that a given triangle can be more than one type at the same time.

Scalene Triangle : A triangle where all three sides are different in length.

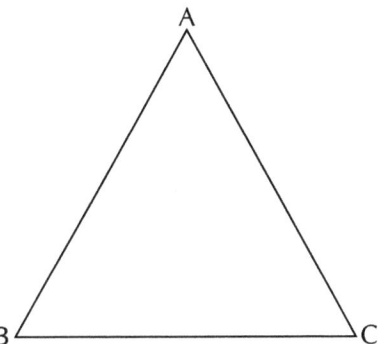

Isosceles Triangle : A triangle which has two of its sides equal in length.

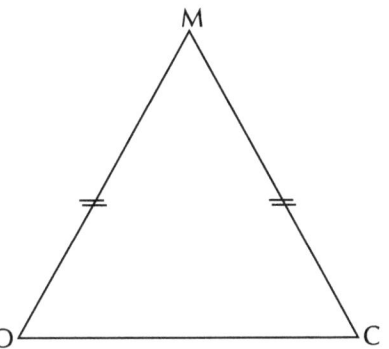

Equilateral Triangle : A triangle which has all three of its sides equal in length.

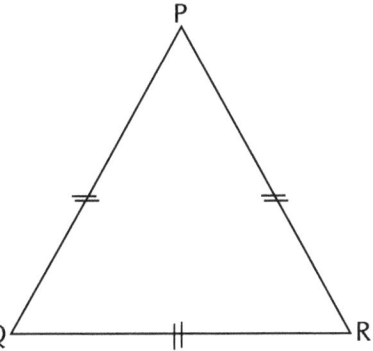

Right Triangle : A triangle where one of its interior angle is a right angle. (90°).

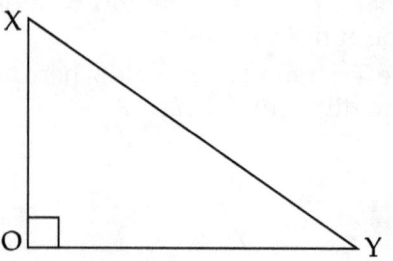

Obtuse Triangle : A triangle where one of the internal angles is greater than 90°.

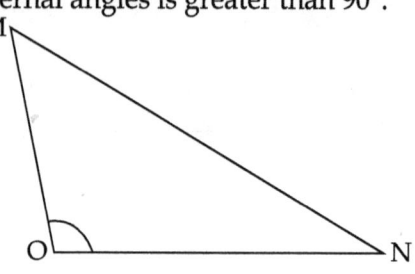

Acute Triangle : A triangle where all three internal angles are acute (less than 90°).

Two Types of Right Angled Triangles
There are two types of right angled triangle :

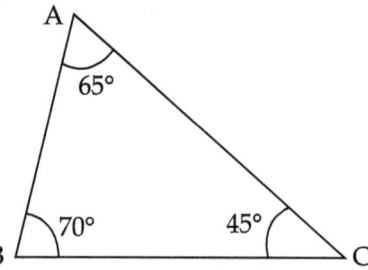

Scalene right angled triangle
- One right angle
- Two other unequal angles
- No equal sides

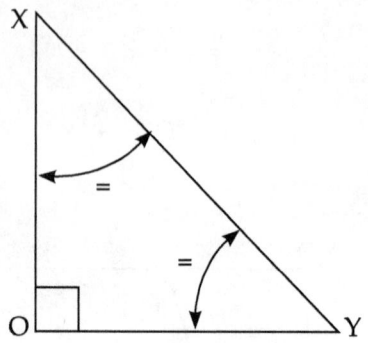

Isosceles right angled triangle
- One right angle
- Two other equal angles always of 45°
- Two equal sides

Example : The 3, 4, 5 Triangle

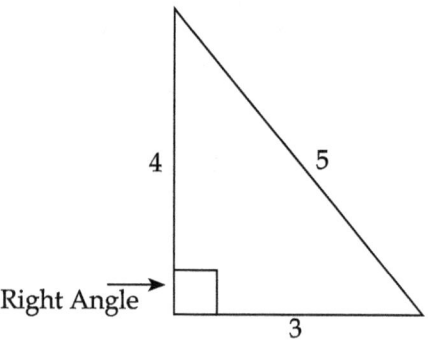

The "3, 4, 5 Triangle" has a right angle in it. It has no equal sides so it is a scalene right angled triangle.

Do you know?
Architecture is based on angles and lines. They use concept of angles to design buildings.

Reflection
When we see our image in a plane mirror, we find:
(i) the distance of image behind the mirror is same as the distance of object in front by us.
(ii) The line joining the image and object is always perpendicularly bisected by the mirror.

In the below diagram, AB is a plane mirror and P′ is the image of P in the mirror AB. Clearly OP = OP′. and ∠AOP = 90°.

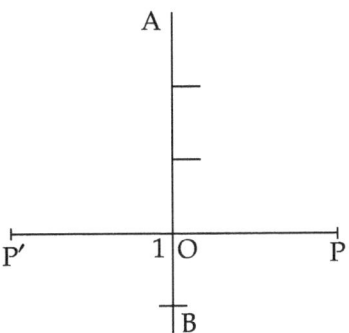

Reflections are everywhere ... in mirrors, glass, and here in a lake.

The reflection has the same size as the original image.

The central line is called the Mirror Line. Every point is the same distance from the central line.

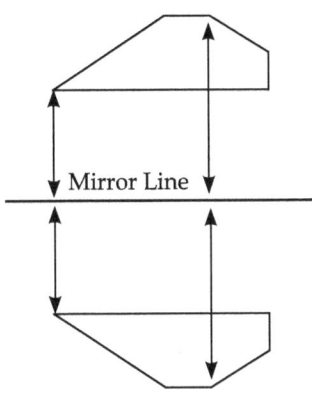

In fact Mirror Lines can be in any direction. Imagine turning the photo at the top in different directions. The reflected image is always the same size; it just faces the other way :

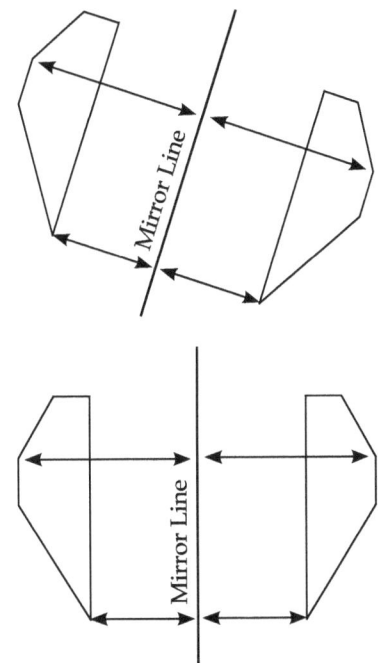

A reflection is a flip over a line.

Rotation

"Rotation" means turning around a center. The distance from the center to any point on the shape stays the same. Every point makes a circle around the center.

Geometrical Shapes and Angles

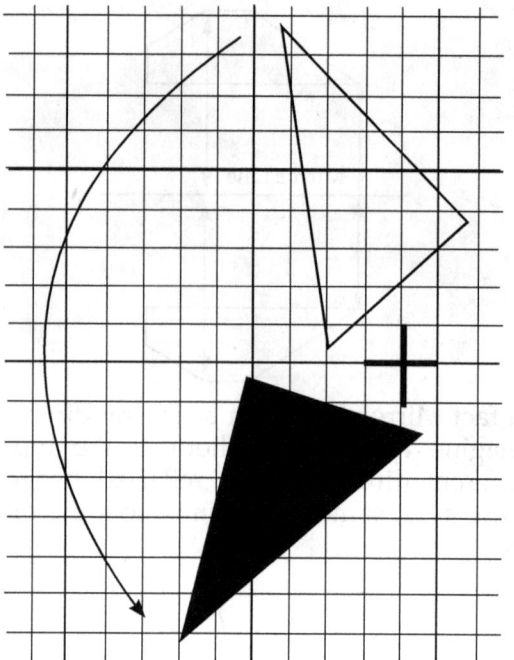

Here a triangle is rotated around the point marked with a "+".

Symmetry

Symmetry is when one shape becomes exactly like another if you flip, slide or turn it. 3D shapes have faces (sides), vertices and edges (corners). A net of a 3D shape is a figure which folds up to form 3D shape.

The exception is the sphere which has no edges or vertices.

The net of a 3D shape is what it looks like if it is opened out flat. A net can be folded up to make a 3D shape.

There may be several possible nets for one 3D shape.

Here are some examples:

Net of a cube

Net of a cuboid

Net of a square-based pyramid

Net of a triangle-based pyramid

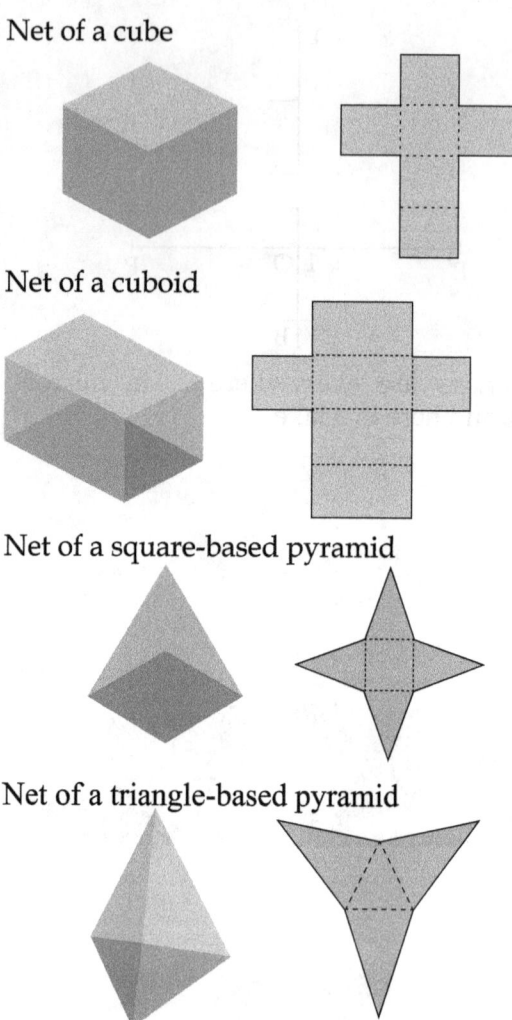

Reflection Symmetry

The simplest symmetry is Reflection Symmetry (sometimes called Line Symmetry or Mirror Symmetry). It is easy to see, because one half is the reflection of the other half.

Here a dog has her face made perfectly symmetrical with a bit of photo magic. The white line down the center is the Line of Symmetry.

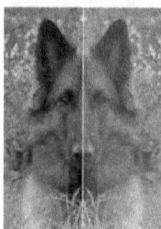

The Line of Symmetry does not have to be up-down or left-right, it can be in any direction.

Rotational Symmetry

With Rotational Symmetry, the image is rotated (around a central point) so that it appears 2 or more times. How many times it appears is called the Order.

Here are some examples.

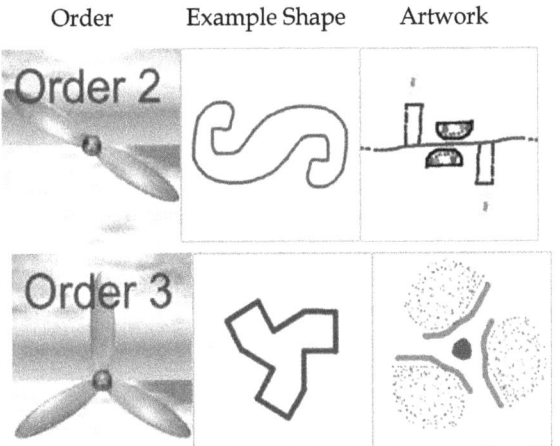

Point Symmetry

Point Symmetry is when every part has a matching part :
- the same distance from the central point
- but in the opposite direction

It is also the same as "Rotational Symmetry of Order 2" above.

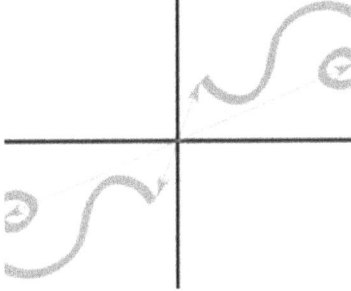

Did you know?
The line of symmetry divides the objects such that it forms two parts that are mirror image of each other.

MUST REMEMBER

- The corner point of an angle is called the vertex and the two straight sides are called arms.
- A positive angle goes counterclock-wise (opposite direction that clocks go)
- A negative angle goes clockwise.
- A right angle measures 90°.
- An Obtuse Angle is more than 90° but less than 180°.
- A straight angle measures 180 degrees.
- A reflex angle measures more than 180° but less than 360°.
- The reflection has the same size as the original image.
- "Rotation" means turning around a center. The distance from the center to any point on the shape stays the same.

Geometrical Shapes and Angles

MULTIPLE CHOICE QUESTIONS

1. The angle 89° is :
   (a) Acute (b) Right
   (c) Obtuse (d) Reflex

2. The angle 234° is :
   (a) Acute (b) Obtuse
   (c) Straight (d) Reflex

3. Which is closest to the size of angle AOB?

   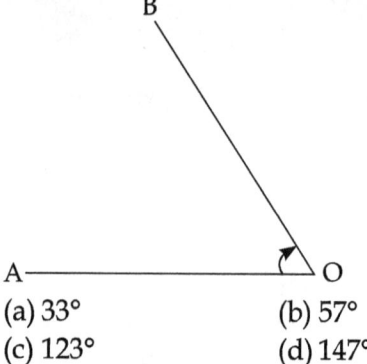

   (a) 33° (b) 57°
   (c) 123° (d) 147°

4. Which is closest to the size of reflex angle FOE?

   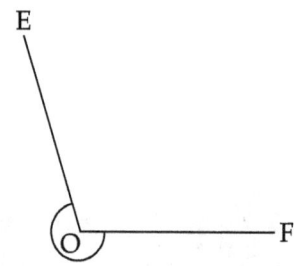

   (a) 106° (b) 164°
   (c) 254° (d) 286°

5. For the angle shown in the diagram, the arrow points to its :

   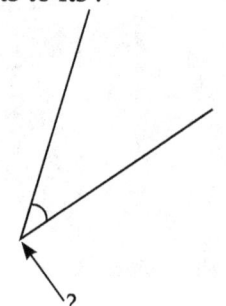

   (a) Arm (b) Corner
   (c) Vertex (d) Bend

6. By using the three letters on the shape that define the angle, angle α is written as :

   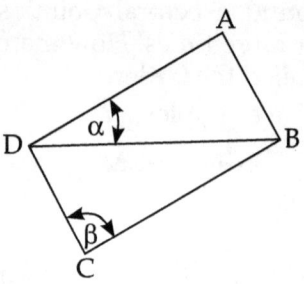

   (a) ∠ABD (b) ∠ADB
   (c) ∠BAD (d) ∠BDC

7. By using the three letters on the shape that define the angle, angle β is written as:

   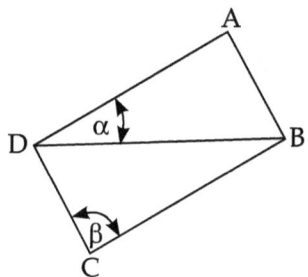

   (a) ∠DCB (b) ∠BDC
   (c) ∠CBD (d) ∠ACB

8. If two acute angles are added together, which of the following is NOT possible for their sum :
   (a) Acute
   (b) Right
   (c) Obtuse
   (d) Straight

9. Which one of the following angles is acute?
   (a) Half a right angle
   (b) A right angle
   (c) One and a half right angles
   (d) Two right angles

10. How many acute angles are there in the diagram?

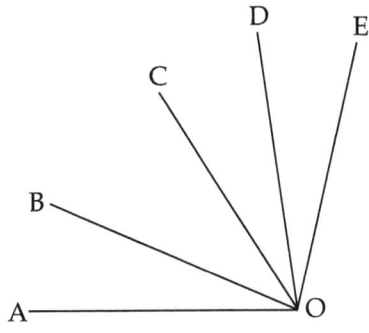

(Think of all possibilities).
(a) 10 (b) 9
(c) 7 (d) 4

11. How many acute angles are there in this pentagram?

(a) 5 (b) 10
(c) 15 (d) 20

12. How many acute angles are there in the diagram?

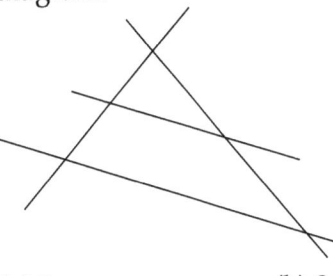

(a) 5 (b) 8
(c) 9 (d) 10

13. How many acute angles are there in the diagram?

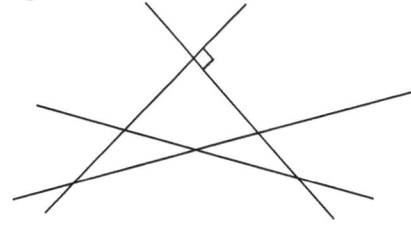

(a) 5 (b) 10
(c) 12 (d) 14

14. How many right angles are there in the diagram?

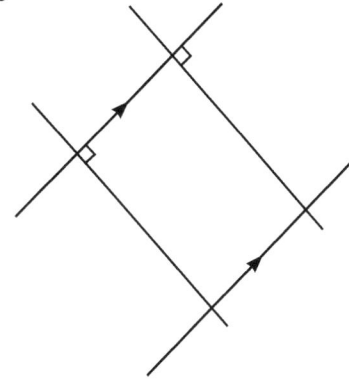

(a) 2 (b) 4
(c) 8 (d) 16

15. How many right angles make two full rotations?
(a) 4 (b) 6
(c) 8 (d) 10

16. How many obtuse angles are there in the diagram?

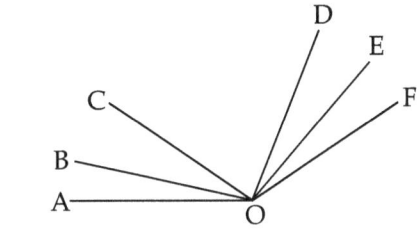

(a) 7 (b) 8
(c) 9 (d) 10

17. Which one of the following angles is obtuse?
(a) Half a right angle
(b) One right angle
(c) One and a half right angles
(d) Two right angles

18. How many straight angles are there in three full rotations?
(a) 3 (b) 4
(c) 6 (d) 8

Geometrical Shapes and Angles

19. Which one of the following angles is not reflex?
    (a) 178° (b) 182°
    (c) 270° (d) 359°
20. Which one of the following angles is reflex?

    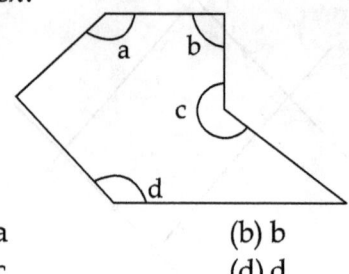

    (a) a (b) b
    (c) c (d) d
21. If angle AOB = 67°, what is the size of reflex angle AOB?

    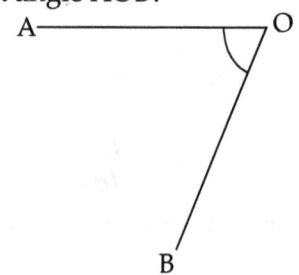

    (a) 113° (b) 247°
    (c) 293° (d) 427°
22. What is the least number of 33° angles you would need to make a reflex angle?
    (a) 2 (b) 5
    (c) 6 (d) 7
23. Which of the following describes the triangle shown above?

    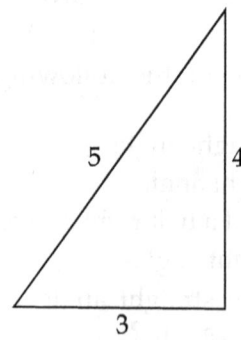

    (a) A scalene right angled triangle
    (b) A scalene obtuse angled triangle
    (c) A scalene acute angled triangle
    (d) An isosceles right angled triangle
24. A triangle is isosceles and right angled. Which of the following statements must be false?
    (a) The triangle has angles 45°, 45° and 90°
    (b) The triangle has two of its sides equal
    (c) The triangle has one line of symmetry
    (d) The triangle has sides of lengths 3, 4 and 5
25. Shraddha made two copies of the right angled triangle shown and cut them out.

    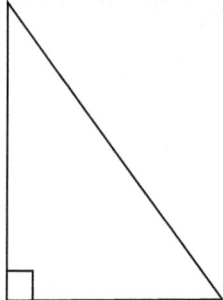

    She then joined edges of the triangles together to make shapes. Which of the following shapes was not possible for Shraddha to make?
    (a) A square
    (b) A kite
    (c) A parallelogram
    (d) An isosceles triangle
26. Shraddha made two copies of the following isosceles right angled triangle and cut them out. She then joined edges of the triangles together to make shapes.

    Which of the following shapes was it NOT possible for Shraddha to make?

    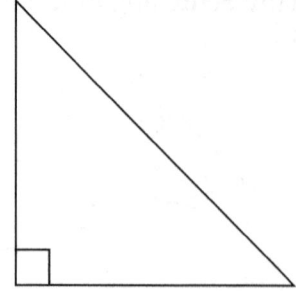

(a) A square
(b) An equilateral triangle
(c) A parallelogram
(d) An isosceles triangle

27. The square is turned one complete rotation about the point O. Which of the rotation following shows the new position of the square?

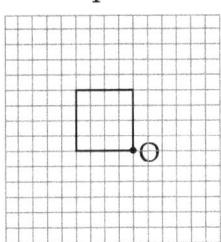

(a)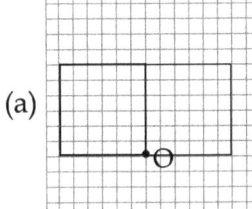

(b)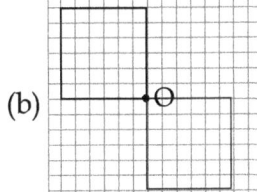

(c)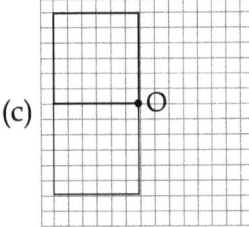

(d)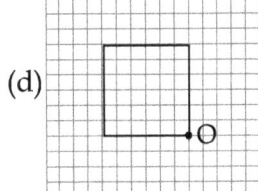

28. How many lines of symmetry does this star have?

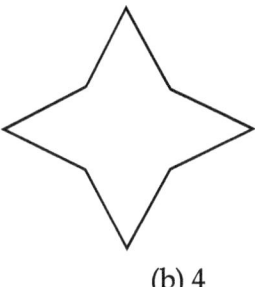

(a) 2   (b) 4
(c) 6   (d) 8

29. What is the order of rotational symmetry of this star?

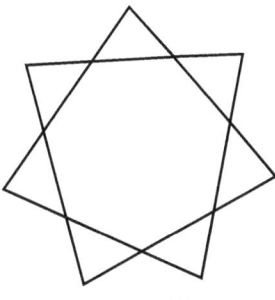

(a) 5   (b) 6
(c) 7   (d) 8

30. What is the order of rotational symmetry of this shape?

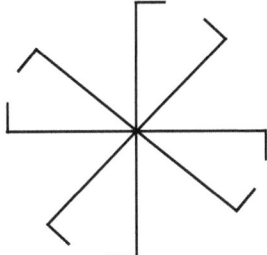

(a) 2   (b) 4
(c) 8   (d) 16

Geometrical Shapes and Angles

HOTS

1. Which figure has no line of symmetry?

   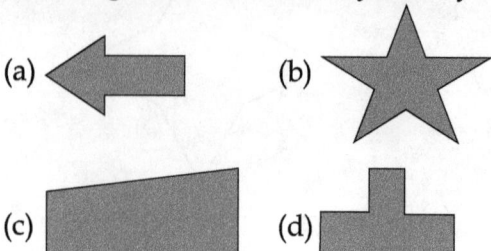

   (a) (b) (c) (d)

2. How many right angles are there in $2\frac{1}{2}$ complete turns?
   (a) 8 (b) 10
   (c) 12 (d) 14

3. Angle X is equal to _____ right angle(s).

   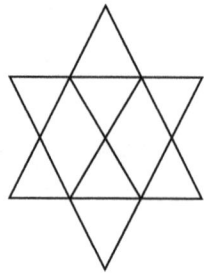

   (a) 1 (b) 2
   (c) 3 (d) 4

4. Count the number of triangles in the given figure.

   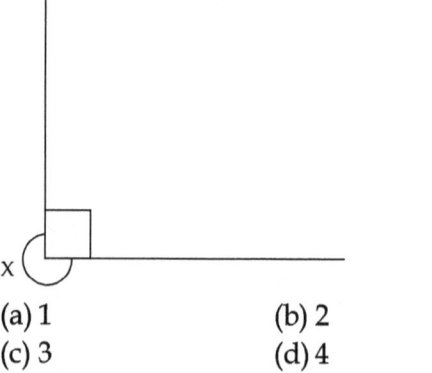

   (a) 8 (b) 10
   (c) 14 (d) None of these

5. Which of the following figure/net folds up to form a cube?

   (a)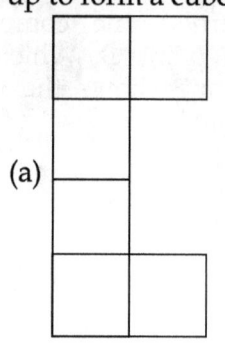

   (b)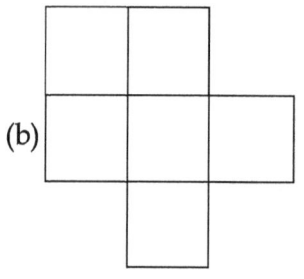

   (c)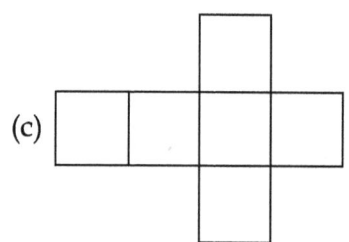

   (d)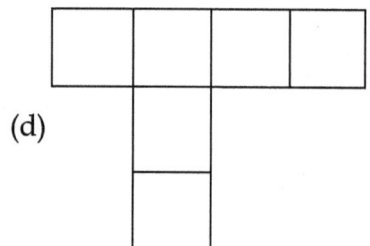

SUBJECTIVE QUESTIONS

1. Bunny makes some frame boards. In which board has he identified angle less than 90°?

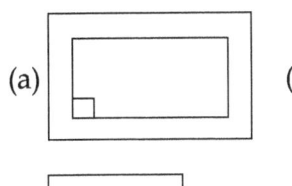
(a) (b)

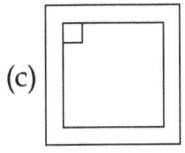
(c)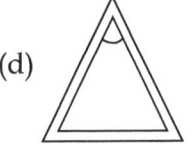
(d)

Solution
(a) Option (a) has all right angles.
(b) Option (b) has obtuse angle.
(c) Option (c) has right angle.
(d) Option (d) has acute angle i.e. less than 90°.

2. Sneha runs around a field of the shape given below. Which is true for the angles formed by the corners of the field?

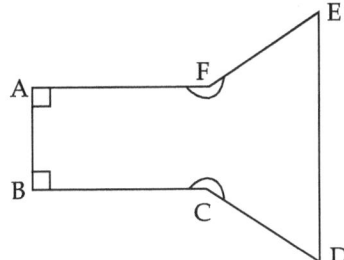

Solution:
∠A = ∠B = 90° (Right angles)
∠F & ∠C > 90° (Obtuse angles)
∠E & ∠D < 90° (Acute angles)

3. The angles of a triangle are in the ratio 2: 3: 4. Find the measures of all angles.
Solution:
$2x + 3x + 4x = 180°$
$9x = 180°$
$x = (180°)/9 = 20°$
Then, $2x = 2 × 20° = 40°$
$3x = 3 × 20° = 60°$ $4x = 4 × 20° = 80°$
Hence, angles of triangle are 40°, 60° and 80°.

4. If the sum of two angles in a triangle equals third angle, then the triangle will be _____?
Solution:
Let angles are x, y and z.
$x + y = z$
In any Δ, sum of interior angles is equal to 180°
Hence, $x + y + z = 180°$
$z + z = 180°$
$2z = 180°$
$z = 90°$
Therefore, the triangle is right angled Δ.

5. Find the number of triangles in the following figure and name them.

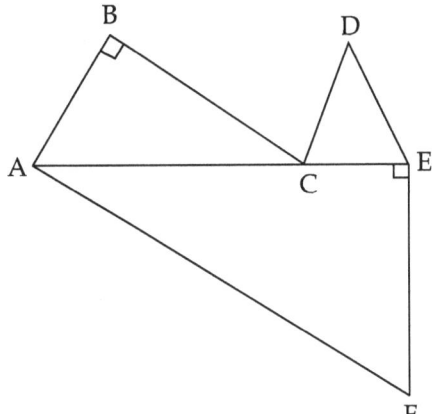

Solution:
Number of triangles = 3
They are = triangle ABC, triangle CDE, triangle AEF
triangle ABC = Right angle triangle
triangle CDE = Isosceles Triangle
triangle AEF = Right Angle Triangle

SECTION 2
LOGICAL REASONING

Series and Pattern

Learning Objectives : In this chapter, students will learn about:
- ✓ Completion of series
- ✓ Odd one out
- ✓ Figure Pattern
- ✓ Figure Matrix

CHAPTER SUMMARY

Series
The well arranged order of numbers/letters placed in a particular group is called series. A particular place is left blank in the series. These terms (numbers or letters) follow a certain pattern. You are required to recognize this pattern and complete the series or identify the wrong member of that series. This includes the completion of incomplete numbers, letters, figures and their combination.

These types of questions can be categorized into two types :

Type I : Completion of Series
Directions :
Identify next number in the given series :

Example 1 : 4, 6, 9, 13, ...
(a) 17 (b) 18
(c) 21 (d) 25
Sol. (b)
The difference between the two consecutive numbers is increasing in the order of + 2, +3 + 4, +5, etc. Hence, required answer = 13 + 5 = 18.

Example 2 : 120, 99, 80, 63, 48, ?
(a) 34 (b) 36
(c) 35 (d) 25
Sol. (c)
The given series is

120 99 80 63 48
  ↘↗ ↘↗ ↘↗ ↘↗
  −21 −19 −17 −15

So, missing term = 48 − 13 = 35.

Example 3 : 125, 80, 45, 20, ?
(a) 3 (b) 6
(c) 5 (d) 5
Sol. (d)
The given series is

125   80   45   20
  ↘↗ ↘↗ ↘↗
  −45 −35 −25

So, missing term = 20 − 15 = 5.

Example 4 : 1, 1, 2, 6, 24, ?, 720
(a) 108 (b) 100
(c) 10 (d) 120
Sol. (d)
The given series is

$1 \xrightarrow{\times 1} 1 \xrightarrow{\times 2} 2 \xrightarrow{\times 3} 6 \xrightarrow{\times 4} 24 \xrightarrow{\times 5}$

$120 \xrightarrow{\times 6} 720$

So, missing term = 120.

Type II : Odd One Out
In each of the following examples, one term in the number series is wrong.
Find out the wrong term in the given series.

Example 5 : 24, 27, 31, 33, 36
(a) 24 (b) 27
(c) 31 (d) 36

Series and Pattern

Sol. The given series is :

24   27   30   33   36
  +3   +3   +3   +3

Hence, 31 is wrong term (odd one out).

Example 6 : 1, 4, 8, 16, 31, 64, 127, 256
(a) 1 (b) 8
(c) 16 (d) 127

Sol. The given series is

$1 \xrightarrow{\times 2+2} 4 \xrightarrow{\times 2-1} 7 \xrightarrow{\times 2+2} 1\!6 \xrightarrow{\times 2-1} 31$

Hence 8 is wrong term.

Pattern

There are many patterns in our everyday life. For example, first you sell one chocolate for the price of ₹ 5, and then two chocolates for price ₹ 10. In this example, the pattern increases by 5. See the pattern of bricks in a wall. Patterns can also be in number form.

In this type of questions a set of terms following a certain pattern is given. We are required to identify the pattern followed in the given terms. Determine if the order of numbers is ascending (getting larger in value) or descending (becoming smaller in value). Also find the difference between numbers that are next to each other. We can also use the difference between numbers to find the missing number.

Example 7 : Find the missing number :
15, 13, ?, 9
(a) 14 (b) 12
(c) 10 (d) 11

Sol. (d)
The given series is as follows :

$15 \xrightarrow{-2} 13 \xrightarrow{-2} 11 \xrightarrow{-2} 9$

∴ Required number = 11

Example 8 : Find the missing number
30, 23, ?, 9
(a) 15 (b) 12
(c) 20 (d) 16

Sol. (d)
The order of numbers in given series is going down or descending.
The difference between numbers is

30 – 23 = 7
Since the order is descending subtract 7 from 23. The missing number may be 16.
The missing number is 16 since it is 7 more than the last number 9.

Figure Pattern

In this type of pattern we deal with some questions in which there are some guest figure followed by answer figures. We are required to recognize the pattern followed by question figures.

Movement of figures

The figures/symbols can move in two directions

(*i*) Clockwise direction

(*ii*) Anti-clockwise direction

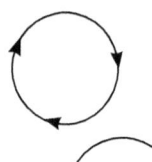

Rotation of figures

The figures/symbols can rotate at a specific angle either in clockwise or anti-clockwise direction.

Figure Matrix

In this type of pattern, the picture and number figures or shapes of objects or activities are given. Here sets of figures follow the same rule either row-wise or column-wise. You have to analyse the set of figures and find out the pattern followed by them.

Example 9 : Which of the following is the missing figure?

Problem Figure

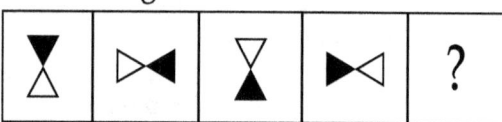

Answer Figure

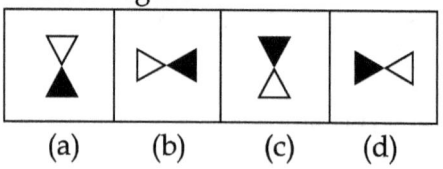
(a)   (b)   (c)   (d)

Sol. (c)

In this example, the question figure is rotated clockwise through 90 degrees each time. The answer is therefore option C which represents the last shape rotated through a further 90 degrees.

Example 10 : Select a suitable figure from the four alternatives that would complete the figure matrix.

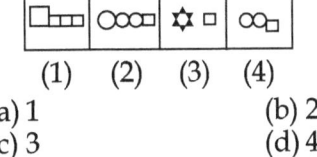

(a) 1   (b) 2
(c) 3   (d) 4

Sol. (a)

In each row, the second figure is obtained from the first figure by increasing the number of smaller elements by one and the third figure is obtained from the second figure by increasing the number of smaller elements by one. Hence A is the required answer.

Example 11 : Select a suitable figure from the four alternatives that would complete the figure matrix.

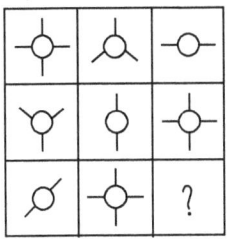

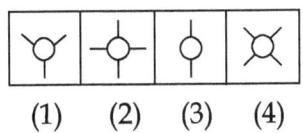

(a) 1   (b) 2
(c) 3   (d) 4

Sol. (a)

Each row (as well as each column) contains a figure consisting of a circle and two line segments, a figure consisting of a circle and three line segments and a figure consisting of a circle and four line segments. Hence A (Circle and three line segments) is the required answer.

Example 12 : Select a suitable figure from the four alternatives that would complete the figure matrix.

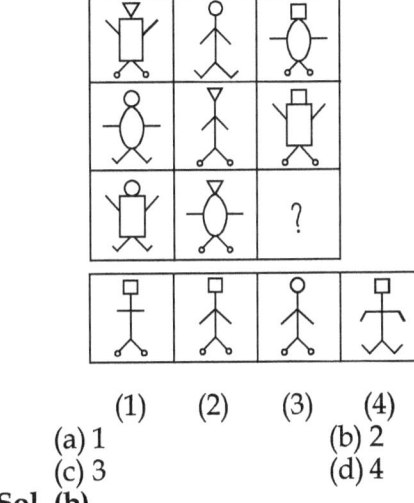

(a) 1   (b) 2
(c) 3   (d) 4

Sol. (b)

There are 3 types of faces, 3 types of bodies, 3 types of hands and 3 types of legs, each of which is used only once in a single row. So, the features which have not been used in the first two figures of the third row would combine to produce the missing figure. Hence B is the correct answer.

Series and Pattern

MULTIPLE CHOICE QUESTIONS

1. Complete the series
   __ op ___ mo ___ n ___ ___ pnmop___
   (a) npmon (b) pnmo
   (c) mnpmon (d) nomp

2. Complete the series
   ba____ba____bac____acb____cbac
   (a) acbc (b) bcab
   (c) cbab (d) ccba

3. Complete the series
   m___nm___n___an___
   (a) amnn (b) anma
   (c) mnam (d) aamm

4. Complete the series
   R___MR___M___ ___M
   (a) AA AA (b) AA RR
   (c) AA RA (d) RR AA

5. Complete the series
   bca____b____aabc ____a____caa
   (a) acab (b) bcbb
   (c) cbab (d) ccab

6. Complete the series
   a____ba____b____b____a____b
   (a) abaab (b) abbab
   (c) aabba (d) bbabb

7. Complete the series
   ____nmmn____mmnn____mnnm____
   (a) nmmn (b) mnnm
   (c) nnmm (d) nmnm

8. Complete the series
   cccbb____aa____cc____bbbaa____c
   (a) aebe (b) baca
   (c) baba (d) acba

9. Complete the series
   ab____d____aaba____na____badna___b
   (a) andaa (b) babda
   (c) badna (d) dbanb

10. Find the next two elements in series: A/2, B/4, C/6, D/8
    (a) E/8, F/10 (b) E/12, F/14
    (c) E/10, F/12 (d) D/10, E/10

11. Find the missing element:
    2Z5, 7Y7, 14X9, 23W11, 34V13, ?
    (a) 27U24 (b) 47U15
    (c) 45U15 (d) 47V14

12. Find the missing element:
    P3C, R5F, T8I, V12L, ?
    (a) Y17O (b) X17M
    (c) X17O (d) X16O

13. Find the missing element:
    J2Z, K4X, 17V, ?, H16R, M22P
    (a) L11S (b) L12T
    (c) L11T (d) L12S

14. Find the missing element:
    3F, 6G, 11I, 18L, ?
    (a) 21O (b) 25N
    (c) 27P (d) 27Q

15. Find the missing element:
    D-4, F-6, H-8, J-10, ?, ?
    (a) K-12, M-13 (b) L-12, M-14
    (c) L-12, N-14 (d) K-12, M-14

16. Find the missing element:
    A-26, B-25, C-24, D-23, ?, ?
    (a) E-21, F-20 (b) E-24, F-22
    (c) E-22, F-21 (d) E-21, F-20

17. Find the missing element:
    2A11, 4D13, 12G17, ?
    (a) 36I19 (b) 48J21
    (c) 36J21 (d) 48J23

18. Find the missing element:
    C4X, F9U, I16R, ?
    (a) K25P (b) Y44B
    (c) L25O (d) Z88B

19. Find the missing element:
    BAZ, DCY, FEX, ?
    (a) FXW (b) EFX
    (c) FEY (d) HGW

20. Find the missing element:
    FLP, INS, LPV, ?
    (a) ORY (b) UXZ
    (c) VXY (d) SVW

21. Find the missing element:
    M, N, O, L, R, I, V, ?
    (a) A (b) E
    (c) F (d) H

22. Find the missing element:
    BAS, ?, DCQ, DDP, FEO
    (a) CBT (b) ABR
    (c) BCT (d) BBR

23. Find the missing element:
    DEF, HIJ, MNO, ?
    (a) STU (b) RTV
    (c) SRQ (d) TUV
24. Find the missing element:
    BYW, DUX, FQY, ?
    (a) HZM (b) HCZ
    (c) HMZ (d) HZC
25. Find the missing element:
    DFE, JIH, MLN, ?, VUT
    (a) OQP (b) PSR
    (c) PRQ (d) RSP
26. Find the missing element:
    EJO, TYD, INS, XCH, ?
    (a) NRW (b) MRW
    (c) MSX (d) NSX
27. Find the picture that follows logically from the diagrams to the right.
    (a) (b) (c) (d)
28. Find the picture that follows logically from the diagrams to the right.
    (a) (b) (c) (d)
29. Find the next term
    4, 5, 8, 17, 44,
    (a) 80   (b) 125
    (c) 112 (d) 60
    (e) 84
30. Find the next term
    13, 57, 911, 1315, 1719
    (a) 2123 (b) 1879
    (c) 3002 (d) 5004
    E. 1784

Direction (31-35) : In each of the following questions, one number is wrong in the series. Find out the wrong number.

31. 3, 5, 12, 39, 154
    (a) 5   (b) 3
    (c) 39 (d) 12
32. 4, 16, 36, 49, 64
    (a) 4   (b) 49
    (c) 36 (d) 64
33. 1, 3, 5, 7, 8
    (a) 1   (b) 3
    (c) 5   (d) 8
34. 5, 10, 15, 20, 25, 34
    (a) 5   (b) 10
    (c) 20 (d) 34
35. Which of the diagrams follows?

    ↔ ∞ 王 :: 干 ∞ ⊤ ⊥

    (a) (b) (c) (d)

36. Identify the figure that completes the pattern.
    (X) (a) (b) (c) (d)
37. Identify the figure that completes the pattern.
    (X) (a) (b) (c) (d)
38. Identify the figure that completes the pattern.
    (X) (a) (b) (c) (d)
39. Identify the figure that completes the pattern.
    (X) (a) (b) (c) (d)
40. Identify the figure that completes the pattern.
    (X) (a) (b) (c) (d)

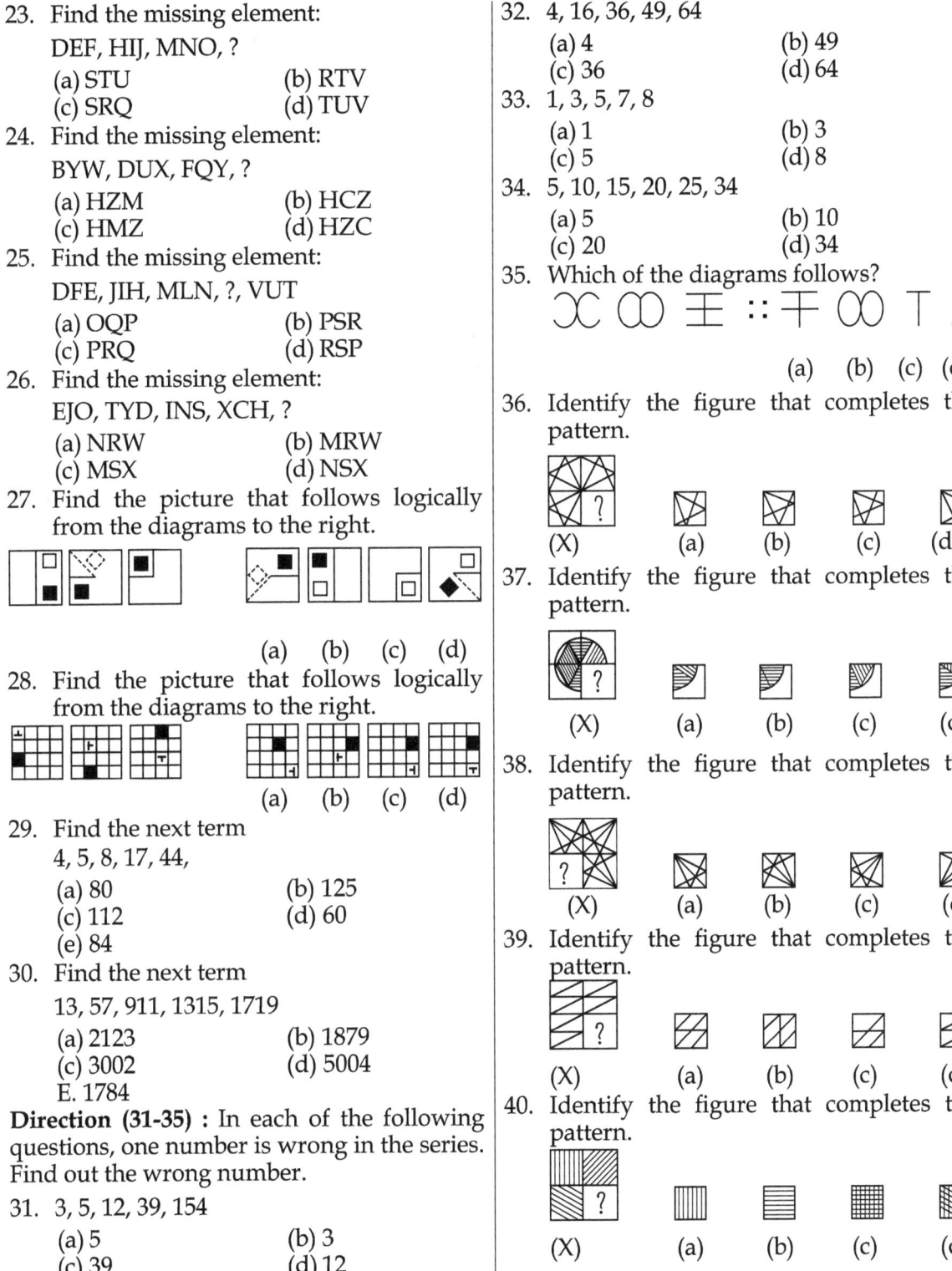

HOTS

1. Find the missing element: Q1F, S2E, U6D, W21C, ?
   (a) Y88B (b) Y77B
   (c) Z88B (d) Y84B

2. Find the missing element: C4X, F9U, I16R, ?
   (a) K25P (b) Y44B
   (c) L25O (d) Z88B

3. One number is wrong in the series. Find out the wrong number.
   4, 16, 36, 64, 99
   (a) 99 (b) 4
   (c) 36 (d) 64

4. What is the next number in the number pattern?

   | 1 | 6 | 15 | ? | 45 | 66 | 91 |

   (a) 22 (b) 28
   (c) 34 (d) 27

5. The missing number below is _____.
   737629, 717629, ? , 677629, 657629
   (a) 687629 (b) 607629
   (c) 707629 (d) 697629

Analogy

Learning Objectives : In this chapter, students will learn about:
- ✓ Relationship between words
- ✓ Relationship between events
- ✓ Relationship between objects or alphabet sets

CHAPTER SUMMARY

Analogy

Analogy means similarity. Analogy specifies a relationship between given words, events, objects or alphabet sets which has to be recognised. In this type of questions, two terms/figures related in some way are given and third term/figure is also given with four or five alternatives. It is the process of reasoning on the basis of parallel events or objects.

Example 1 : 'Nun' is related to 'Convent' in the same way as 'Hen' is related to :
- (a) Nest
- (b) Shed
- (c) Cell
- (d) Cote

Sol. (d)
As dwelling place of 'Nun' is 'Convent' similarly the dwelling place of 'Hen' is 'Cote'.

Example 2 : 'College' is related to 'Teachers' in the same way as 'Hospital' is related to :
- (a) Doctors
- (b) Patients
- (c) Medicine
- (d) Beds

Sol. (a)
As teaching is done by 'Teachers' in the 'College' similarly treatment is done by 'Doctors' in the 'Hospital'.

Example 3 : 'Flower' is related to 'Bud' as 'Fruit' is to :
- (a) Seed
- (b) Tree
- (c) Flower
- (d) Stem

Sol. (c)
As 'Flower' is made from 'Bud' similarly 'Fruit' is made from 'Flower'.

Direction (4-9) : In the following questions, choose the missing word in place of sign(?) on the basis of the relationship between the words given on the left/right hand side of sign ::

Example 4 : Food : Stomach : : Fuel : ?
- (a) Engine
- (b) Automobile
- (c) Rail
- (d) Aeroplane

Sol. (a): 'Food' is consumed in the 'stomach' and 'Fuel' is consumed in 'Engine'.

Example 5 : Water : Sand : : Ocean : ?
- (a) River
- (b) Engine
- (c) Desert
- (d) Waves

Sol. (c): 'Water' is contained in 'Ocean'. Likewise 'Sand' is contained in 'Desert'.

Example 6 : Curd: Milk :: Shoe : ?
- (a) Leather
- (b) Cloth
- (c) Jute
- (d) Silver

Sol. (a)
As curd is made from milk similarly shoe is made from leather.

Example 7 : ABC : ZYX :: CBA : ?
- (a) XYZ
- (b) BCA
- (c) YZX
- (d) ZXY

Sol. (a)
CBA is the reverse of ABC similarly XYZ is the reverse of ZYX.

Example 8 : 4 : 18 :: 6 : ?
   (a) 32   (b) 38
   (c) 11   (d) 37

Sol. (b)
As, $(4)^2 + 2 = 16 + 2 = 18$
Similarly, $(6)^2 + 2 = 36 + 2 = 38$.

Example 9 : 5 : 125 :: 10 : ?
   (a) 100   (b) 1000
   (c) 10   (d) 250

Sol. (b)
As $5^3 = 125$
Similarly $10^3 = 1000$

Direction (10-14) : In the following questions, find the pair of words which holds the same relation as given at the top of every pair/group.

Example 10 : Malaria : Mosquito :: ? : ?
   (a) Poison : Death
   (b) Cholera : Polluted Water
   (c) Rat : Plague
   (d) Medicine : Disease

Sol. (b)
Malaria is caused due to mosquito. Similarly 'cholera' is caused due to polluted water.

Example 11 : Glove: Hand :: ? : ?
   (a) Neck : Collar   (b) Tie : Shirt
   (c) Socks : Feet   (d) Coat : Pocket

Sol. (c)
As Glove is worn in Hands similarly Socks are worn on feet.

Example 12 : Lawyer : Court :: ? : ?
   (a) Chemist : Medical shop
   (b) Businessman : Office
   (c) Labour : Factory
   (d) Athlete : Olympics

Sol. (a)
As the working field of lawyer is Court, similarly the working field of chemist is medical shop.

Example 13 : Letter : Word :: ? : ?
   (a) Page : Book
   (b) Product : Factory
   (c) Club : People
   (d) Home work : School

Sol. (a)
As Word is a group of letters similarly Book is a group of pages.

Example 14 : Lively : Dull:: ? : ?
   (a) Employed : Jobless
   (b) Flower : Bud
   (c) Factory : Labour
   (d) Happy : Gay

Sol. (a)
First word is opposite to the second word.

MULTIPLE CHOICE QUESTIONS

1. Sword is related to Slaughter in the same way as Scalpel is related to
   (a) Murder (b) Stab
   (c) Surgery (d) Chopping

2. Life is related to Autobiography in the same way as Witness is related to
   (a) Papers (b) Truth
   (c) Documents (d) Acceptance

3. Chef is related to Restaurant in the same way as Druggist is related to
   (a) Medicine (b) Pharmacy
   (c) Store (d) Chemist

4. Jade is related to Green in the same way as Garnet is related to
   (a) Blue (b) Orange
   (c) Red (d) Yellow

5. Dancer is related to Stage in the same way as Priest is related to
   (a) Pulpit (b) Assembly
   (c) Parliament (d) State

6. Birds are related to Aviary in the same way as Bees are related to
   (a) Aquarium (b) Hive
   (c) Brewery (d) Apiary

7. Resign is related to Politician in the same way as Abdicate is related to
   (a) Prince (b) King
   (c) Realm (d) Throme

8. Scissors is related to Cloth in the same way as Scythe is related to
   (a) Wood (b) Steel
   (c) Grass (d) Paper

9. Gardener is related to Trowel in the same way as Seamstress is related to
   (a) Saw (b) Scissors
   (c) Sneakers (d) Crowbar

10. Prose is to Writing as Lisp is to
    (a) Reading (b) Music
    (c) Speech (d) Drawing

11. Anthropology is related to Man in the same way as Anthology is related to
    (a) Nature (b) Trees
    (c) Apes (d) Poems

12. What is related to Leaves in the same way as Chatter is related to Teeth?
    (a) Whistle (b) Ripple
    (c) Rustle (d) Cackle

13. Lion is related to Prowl in the same way as Bear is related to?
    (a) Frisk (b) Lumber
    (c) Stride (d) Bound

14. Mirror is related to Reflection in the same way as Water is related to
    (a) Conduction (b) Dispersion
    (c) Immersion (d) Refraction

15. Firm is related to Flabby in the same way as Piquant is related to
    (a) Bland (b) Salty
    (c) Pleasant (d) Small

16. Happiness is related to Sorrow in the same way as Comfort is related to
    (a) Hardship (b) Rest
    (c) Poverty (d) Difficulty

Direction (17-25): In the following questions, choose the missing word in place of sign?

17. Appreciation : Reward :: Disgrace : ?
    (a) Crime (b) Guilt
    (c) Allegation (d) Punishment

18. Naphthalene : Woollen :: Antibiotics ?
    (a) Germs (b) Immunity
    (c) Diseases (d) Body

19. Retirement: Service :: Dismissal : ?
    (a) Agreement (b) Communication
    (c) Employment (d) Ad

20. Drummer : Orchestra :: Minister : ?
    (a) Voter (b) Constituency
    (c) Cabinet (d) Department

Analogy

21. Physiology : Biology :: Metaphysics : ?
    (a) Physics (b) Statistics
    (c) Mathematics (d) Philosophy
22. Highbrow : Cultivated :: Suave : ?
    (a) Elegant (b) Urbane
    (c) Stylish (d) Broad-minded
23. Affirm : Hint :: Charge : ?
    (a) Insinuate (b) Reject
    (c) Convince (d) Deny
24. Author : Book :: Choreographer : ?
    (a) Drama (b) Ballet
    (c) Masque (d) Opera
25. Thick : Thin :: Idle : ?
    (a) Virtuous (b) Business
    (c) Industrious (d) Activity
26. Coherent is related to Consistent in the same way as Irate is related to?
    (a) Unreasonable (b) Unhappy
    (c) Irritated (d) Angry
27. Book is related to Magazine in the same way as Newspaper is related to?
    (a) Journal (b) News
    (c) Article (d) Headline
28. Tungsten is related to Filament in the same way as Bronze is related to?
    (a) Copper (b) Ships
    (c) Tin (d) Ornaments
29. Claymore is related to Sword in the same way as Beretta is related to?
    (a) Club (b) Axe
    (c) Knife (d) Gun
30. Indolence is related to Work in the same way as Taciturn is related to?
    (a) Observe (b) Speak
    (c) Cheat (d) Act
31. Gill is related to Lamellae in the same way as Lung is related to?
    (a) Ribs (b) Trachea
    (c) Alveoli (d) Pharynx
32. Dwell is related to Denizen in the same way as Inherit is related to?
    (a) Acquire (b) Successor
    (c) Outcast (d) Heir
33. Solicitous is related to Concern in the same way as Verbose is related to?
    (a) Tiredness (b) Wordiness
    (c) Speech (d) Deafness
34. Mouse is related to Cat in the same way as Fly is related to?
    (a) Animal (b) Horse
    (c) Spider (d) Rat
35. Brain is related to Cranium in the same way as Pearl is related to?
    (a) Box (b) Oyster
    (c) Sand (d) Shore
36. Horse is related to Hay in the same way as Cow is related to?
    (a) Leaves (b) Fodder
    (c) Milk (d) Trees
37. Abduction in related to Kidnapping in the same way as Larceny is related to?
    (a) Theft (b) Crime
    (c) Blackmail (d) Sin
38. Street is related to Lane in the same way as Road is related to?
    (a) Footpath (b) Junction
    (c) Avenue (d) Highway
39. Concert is related to Theatre in the same way as wedding is related to?
    (a) Hotel (b) Party
    (c) Feast (d) Supper
40. Statue is related to Shape in the same way as Song is related to?
    (a) Beauty (b) Sing
    (c) Tune (d) Poetry
41. Estonia is related to Rouble in the same way as Chile is related to?
    (a) Dinar (b) Peso
    (c) Peseta (d) Franc

42. Engineer is related to Machine in the same way as Doctor is related to?
    (a) Hospital   (b) Mind
    (c) Disease   (d) Medicine
43. Neck is related to Tie in the same way as Waist is related to?
    (a) Watch   (b) Belt
    (c) Ribbon   (d) Shirt
44. Oriya is related to Orissa in the same way as Dogri is related to?
    (a) Himachal Pradesh (b) Sikkim
    (c) Jammu   (d) Assam
45. Satyajit Ray is related to Films in the same way as Picasso is related to?
    (a) Literature   (b) Drama
    (c) Poetry   (d) Painting
46. South is related to North-West in the same way as West is related to?
    (a) South-West   (b) East
    (c) North-East   (d) South
47. Bull is related to Draught in the same way as Cow is related to?
    (a) Livestock   (b) Milch
    (c) Farm   (d) Fodder
48. Summit is related to Apex in the same way as Summon is related to?
    (a) Court   (b) Judge
    (c) Witness   (d) Beckon
49. Distil is related to Whisky in the same way as Brew is related to?
    (a) Ferment   (b) Gin
    (c) Beer   (d) Sugar
50. DDT is related to Abbreviation in the same way as LASER is related to?
    (a) Antithesis   (b) Acronym
    (c) Epigram   (d) Epithet

HOTS

1. QIOK : MMKO :: YAWC : ?
   (a) UVES   (b) UESG
   (c) UGSA   (d) UEGA
2. Select the related word/number from the given alternatives.
   FGHI : OPQR :: BCDE : ?
   (a) UVIW   (b) PQRS
   (c) TUVW   (d) KLMN
3. Fill in the blank. Never: Always:: Hate: _____
   (a) Do   (b) Eat
   (c) Reply   (d) Love
4. '12' is to '3' as '61' is to _____
   (a) 7   (b) 5
   (c) 31   (d) 15
5. Car: Wheel is related to which of the following?
   (a) Computer: Bicycle
   (b) Computer: Train
   (c) Computer: Aeroplane
   (d) Computer: Hard Disk

Odd One Out   3

Learning Objectives: In this chapter, students will learn about:
- ✓ Odd word
- ✓ Number alphabet

CHAPTER SUMMARY

Odd One Out

In this type of questions some numbers/words or alphabets are given in such a way that one item does not belong to that group of which the rest are members. The word/number or alphabet which does not belong to that group is called an odd word/number alphabet. Candidate have to select the odd number/word.

Example 1 : Find the odd man out.
- (a) Violet
- (b) Yellow
- (c) Red
- (d) Black

Sol. (d)
Except 'Black' all the others are different colours of rainbow.

Example 2 : Which one is different from the other three?
- (a) Mother
- (b) Father
- (c) Grand father
- (d) Wife

Sol. (d)
Except wife all others are blood relatives.

Example 3 : Find the odd one out.
- (a) A
- (b) E
- (c) I
- (d) D

Sol. (d)
Except D all other letters are vowels.

Example 4 : Find the odd one out.
- (a) 144
- (b) 64
- (c) 27
- (d) 216

Sol. (a)
Except 144 all others are perfect cube.

MULTIPLE CHOICE QUESTIONS

Direction (1-36): Find the odd one out.

1. (a) Onion (b) Tomato (c) Potato (d) Garlic
2. (a) Moscow (b) London (c) Paris (d) New York
3. (a) Bang (b) Hiss (c) Whistle (d) Wink
4. (a) Sparrow (b) Parrot (c) Cuckoo (d) Duck
5. (a) Gold (b) Silver (c) Bronze (d) Iron
6. (a) Sympathy (b) Hatred (c) Help (d) Adoration
7. (a) Unicorn (b) Rhino (c) Fox (d) Antepole
8. (a) Swan (b) Orange (c) Cotton (d) Snow
9. (a) Blackmail (b) Smuggling (c) Snobbery (d) Forgery
10. (a) Yen (b) Lira (c) Dollar (d) Ounce
11. (a) Moon (b) Saturn (c) Earth (d) Dog
12. (a) Complicated (b) Tricky (c) Complex (d) Contrast
13. (a) Book (b) Pages (c) Index (d) Chapters
14. (a) Huge (b) Massive (c) Heavy (d) Small
15. (a) Spring (b) Heat (c) Winter (d) Autumn
16. (a) Sky (b) Star (c) Planet (d) Comet
17. (a) Rigveda (b) Yajurveda (c) Atharveda (d) Ayurveda
18. (a) Teeth (b) Tongue (c) Palate (d) Chin
19. (a) Ink (b) Pen (c) Pencil (d) Brush
20. (a) Cooperate (b) Coordinate (c) Correlate (d) Combat
21. (a) Conscience (b) Morality (c) Conduct (d) Weight
22. (a) Guitar (b) Piano (c) Harmonium (d) Banjo
23. (a) Secretary (b) Council (c) Panel (d) Cabinet
24. (a) Topple (b) Tumble (c) Slip (d) Skip
25. (a) Freeze (b) Simmer (c) Bake (d) Boil
26. (a) Mother (b) Sister (c) Brother (d) Aunt
27. (a) Jack (b) King (c) Ace (d) Minister
28. (a) Hawk (b) Parrot (c) Falcon (d) Eagle
29. (a) Lemon (b) Orange (c) Citron (d) Banana
30. (a) Premchand (b) Kalidas (c) Shakespeare (d) G.B. Shaw
31. (a) Manganese (b) Rubber (c) Salt (d) Gold
32. (a) Rectangle (b) Rhombus (c) Square (d) Circle
33. (a) Bark (b) Cry (c) Chirp (d) Roar
34. (a) Aluminium (b) Copper (c) Brass (d) Brick
35. (a) Metre (b) Yard (c) Litre (d) Inch

Odd One Out

HOTS

1. Identify the one that does not belong to the group.
   (a) DEF (b) LNQ
   (c) ART (d) HOW

2. Find the odd one out.
   (a) Speaker (b) Piano
   (c) Harmonium (d) Banjo

3. Find the odd one out.
   (a) Sympathy (b) Hate
   (c) Help (d) Love

4. Find the odd one out
   (a) Kanpur (b) Allahabad
   (c) Varanasi (d) Alwar

5. In this type, pairs are given with minimum 3 digit or object which are correlated to each other with any specific property
   (a) (3, 9, 27) (b) (9, 18, 278)
   (c) (5, 25, 125) (d) (6, 36, 216)

Coding and Decoding   4

Learning Objectives : In this chapter, students will learn about:
- ✓ Letter Coding
- ✓ Number coding
- ✓ Number to Letter Coding
- ✓ Substitution Coding

CHAPTER SUMMARY

Coding and Decoding

The Coding and Decoding Test is set up to judge the candidate's ability to decipher the rule that codes a particular word / message and break the code to decipher the message.

A CODE is a 'system of signals'. Therefore, Coding is a method of transmitting a message between the sender and the receiver without a third person understanding it. Decoding is a process to understand a code language.

Type-I : Letter Coding

In this type of questions, the real alphabets in a word are replaced by certain other alphabets according to a specific rule to form its code. You are required to detect the common rule and answer the given questions accordingly.

Example 1 : If in a certain language, MADRAS is coded as NBESBT, how is BOMBAY coded in that code?

(a) CPNCBX (b) CPNCBZ
(c) CPOCBZ (d) CQOCBZ
(e) None of these

Ans. (b)

Each letter in the word is moved one step forward to obtain the corresponding letter of the code.

i.e. M A   D   R   A   S
     +1↓+↓ +1↓ +1↓ +1↓ +↓
      N B   E   S   B   T

Then B O   M   B   A   Y
     +1↓+↓ +1↓ +1↓ +1↓ +1↓
      C P   N   C   B   Z

Example 2 : In a certain code, TRIPPLE is written as SQHOOKD. How is DISPOSE written in that code?

(a) CHRONRD (b) DSOESPI
(c) ESJTPTF (d) ESOPSID
(e) None of these

Ans. (a)

Each letter in the word is moved one step back to obtain the corresponding letter of the code.

Here, T R I P P L E
     -1↓ -1↓ -1↓ -1↓ -1↓ -1↓ -1↓
      S Q H O O K D

Then, D I S P O S E
     -1↓ -1↓ -1↓ -1↓ -1↓ -1↓ -1↓
      C H R O N R D

Example 3 : If in a code language, COULD is written as BNTKC and MARGIN is written as LZQFHM, how will MOULDING be written in that code?

143

(a) CHMFINTK (b) LNKTCHMF
(c) LNTKCHMF (d) NITKHCMF
(e) None of these

Ans. (c)
Each letter in the word is moved one step back to obtain the corresponding letter of the code.
Hence M O U L D I N G
      -1↓ -1↓ -1↓ -1↓ -1↓ -1↓ -1↓ -1↓
       L N T K C H M F

Example 4 : In a certain code, MONKEY is written as XDJMNL. How is TIGER written in that code?
(a) QDFHS (b) SDFHS
(c) SHFDQ (d) UJHFS
(e) None of these

Ans. (a)
The letters of the word is written in reverse order and then each letter is moved one step back to obtain the code.

Hence MONKEY→ Y E K N O M
              -1↓ -1↓ -1↓ -1↓ -1↓ -1↓
               X D J M N L
then TIGER→ R E G I T
              -1↓ -1↓ -1↓ -1↓ -1↓
               Q D F H S

Example 5 : In a certain code, COMPUTER is written as RFUVQNPC. How is MEDICINE written in the same code?
(a) EOJDJEFM (b) EOJDEJFM
(c) MFEJDJOE (d) MFEDJJOE
(e) None of these

Ans. (a)
The letters of the word is written in a reverse order and each letter, except the first and the last one, is moved one step forward, to obtain the code.
COMPUTER→ R E T U P M O C
           +1↓ +1↓ +1↓ +1↓ +1↓ +1↓
            R F U V Q N P C
then MEDICINE→ E N I C I D E M
               +1↓ +1↓ +1↓ +1↓ +1↓ +1↓
                E O J D J E F M

Type-II : Number Coding

In this type of questions, either numerical code values are assigned to a word or alphabetical code letters are assigned to the numbers. We are required to analyse the code as per the directions.

Example 6 : If DELHI is coded as 73541 and CALCUTTA is coded as 82589662, how will CALICUT be coded in that language?
(a) 5279431 (b) 5978213
(c) 8251896 (d) 8543691

Ans. (c)
The alphabets are coded as follows:

D	E	L	H	I	C	A	U	T
7	3	5	4	1	8	2	9	6

So, in CALICUT,
C is coded as 8,
A is coded as 2,
L is coded as 5,
I is coded as 1,
U is coded as 9 and
T is coded as 6.
Thus, the code for CALICUT is 8251896.

Example 7 : In a certain code, RIPPLE is written as 613382 and LIFE is written as 8192. How is PILLER written in that code?
(a) 318826 (b) 318286
(c) 618826 (d) 338816

Ans. (a)
The alphabets are coded as shown:

R	I	P	L	E	F
6	1	3	8	2	9

So, in PILLER,
P is coded as 3,
I is coded as 1,
L is coded as 8,
E is coded as 2 and
R is coded as 6.
Thus, the code for PILLER is 318826.

Example 8 : If ROSE is coded as 6821, CHAIR is coded as 73456 and PREACH is coded as 961473, what will be the code for SEARCH?
(a) 246173
(b) 214673
(c) 214763
(d) 216473

Ans. (b)

The alphabets are coded as shown :

R	O	S	E	C	H	A	I	P
6	8	2	1	7	3	4	5	9

So, in SEARCH,
S is coded as 2,
E is coded as 1,
A is coded as 4,
R is coded as 6,
C is coded as 7,
H is coded as 3.
Thus, the code for SEARCH is 214673.

Example 9 : If in a certain code, TWENTY is written as 863985 and ELEVEN is written as 323039, how is TWELVE written in that code?
(a) 863203
(b) 863584
(c) 863903
(d) 863063

Ans. (a)

The alphabets are coded as shown :

T	W	E	N	Y	L	V
8	6	3	9	5	2	0

So, in TWELVE,
T is coded as 8,
W is coded as 6,
E is coded as 3,
L is coded as 2,
V is coded as 0.
Thus, the code for TWELVE is 863203.

Example 10 : If the letters in PRABA are coded as 27595 and THILAK are coded as 368451, how can BHARATHI be coded?
(a) 37536689
(b) 57686535
(c) 96575368
(d) 96855368

Ans. (c)

The alphabets are coded as shown :

P	R	A	B	T	H	I	L	K
2	7	5	9	3	6	8	4	1

So, B is coded as 9,
H is coded as 6,
A is coded as 5,
R is coded as 7,
T is coded as 3 and
I is coded as 8.
Thus, the code for BHARATHI is 96575368.

Type-III : Number To Letter Coding

Sometimes numbers/symbols are assigned to words.

Example 11 : In a certain code, 15789 is written as EGKPT and 2346 is written as ALUR. How is 23549 written in that code?
(a) ALEUT
(b) ALGTU
(c) ALGUT
(d) ALGRT

Ans. (c)

In the given codes, the numbers are coded as shown:

1	5	7	8	9	2	3	4	6
E	G	K	P	T	A	L	U	R

Obviously 2 is coded as A,
3 is coded as L,
5 is coded as G,
4 is coded as U and
9 is coded as T.
So, 23549 is coded as ALGUT.

Example 12 : In a certain code, a number 13479 is written as AQFJL and 5268 is written as DMPN. How is 396824 written in that code?
(a) QLPNKJ
(b) QLPNMF
(c) QLPMNF
(d) QLPNDF

Ans. (b)

In the given codes, the numbers are coded as shown:

1	3	4	7	9	5	2	6	8
A	Q	F	J	L	D	M	P	N

Clearly 3 is coded as Q,
9 is coded as L,
6 is coded as P,
8 is coded as N,
2 is coded as M and
4 is coded as F.
Hence, 396824 is coded as QLPNMF.

Example 13 : The number in the question below is to be codified as per the following code:

Digit	7	2	1	5	3	9	8	6	4
Letter	W	L	M	S	I	N	D	J	B

How is 184632 written in that code?
(a) MDJBSI   (b) MDJBIL
(c) MDJBWL   (d) MDBJIL

Ans. (d)
As given, 1 is coded as M,
8 is coded as D,
4 is coded as B,
6 is coded as J,
3 is coded as I and
2 is coded as L.
So, 184632 is coded as MDBJIL.

Example 14 : The number in the question below is to be codified as per the following code:

Digit	7	2	1	5	3	9	8	6	4
Letter	W	L	M	S	I	N	D	J	B

How is 879341 written in that code?
(a) DWNIBS   (b) DWNBIM
(c) DWNIBM   (d) NDWBIM

Ans. (c)
As given, 8 is coded as D,
7 is coded as W,
9 is coded as N,
3 is coded as I,
4 is coded as B and
1 is coded as M.
So, 879341 is coded as DWNIBM.

Example 15 : The number in the question below is to be codified as per the following code:

Digit	7	2	1	5	3	9	8	6	4
Letter	W	L	M	S	I	N	D	J	B

How is 64928 written in that code?
(a) JBNLD   (b) JBLND
(c) BJNLD   (d) DBNLS

Ans. (a)
As given, 6 is coded as J,
4 is coded as B,
9 is coded as N,
2 is coded as L and
8 is coded as D.
So, 64928 is coded as JBNLD.

Type-IV : Substitution Coding

In this type of questions, some particular objects are assigned code names. Then a question is asked that is to be answered in the code language.

Example 16 : If white is called blue, blue is called red, red is called yellow, yellow is called green, green is called black, black is called violet and violet is called orange, what would be the colour of human blood?
(a) Red   (b) Green
(c) Yellow   (d) Violet
(e) Orange

Ans. (c)
The colour of the human blood is 'red' and given that 'red' is called 'yellow'.
So, the colour of human blood is 'yellow'.

Example 17 : If orange is called butter, butter is called soap, soap is called ink, ink is called honey and honey is called orange, which of the following is used for washing the clothes?
(a) Honey (b) Butter
(c) Orange (d) Soap
(e) Ink

Ans. (e)
Clearly, 'soap' is used for washing the clothes. But, 'soap' is called 'ink'. So, 'ink' is used for washing the clothes.

Example 18 : If the animals which can walk are called swimmers, animals who crawl are called flying, those living in water are called snakes and those which fly in the sky are called hunters, then what will a lizard be called?
(a) Swimmers (b) Snakes
(c) Flying (d) Hunters
(e) None of these

Ans. (c)
Clearly, a lizard crawls and the animals that crawl are called 'flying'.
So, 'lizard' is called 'flying'.

Example 19 : If air is called green, green is called blue, blue is called sky, sky is called yellow, yellow is called water and water is called pink, then what is the colour of clear sky?

(a) Blue (b) Sky
(c) Yellow (d) Water
(e) Pink

Ans. (b)
The colour of clear sky is 'blue' and given that 'blue' is called 'sky'. So, the colour of clear sky is 'sky'.

Example 20 : If sky is called sea, sea is called water, water is called air, air is called cloud and cloud is called river, then what do we drink when thirsty?
(a) Sky (b) Air
(c) Water (d) Sea
(e) Cloud

Ans. (b)
One drinks 'water' when thirsty and given that 'water' is called 'air'.

Example 21 : If man is called girl, girl is called woman, woman is called boy, boy is called butler and butler is called rogue, who will serve in a restaurant?
(a) Butler (b) Girl
(c) Man (d) Woman
(e) Rogue

Ans. (a)
A 'butler' serves in a restaurant but 'butler' is called 'rogue'. So 'rouge' will serve in the restaurant.

MULTIPLE CHOICE QUESTIONS

1. If GIVE is coded as 5137 and BAT is coded as 924, how is GATE coded?
   (a) 5427   (b) 2547
   (c) 5247   (d) 5724

2. If in a certain code, LUTE is written as MUTE and FATE is written as GATE, then how will BLUE be written in that code?
   (a) CLUE   (b) GLUE
   (c) FLUE   (d) SLUE

3. In a certain code, INSTITUTION is written as NOITUTITSNI. How is PERFECTION written in that code?
   (a) NOICTEFREP   (b) NOITCEFERP
   (c) NOITCEFREP   (d) NOITCEFPER

4. In a certain code, GIGANTIC is written as GIGTANCI. How is MIRACLES written in that code?
   (a) MIRLCAES   (b) MIRLACSE
   (c) RIMCALSE   (d) RIMLCAES

5. In a certain code, GOODNESS is written as HNPCODTR. How is GREATNESS written in that code?
   (a) HQFZUODTR   (b) HQFZUMFRT
   (c) HQFZSMFRT   (d) FSDBSODTR

6. If in a certain language MADRAS is coded as NBESBT, how is BOMBAY coded in that language?
   (a) CPNCBX   (b) CPNCPZ
   (c) CPNCBZ   (d) CQOCBZ

7. If FISH is written as EHRG in a certain code, how would JUNGLE be written in that code?
   (a) ITMFKD   (b) ITNFKD
   (c) KVOHMF   (d) TIMFKD

8. In a certain code, TWINKLE is written as SVHOJKD, then how would FILTERS be written in the same code?
   (a) EHKSDQR   (b) EHKUDQR
   (c) EGKUDQR   (d) GJMSFSR

9. In a certain code, ROAD is written as URDG. How is SWAN written in that code?
   (a) VXDQ   (b) VZDQ
   (c) VZCP   (d) UXDQ

10. In a certain code, FAVOUR is written as EBUPTS. How is DANGER written in that code?
    (a) CBFFDS   (b) CBMHDS
    (c) EBFHDS   (d) EBHHFS

11. In a certain code, PRODUCTIONS is written as QQPCVEUHPMT. How is ORIENTATION written in that code?
    (a) PQJDOVBSJNO
    (b) PQJDOUBUJPO
    (c) PSJFOVBSJNO
    (d) NSHFMVBSJNO

12. If in a code, MIND becomes KGLB and ARGUE becomes YPESC, then what will DIAGRAM be in that code?
    (a) BGYEPYK   (b) BGYPYEK
    (c) GLPEYKB   (d) LKBGYPK

13. In a certain language SIGHT is written as FVTUG. How is REVEAL written in the same language?
    (a) YNRIRE   (b) DQHQMX
    (c) FSJSOZ   (d) ERIRNY

14. If in a certain language, MIRACLE is coded as NKUEHRL, then how is GAMBLE coded in that language?
    (a) JDOCMF   (b) CLEMNK
    (c) HCPFQK   (d) AELGMN

15. If in a certain code, BELIEF is written as AFKKDI. How is SELDOM written in that code?
    (a) RDKCNL   (b) RFKENM
    (c) RFKFNP   (d) TFKENP

16. In a certain code, TRIPPLE is written as SQHOOKD. How is DISPOSE written in that code?
    (a) CHRONRD (b) DSOESPI
    (c) ESJTPTF (d) ESOPSID
17. If in a code language, COULD is written as BNTKC and MARGIN is written as LZQFHM, how will MOULDING be written in that code?
    (a) CHMFINTK (b) LNKTCHMF
    (c) LNTKCHMF (d) NITKHCMF
18. In a certain code, MONKEY is written as XDJMNL. How is TIGER written in that code?
    (a) QDFHS (b) SDFHS
    (c) SHFDQ (d) UJHFS
19. In a certain code, COMPUTER is written as RFUVQNPC. How is MEDICINE written in the same code?
    (a) EOJDJEFM (b) EOJDEJFM
    (c) MFEJDJOE (d) MFEDJJOE
20. If VICTORY is coded as YLFWRUB, how can SUCCESS be coded?
    (a) VXEEIVV (b) VXFFHVV
    (c) VYEEHVV (d) VYEFIVV
21. In a certain code, TOGETHER is written as RQEGRJCT. In the same code, PAROLE will be written as
    (a) NCPQJG (b) NCQPJG
    (c) RCPQJK (d) RCTQNC
22. If BOMBAY is written as MYMYMY, how will TAMILNADU be written in that code?
    (a) TIATIATIA
    (b) MNUMNUMNU
    (c) IATIATIAT
    (d) ALDALDALD
23. If FRIEND is coded as HUMJTK, how is CANDLE written in that code?
    (a) EDRIRL (b) DCQHQK
    (c) ESJFME (d) FYOBOC
24. If in a certain language, COUNSEL is coded as BITIRAK, how is GUIDANCE written in that code?
    (a) EOHYZKBB (b) FOHYZJBB
    (c) FPHZZKAB (d) HOHYBJBA
25. If DELHI is coded as 73541 and CALCUTTA as 82589662, how can CALICUT be coded?
    (a) 5279431 (b) 5978213
    (c) 8251896 (d) 8543691
26. If ROSE is coded as 6821, CHAIR is coded as 73456 and PREACH is coded as 961473, what will be the code for SEARCH?
    (a) 246173 (b) 214673
    (c) 214763 (d) 216473
27. If in a certain code, TWENTY is written as 863985 and ELEVEN is written as 323039, how is TWELVE written in that code?
    (a) 863203 (b) 863584
    (c) 863903 (d) 863063
28. If the letters in PRABA are coded as 27595, and the letter in THILAK are coded as 368451, how can BHARATHI be coded?
    (a) 37536689 (b) 57686535
    (c) 96575368 (d) 96855368
29. If GIVE is coded as 5137 and BAT is coded as 924, how is GATE coded?
    (a) 5427 (b) 5724
    (c) 5247 (d) 2547
30. If in a certain language ENTRY is coded as 12345 and STEADY is coded as 931785, then state which is the correct code for below word.
    NEATNESS
    (a) 25196577 (b) 21732199
    (c) 21362199 (d) 21823698

31. If in a certain language ENTRY is coded as 12345 and STEADY is coded as 931785, then state which is the correct code for below word
    SEDATE
    (a) 918731 (b) 954185
    (c) 814195 (d) 614781

32. If in a certain language if ENTRY is coded as 12345 and STEADY is coded as 931785, then state which the correct code for below word is. ARREST
    (a) 744589 (b) 744193
    (c) 166479 (d) 745194

33. If in a certain language if ENTRY is coded as 12345 and STEADY is coded as 931785, then state which the correct code for below word is. ENDEAR
    (a) 524519 (b) 174189
    (c) 128174 (d) 124179

34. If ENGLAND is written as 1234526 and FRANCE is written as 785291. How is GREECE coded?
    (a) 381171 (b) 381191
    (c) 832252 (d) 835545

35. In a certain code, a number 13479 is written as AQFJL and 5268 is written as DMPN. How is 396824 written in that code?
    (a) QLPNKJ (b) QLPNMF
    (c) QLPMNF (d) QLPNDF

36. If white is called blue, blue is called red, red is called yellow, yellow is called green, green is called black, black is called violet and violet is called orange, what would be the colour of human blood?
    (a) Red (b) Green
    (c) Yellow (d) Violet

37. If orange is called butter, butter is called soap, soap is called ink, ink is called honey and honey is called orange, which of the following is used for washing clothes?
    (a) Honey (b) Butter
    (c) Orange (d) Soap
    (e) Ink

38. If the animals which can walk are called swimmers, animals who crawl are called flying, those living in water are called snakes and those which fly in the sky are called hunters, then what will a lizard be called?
    (a) Swimmers (b) Snakes
    (c) Flying (d) Hunters
    (e) None

39. If air is called green, green is called blue, blue is called sky, sky is called yellow, yellow is called water and water is called pink, then what is the colour of clear sky?
    (a) Blue (b) Sky
    (c) Yellow (d) Water
    (e) Pink

40. If sky is called sea, sea is called water, water is called air, air is called cloud and cloud is called river, then what do we drink when thirsty?
    (a) Sky (b) Air
    (c) Water (d) Sea

41. If man is called girl, girl is called woman, woman is called boy, boy is called butler and butler is called rogue, who will serve in a restaurant?
    (a) Butler (b) Girl
    (c) Man (d) Woman
    (e) Rogue

42. If train is called bus, bus is called tractor, tractor is called car, car is called scooter, scooter is called bicycle, bicycle is called moped, which is used to plough a field?
    (a) Train (b) Bus
    (c) Tractor (d) Car
    (e) Moped

43. If lead is called stick, stick is called nib, nib is called needle, needle is called rope and rope is called thread, what will be fitted in a pen to write with it?
    (a) Stick   (b) Lead
    (c) Needle   (d) Nib
    (e) Thread

44. If rose is called popy, popy is called lily, lily is called lotus and lotus is called glandiola, which is the king of flowers?
    (a) Rose   (b) Lotus
    (c) Popy   (d) Lily
    (e) Glandiola

45. If 'ish lto inm' stands for 'neat and tidy'; 'qpr inm sen' stands for 'small but neat' and 'hsm sen rso' stands for 'good but erratic', what would 'but' stand for?
    (a) inm   (b) qpr
    (c) sen   (d) hsm

46. In a certain code, 'bi nie pie' means 'some good jokes' : 'nie bat lik' means 'some real stories' ; and 'pie lik tol' means 'many good stories'. Which word in that code means 'jokes'?
    (a) bi
    (b) nie
    (c) pie
    (d) Can't be determined

47. In a certain code language, (A) 'pit dar na' means 'you are good' (B) 'dar tok pa' means 'good and bad' (C) 'tim na tok' means 'they are bad' In that language, which word stands for 'they'?
    (a) na   (b) tok
    (c) tim   (d) pit

48. In a certain code language, (A) 'pit dar na' means 'you are good' (B) 'dar tok pa' means 'good and bad' (C) 'tim na tok' means 'they are bad' To find the answer to the above questions, which of the following statements can be dispensed with?
    (a) Only A   (b) Only B
    (c) A or B   (d) B and C
    (e) None of these

49. In a certain code language, (A) 'pic vic nic' means 'winter is cold' (B) 'to nic re' means 'summer is hot' (C) 're pic boo' means 'winter and summer' (D) 'vic tho pa' means 'nights are cold' Which word in that language means 'summer'?
    (a) nic   (b) re
    (c) to   (d) pic
    (e) vic

50. In a certain code language, (A) 'pit na som' means 'bring me water' (B) 'na ja tod' means 'water is life' (C) 'tub od pit' means 'give me toy' (D) 'jo lin kot' means 'life and death' Which of the following represents 'is' in that language?
    (a) jo   (b) na
    (c) tod   (d) lin
    (e) None of these

HOTS

1. If 'Sugar' is called 'Book'; 'Book' is called 'Salt' and 'Salt' is called 'Sweet' then what do we read?
   (a) Sugar (b) Sweet
   (c) Book (d) Salt

2. In a certain code language 'i will go' is written as 'ta ma ra' and 'i will eat' is written as 'ta ma ga', then code for 'eat' is.........
   (a) ta (b) ga
   (c) ok (d) ar

3. In a certain code, FINGER is written is NIFREG, how is WINDOW written in the same code?
   (a) WINDOW (b) WINWOD
   (c) NIWWOD (d) NIWDOW

4. In a certain code, 32974 is written as 10752. How is 46295 written in the same code?
   (a) 20077 (b) 86407
   (c) 47447 (d) 24073

5. In a certain code, INACTIVE is written as VITCANIE, how is COMPUTER written in the same code?
   (a) ETTPOPCOR (b) RETURNOC
   (c) ETUPMOCR (d) UPTCMORE

Number Ranking and Alphabet Test   5

Learning Objectives : In this chapter, students will learn about:
- ✓ Various objects included in Ranking
- ✓ Alphabetical Order of Words
- ✓ Letter-Word Problems

CHAPTER SUMMARY

Number Ranking

In this type of questions a set of information is given. The information given shows relationship among rank and candidates are required to answer the questions based on the information given. The term ranking may include various objects such as age, height, marks, salary, weight etc.

Example 1 : P, Q, R and S are four men. P is the oldest but not the poorest. R is the richest but not the oldest and is older than S and Q. P is richer than Q but not than S and Q is older than S. The four man can be ordered descending in respect of age as.

(a) PQRS (b) PRQS
(c) PRSQ (d) PRQS

Sol. According to given information P> R > Q > S. Hence option B is correct.

Example 2 : Five girls took part in a race. Sonam finished before Neha but behind Puja. Shivani finished before Anjuman but behind Neha. Who won the race?

(a) Sonam (b) Puja
(c) Neha (d) Shivani

Sol. According to the given information the arrangement of five girls is as follows:
Puja > Sonam > Neha > Shivam > Anjuman
Hence option B is correct.

Alphabet Test

In alphabet test, the questions are based on the understanding of the position of letters in English alphabet. In a dictionary the words are arranged in the alphabetical order. The words beginning with the same letter are again arranged alphabetically with respect to the second letter in the word and so on. In order to solve questions on order arrangement we may have to compare all the letters sequentially.

Alphabetical Order of Words

In these type of questions, certain words are given. The candidate are required to arrange them in an order in which they shall be arranged in a dictionary and then state the word which is placed in the desired place. Knowledge of the English alphabets and dictionary usage is required for this test. In a dictionary, the words are put in an alphabetical order with respect to the second alphabet of the words and so on.

Example 3 : Arrange the given words in alphabetical order and choose the one that comes first.

(a) Wasp (b) Waste
(c) War (d) Wrinkle
(e) Wrist

Sol. (c)

The given words can be arranged in the alphabetical order as

War, Wasp, Waste, Wrinkle, Wrist.
  I   II   III   IV   V

Example 4 : Arrange the given words in alphabetical order and choose the one that comes first.
(a) Science (b) Scrutiny
(c) Scripture (d) Scramble
(e) Script

Sol. (a)

The given words can be arranged in the alphabetical order as:

Science, Scramble, Script, Scripture, Scrutiny
   I   II   III   IV   V

Example 5 : Arrange the given words in alphabetical order and tick the one that comes at the second place.
(a) Intense (b) Intellect
(c) Intend (d) Intelligent
(e) Integument

Sol. (b)

The given words can be arranged in the alphabetical order as.

Integument, Intellect, Intelligent, Intend, Intense
     I   II   III   IV   V

Example 6 : Arrange the given words in alphabetical order and choose the one that comes first.
(a) Nature (b) Native
(c) Narrate (d) Nascent
(e) Naughty

Sol. (c)

The given words can be arranged in the alphabetical order as.

Narrate, Nascent, Native, Nature, Naughty
   I   II   III   IV   V

Example 7 : Which of the following words will come fourth in the English dictionary?
(a) Didactic (b) Dictum
(c) Dictionary (d) Diastole
(e) Dictate

Sol. (b)

The given words can be arranged in the alphabetical order as.

Diastole, Dictate, Dictionary, Dictum, Didactic
    I   II   III   IV   V

Letter-Word Problems

In letter-word problems, the candidate is required to find out pair of letters in the given word which has as many letters between them in the word as in the English alphabet?

Original Alphabetical Order

A B C D E F G H I J K L M
1 2 3 4 5 6 7 8 9 10 11 12 13

N O P Q R S T U V W X Y Z
14 15 16 17 18 19 20 21 22 23 24 25 26

Example 8 : How many such pairs of letters are there in the word 'BUCKET' which have as many letters between them in the word as in the English alphabet?
(a) One (b) Two
(c) Three (d) Four
(e) More than four

Sol. (a)

Letters in the given word	Letters in the alphabetical order
C K E	C D E

Example 9 : Two letters in the word 'PRESENCE' have as many letters between them in the word as in the alphabet and in the same order. Which one of the two letters comes earlier in the alphabet? (Hint: Do not count the pair EC, because as mentioned in the question, the letters should be in the same order.

(a) C (b) E
(c) R (d) P
(e) None of these
Sol. (d)

Letters in the given word	Letters in the alphabetical order
P R E S	P Q R S

Therefore only one such pair.

Example 10 : How many pairs of letters are there in the word 'CREATIVE' which has as many letters between them in the word as in the alphabet?
(a) 1 (b) 2
(c) 3 (d) 4
(e) None of these
Sol. (c)

Letters in the word	Letters in the alphabetical order
C R E	C D E
A T I V E	A B C D E
T I V	T U V

Therefore there are three such letters in the word creative.

Example 11 : In the word 'PARADISE', how many pairs of letters are there which has as many letters between them in the word as in the English alphabet?
(a) None (b) One
(c) Two (d) Three
(e) Four
Sol. (c)

Letters in the given word	Letters in the alphabetical order
P A R	P Q R
A R A D	A B C D

Example 12 : How many pairs of letters are there in the word 'DABBLE' which has as many letters between them in the word as in the alphabet?
(a) Nil (b) One
(c) Two (d) Three
(e) More than three
Sol. (e)

Letters in the given word	Letters in the alphabetical order
D A B	D C B
B B L E	B C D E
A B	A B
A B B L E	A B C D E

Logical Sequence of Words

In this type of questions, a group of words are given. Student is asked to arrange these words in an order that is meaningful. This can be the sequence of occurrence of events, or sequence of increasing/decreasing number, size, value.

Example: Consider the following series of words: door, key, room, and lock. If you are asked to put these words into a sequence, what will be the answer?
It will be either - room, door, lock and key or the reverse i.e. key, lock, door and room. This is the order a person who is leaving a room or entering a room will follow.

Example 1: Arrange the following in a meaningful sequence:
1. Consultation 2. Illness
3. Doctor 4. Treatment
5. Recovery

Once an Illness occurs, we go to the doctor for consultation who give us treatment and then our recovery starts. So, the sequence will be 2, 3, 1, 4, 5.

Example 2:
1. Birth 2. Death
3. Funeral 4. Marriage
5. Education

The sequence of these events is– birth, education, marriage, death and funeral. Hence the sequence is: 1, 5, 4, 2, 3.

Example 3 :
1. Table
2. Tree
3. Wood
4. Seed
5. Plant

The sequence of these events is– A seed is planted which forms a plant and then the tree. Then, from its wood a table is formed. Hence, the sequence is – 4, 5, 2, 3, 1.

Example 4:
1. College
2. Child
3. Salary
4. School
5. Employment

The sequence of the events is child, school, college, employment and salary as child, first goes to school and then to college. Finally, he/she goes for employment and gets the salary.

MULTIPLE CHOICE QUESTIONS

1. Priti scored more than Rahul. Yamuna scored as much as Divya. Lokita scored less than Manju. Rahul scored more than Yamuna. Manju scored less than Divya. Who scored the least?
   (a) Manju (b) Yamuna
   (c) Lokita (d) Rahul
   (e) None

2. Roshan is taller than Hardik who is shorter than Susheel. Niza is taller than Harry but shorter than Hardik. Sushil is shorter than Roshan. Who is the tallest?
   (a) Roshan (b) Susheel
   (c) Hardik (d) Harry
   (e) Niza

Direction (3-7): Following questions are based on the infor-mation given below. Read the information carefully and answer the questions:
   (i) Seven students P, Q, R, S, T, U and V take a series of tests.
   (ii) No two students get similar marks.
   (iii) V always scores more than P.
   (iv) P always scores more than Q.
   (v) Each time either R scores the highest and T gets the least, or alternatively. S scores the highest and U or Q scores the least.

3. If V is ranked fifth, which of these must be true?
   (a) S scores the highest
   (b) R is ranked second
   (c) T is ranked third
   (d) Q is ranked fourth

4. If R gets the highest, V should be ranked not lower than:
   (a) Second (b) Third
   (c) Fifth (d) Sixth

5. If S is ranked sixth, and Q is ranked fifth, which of the following can be true?
   (a) V is ranked fifth or fourth
   (b) R is ranked second or third
   (c) P is ranked second or fifth
   (d) T is ranked fourth or fifth

6. If R is ranked second and Q is ranked fifth, which of these must be true?
   (a) S is ranked third
   (b) P is ranked third
   (c) V is ranked fourth
   (d) T is ranked sixth

7. Information given in which of the statements is superfluous?
   (a) (ii) (b) (i)
   (c) (iv) (d) None

Direction (8-9): Read the following information and select the best answer given in question.

In a study of five brands of pain relieving tablets P, Q, R, S and T, the brands were tested and ranked against each other as more or less effective per dose. The following results were obtained.
   (i) P was more effective than Q.
   (ii) The effectiveness of R was less than that of S.
   (iii) T was the least effective brand tested.
   (iv) Q and R were equally effective.
   (v) The effectiveness of S was greater than that of Q.

8. If the above statements are true, which of the following must also be true?
   (a) P and S were equally effective.
   (b) P was the most effective.
   (c) S was the most effective.
   (d) R was less effective than P.

9. All the information in the results given above can be derived from which of the following groups of statements?
   (a) Statements i, ii, ii
   (b) Statements i, iii, iv
   (c) Statements ii, iii, iv
   (d) Statements i, ii, iii, iv

Number Ranking and Alphabet Test

Direction (10-12) : Read the following information carefully and answer the questions.

Among A, B, C, D and E, E is taller than D but not as fat as D. C is taller than A but shorter than B. A is fatter than D but not as fat as B. E is thinner than C who is lighter than D. E is shorter than A.

10. If all the persons stood in a line according to their height who would be in the middle?
    (a) A (b) B
    (c) C (d) D

11. Which person is taller than two but thinner than the remaining two?
    (a) A (b) B
    (c) C (d) D

12. In the above question, who is the tallest?
    (a) A (b) B
    (c) C (d) None of these

13. Namita is taller than Pushpa but not as tall as Manish. Reena is taller than Pushpa but not as tall as Namita. Who among them is the tallest ?
    (a) Manish (b) Pushpa
    (c) Namita (d) Reena

14. Arrange the given words in Alphabetical Order and choose the one that comes first.
    (a) Praise (b) Practical
    (c) Prank (d) Prayer
    (e) Practices

15. Arrange the given words in Alphabetical Order and choose the one that comes at the second place.
    (a) Probe (b) Proclaim
    (c) Proceed (d) Problem
    (e) Probate

16. Arrange the given words in Alphabetical Order and choose the one that comes at the second place.
    (a) Guarantee (b) Group
    (c) Grotesque (d) Guard
    (e) Groan

17. Arrange the given words in Alphabetical Order and choose the one that comes first.
    (a) Prominent (b) Prohibit
    (c) Promise (d) Prolong
    (e) Programme

18. Arrange the given words in Alphabetical Order and choose the one that comes at the second place.
    (a) Heredity (b) Hesitate
    (c) Heavy (d) Hedge
    (e) Herald

19. Arrange the given words in Alphabetical Order and choose the one that comes first.
    (a) Exhilarate (b) Ephemeral
    (c) Entrench (d) Enterprise
    (e) Enthusiasm

20. Arrange the given words in Alphabetical Order and choose the one that comes at the third place.
    (a) Filter (b) Homage
    (c) Chastise (d) Charge
    (e) Certify

21. Arrange the given words in Alphabetical Order and choose the one that comes first.
    (a) Tenacious (b) Terminate
    (c) Temperature (d) Temple
    (e) Tenant

22. Arrange the given words in Alphabetical Order and choose the one that comes at the first place.
    (a) Blast (b) Bottle
    (c) Bondage (d) Boisterous
    (e) Bonafide

23. Arrange the given words in Alphabetical Order and choose the one that comes at the second place.
    (a) Grind (b) Growth
    (c) Great (d) Grease
    (e) Greed

24. Arrange the given words in Alphabetical Order and choose the one that comes in the second place.
    (a) Length   (b) Lenient
    (c) Legacy   (d) Legal
    (e) Legible

25. How many pairs of letters are there in the word 'HORIZON' which have as many letters between them in the word as in the English alphabet?
    (a) One
    (b) Two
    (c) Three
    (d) More than three

26. Two letters in the word 'LEMON' have as many letters between them in the word as in the alphabet. Which one of the two letters comes earlier in the alphabet?
    (a) E   (b) L
    (c) M   (d) N
    (e) O

27. How many pairs of letters are there in the word 'CLANGOUR' which have as many letters between them in the word as in the English alphabet?
    (a) One   (b) Two
    (c) Three   (d) Four
    (e) None of these

28. How many pairs of letters are there in the word 'LANGUISH' which have as many letters between them in the word as in the alphabet?
    (a) Nil   (b) One
    (c) Two   (d) Three
    (e) None of these

29. How many pairs of letters are there in the word 'PENCIL' which have as many letters between them in the word as in the alphabet?
    (a) Nil   (b) One
    (c) Two   (d) Three
    (e) None of these

30. How many pairs of letters are there in the word 'CARROT' which have as many letters between them in the word as in the English alphabet?
    (a) 1   (b) 2
    (c) 3   (d) 4
    (e) More than 4

31. How many pairs of letters in the word 'CATASTROPHE' have as many letters between them in the word as in the alphabet?
    (a) One   (b) Two
    (c) Three   (d) Four
    (e) None of these

32. How many pairs of letters are there in the word 'SEQUENTIAL' which have as many letters between them as in the alphabet?
    (a) Nil   (b) One
    (c) Two   (d) Three
    (e) Four

33. How many pairs of letters are there in the word 'REPURCUSSION' which have as many letters between them in the word as in the alphabet and that too in the same order? (Do not consider the pairs 'US' and 'ON'.)
    (a) Nil   (b) One
    (c) Two   (d) Three
    (e) None of these

34. How many pairs of letters are there in the word 'PRESENTMENT' which have as many letters between them in the word as in the alphabet?
    (a) Nil   (b) One
    (c) Two   (d) Three
    (e) None of these

35. How many pairs of letters are there in the word 'ADEQUATELY' which have as many letters between them in the word as in the alphabet?
    (a) One   (b) Two
    (c) Three   (d) Four
    (e) More than four

HOTS

1. Bunny ranks third from the top and sixteenth from the bottom in class. How many students are there in the class?
   (a) 20 (b) 18
   (c) 19 (d) 22

2. How many '8' are followed by even number in following set figures?
   4 8 4 3 8 1 4 8 3 2 8 7 8 4 8 5 6 8 7 8 4 6 8 6
   (a) 3 (b) 2
   (c) 4 (d) 6

3. Chotu remembers that his sister's birthday is after 10th but before 13th of January, while, his sister remembers that her sister's birthday is after 11th but before 16th of January. On which date of January is Chotu's sister birthday?
   (a) 12th (b) 16th
   (c) 19th (d) 15th

4. In the given letter series, which letter is exactly midway between M and J?
   Z A B C Y X L M N D E F G H O P Q R S T I J K U V W
   (a) H (b) O
   (c) P (d) G

5. Arrange the words in a meaningful logical order and then select the appropriate sequence from the options provided below the groups of words.
   1. Trillion   2. Thousand
   3. Billion   4. Hundred
   5. Million
   (a) 1, 2, 4, 3, 5 (b) 1, 5, 3, 1, 4
   (c) 4, 2, 3, 5, 1 (d) 4, 2, 5, 3, 1

Direction Sense Test 6

Learning Objectives : In this chapter, students will learn about:
- Directions and Cardinal directions
- Shadow formation during Sunrise and Sunset

CHAPTER SUMMARY

Direction Sense
The test is meant to judge candidate's ability to sense direction. A successive follow up direction is formulated and the candidate is required to ascertain the final direction.

Before going for questions it is better to have some basics :

Four Directions : There are four directions namely, East, West, North and South.

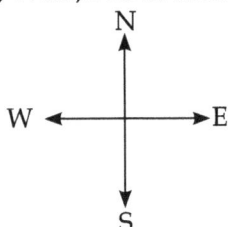

There are four cardinal directions - North-East (N-E), North-West (N-W), South-East (S-E), and South-West (S-W) as shown below :

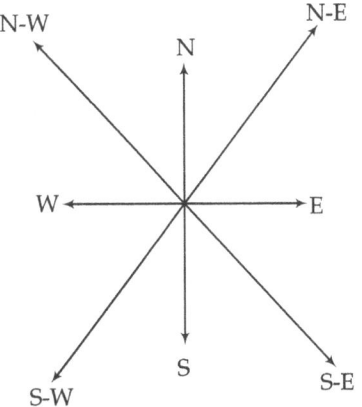

At the Time of Sunrise and Sunset

1. At the time of sunrise if a person stands facing the East, his/her shadow will be towards the West.
2. The shadow of a person or an object at the time of sunset is always in the East.
3. If a man stands facing the North, at the time of sunrise his shadow will be towards his left.
4. If a person stands facing the North, at the time of sunset his shadow will be towards his right.

   At 12:00 noon, the rays of the sun are vertically downward hence there will be no shadow.

Types of Questions on Direction Sense Test

Type 1
Shraddha starting from her house goes 5 km in the East, then she turns to her left and goes 4 km. Finally she turns to her left and goes 5 km. Now how far is she from her house and in what direction?

Sol. From third position it is clear that she is 4 km from her house and is in the North direction.

Direction Sense Test 161

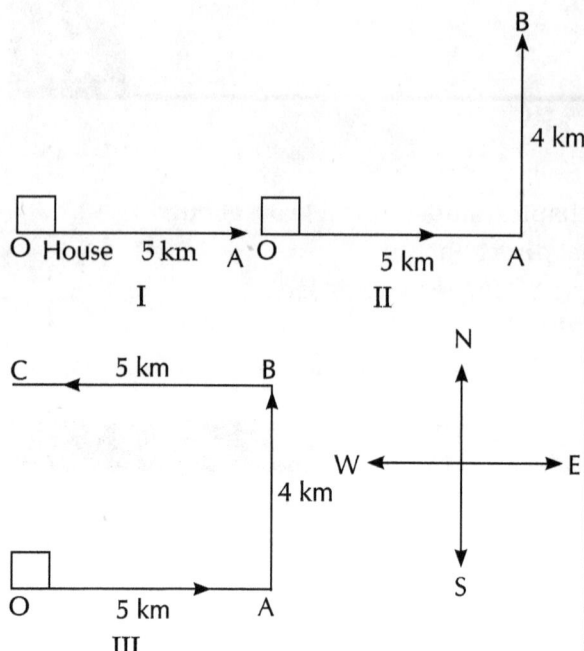

Type 2

Sanjiv starting from his house goes 4 km in the East, then he turns to his right and goes 3 km. What minimum distance should be covered by him to come back to his house?

Sol. Sanjiv's Movement:

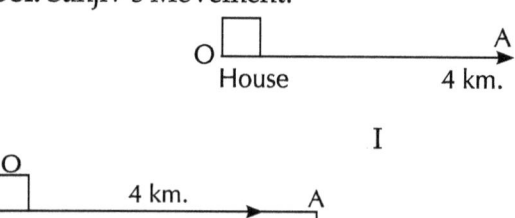

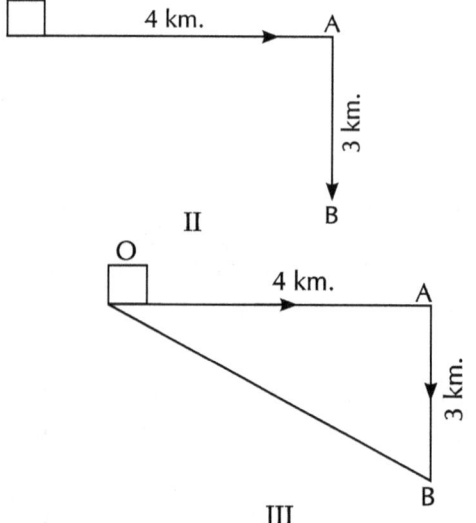

Clearly, minimum distance

$= \sqrt{OA^2 + AB^2} = \sqrt{(4)^2 + (3)^2}$

$= \sqrt{16 + 9}$

$= \sqrt{25}$

$= 5$ km

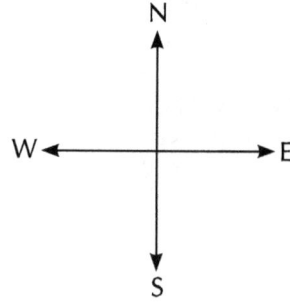

Type 3

One morning after sunrise Ashima, while going to school met Shraddha at road crossing. Shraddha's shadow was exactly to the right of Ashima. If they were face to face, which direction was Shraddha facing?

Sol. In the morning sun rises in the East.

So, in morning the shadow falls towards the West.

Now Shraddha's shadow falls to the right of Ashima. Hence Ashima is facing South, then it means Shraddha is facing North.

Solved Examples

Example 1 : Ayushi walks 1 km to East and then she turns to South and walks 5 km. Again she turns to East and walks 2 km. After this she turns to North and walks 9 km. Now, how far is she from her starting point?

(a) 2 km (b) 3 km
(c) 4 km (d) 5 km

Sol. Ayushi's movement is as shown in figure

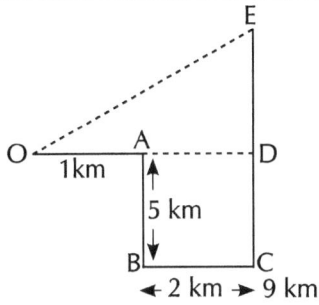

The last position of the Ayushi is E.
Now, AD = BC = 2 km and DE
= EC − DC = 9 − 5 = 4 km

Required distance = OE = $\sqrt{(3^2 + 4^2)}$
OE = $\sqrt{25}$
OE = 5 km.

Example 2 : Sanjiv faces towards North. Turning to his right, he walks 25 meters. He then turns to his left and walks 30 metres. Next, he moves 25 metres to his right. He then turns to his right again and walks 55 metres. Finally, he turns to the right and moves 40 metres. In which direction is he from his starting point?

Sol. Sanjiv's movements are as shown below:

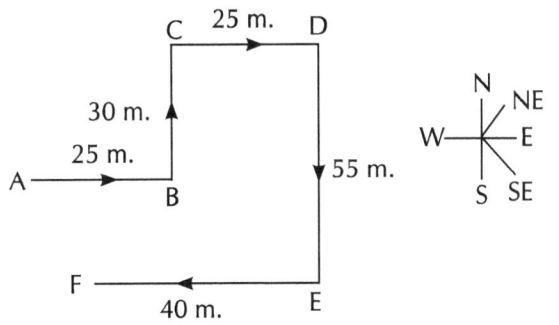

Clearly, Sanjiv is to the South-East from his starting point.

Example 3 : If South-East becomes North and North-East becomes West and all the rest directions are changed in the same manner, then what will be the direction for West?
  (a) South-East   (b) North-East
  (c) North-West   (d) South-West

Sol. If South-east becomes North and North East becomes West, therefore, the whole figure moves through 135°. Hence, West will be South-East.

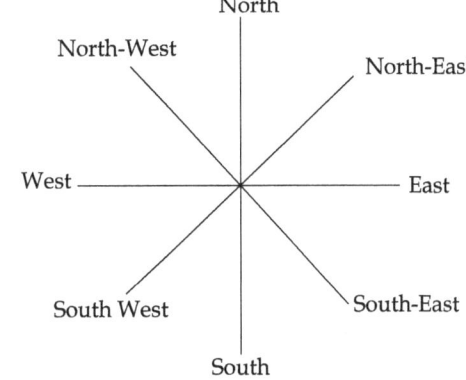

Example 4 : If Swati moves 20 metres in East direction and then turns to her left and then moves 15 metres and then she turns to her right and moves 25 metres. After this she turns to her right and moves 15 metres. Now, how far is she from her starting point?
  (a) 30 m   (b) 45 m
  (c) 55 m   (d) 60 m

Sol. Swati's movements are as shown in the figure:

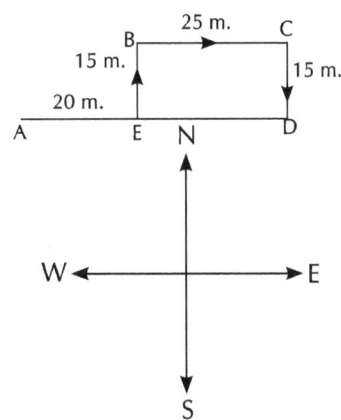

Direction Sense Test

Therefore, the distance of Swati from her starting point, = AD = A E + ED
= 20 + 25
= 45 metres

Example 5 : Golu was facing East. He walked 4 km forward and then after turning to his right walked 3 km. Again he turned to his right and walked 4 km. After this he turned back. Which direction was he facing at that time?

(a) East (b) West
(c) South (d) North

Sol. Golu's movement are as shown in figure:

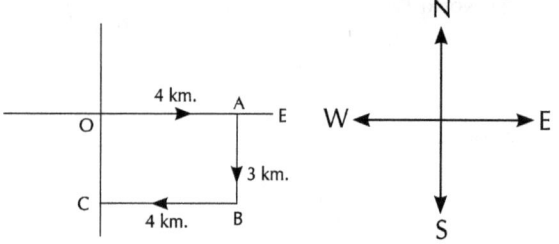

If Golu turned back from final position he must be facing in the direction of East.

Example 6 : A cyclist goes 30 km to North and then turning to East he goes 40 km. Again he turns to his right and goes 20 km. After this he turns to his right and goes 40 km. How far is from his starting point?

(a) 5 km (b) 10 km
(c) 20 km (d) 15 km

Sol. Cyclist's movements are as shown in figure:

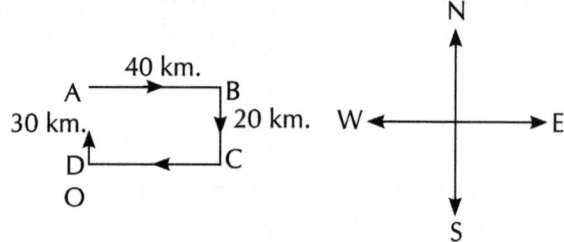

Distance of the Cyclist from his starting point O to end point D = OD = O A − AD = OA − BC
= 30 − 20 = 10 km

MULTIPLE CHOICE QUESTIONS

1. Golu starts from his house towards West. After walking a distance of 30 metres, he turned towards right and walked 20 metres. He then turned left and moving a distance of 10 metres, turned to his left again and walked 40 metres. He now turns to the left and walks 5 metres. Finally he turns to his left. In which direction is he walking now?
   (a) North (b) South
   (c) East (d) South-west

2. A rat runs towards East and turns to right, runs and turns to right, runs and again turns to left, runs and then turns to left, runs and finally turns to left and runs. Now, which direction is the rat facing?
   (a) East (b) West
   (c) North (d) South

3. Suraj walks 10 metres towards the South. Turning to the left, he walks 20 metres and then moves to his right. After moving a distance of 20 metres, he turns to the right and walks 20 metres. Finally, he turns to the right and moves a distance of 10 metres. How far and in which direction is he from the starting point?
   (a) 10 metres North
   (b) 20 metres South
   (c) 20 metres North
   (d) 10 metres South

4. I am facing South. I turn right and walk 20 m. Then I turn right again and walk 10 m. Then I turn left and walk 10 m and then turning right walk 20 m. Then I turn right again and walk 60 m. In which direction am I from the starting point?
   (a) North (b) North-West
   (c) East (d) North-East

5. Anil went 15 kms to the West from my house, then turned left and walked 20 kms. He then turned East and walked 25 kms and finally turning left covered 20 kms. How far was he from his house?
   (a) 5 kms (b) 10 kms
   (c) 40 kms (d) 80 kms

6. Rashmi walks 20 m North. Then she turns right and walks 30 m. Then she turns right and walks 35 m. Then she turns left and walks 15 m. Then she again turns left and walks 15 m. In which direction and how many metres away is she from her original position?
   (a) 15 metres West (b) 30 metres East
   (c) 30 metres West (d) 45 metres East

7. The door of Adi's house faces the East. From the back side of his house, he walks straight 50 metres, then turns to the right and walks 50 metres again. Finally, he turns towards left and stops after walking 25 metres. Now, Adi is in which direction from the starting point?
   (a) South-East (b) North-East
   (c) South-West (d) North-West

8. If A is to the South of B and C is to the East of B, in what direction is A with respect to C?
   (a) North-East (b) North-West
   (c) South-East (d) South-West

9. P, Q, R and S are playing a game of carom. P, R and S, Q are partners. S is to the right of R who is facing West. Then, Q is facing
   (a) North (b) South
   (c) East (d) West

10. The post office is to the East of the school while my house is to the South of the school. The market is to the North of the post office. If the distance of the market from the post office is equal to the distance of my house from the school, in which direction is the market with respect to my school?
    (a) North (b) East
    (c) North-East (d) South-West

Direction Sense Test

11. A watch reads 4.30 if the minute hand points East, in what direction does the hour hand point?
    (a) North   (b) North-West
    (c) South-East   (d) North-East

12. If you are facing North-East and move 10 m forward, turn left and move 7.5 m, then you are in
    (a) North of your initial position
    (b) South of you initial position
    (c) East of your initial position
    (d) 12 m from your initial position

13. One morning after sunrise, Suresh and Ramesh were standing on a lawn with their backs towards each other. Suresh's shadow fell exactly towards his left hand side. Which direction was Ramesh facing?
    (a) East   (b) West
    (c) North   (d) South

Direction (14-15) : Dev, Kumar, Nilesh, Ankur and Pintu are standing facing to the North in a playground such as given below:
- Kumar is at 40 m to the right of Ankur.
- Dev is 60 m in the South of Kumar.
- Nilesh is at a distance of 25 m in the West of Ankur.
- Pintu is at a distance of 90 m in the North of Dev.

14. Which one is in the North-East of the person who is to the left of Kumar?
    (a) Dev   (b) Nilesh
    (c) Ankur   (d) Pintu

15. If a boy starting from Nilesh, walked up to Ankur and then to Kumar and after this he to Dev and then to Pintu and whole the time he walked in a straight line, then how much distance did he cover in total?
    (a) 215 m   (b) 155 m
    (c) 245 m   (d) 185 m

Direction (16-18) : Each of the following questions is based on the following information :
- A # B means B is at 1 metre to the right of A.
- A $ B means B is at 1 metre to the North of A.
- A * B means B is at 1 metre to the left of A.
- A @ B means B is at 1 metre to the South of A.
- In each question first person from the left is facing North.

16. According to X @ B * P, P is in which direction with respect to X?
    (a) North   (b) South
    (c) North-East   (d) South-West

17. According to M # N $ T, T is in which direction with respect to M?
    (a) North-West   (b) North-East
    (c) South-West   (d) South-East

18. According to P # R $ A * U, in which direction is U with respect to P?
    (a) East   (b) West
    (c) North   (d) South

19. From his house, Samrath went 15 km to the North. Then he turned towards West and covered 10 km. Then, he turned South and covered 5 km. Finally, turning to East, he covered 10 km. In which direction is he from his house?
    (a) East   (b) West
    (c) North   (d) South

20. Armaan walks 1 km towards East and then he turns to South and walks 5 km. Again he turns to East and walks 2 km, finally he turns to North and walks 9 km. In which direction is he now with respect to the starting point?
    (a) North-East   (b) South-West
    (c) North   (d) East

HOTS

1. Golu starts walking from his house and comes to a temple which is in South direction from his house. From temple, he takes right turn and goes to the market. What is the direction of market from temple?
   (a) North-East (b) South-East
   (c) West (d) East

2. See the following figure.

   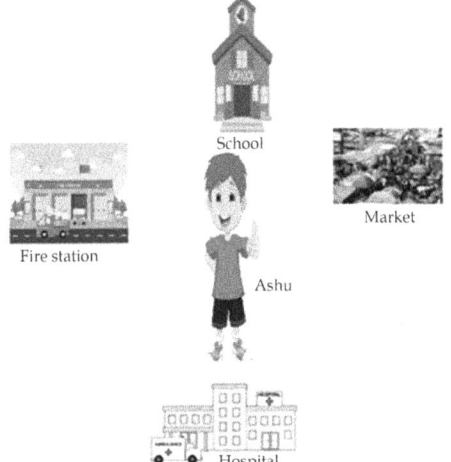

   Suppose Ashu is facing the school. If he turns 90 to his right, then in which direction will he face?
   (a) Market (b) Hospital
   (c) Fire Station (d) School

3. Ankit rode his bicycle towards north, then turned left and rode 1 km and again turned left and rode 2 km. He found himself 1 km west from his starting point. How far did he ride initially towards north?

   (a) 1 km (b) 3 km
   (c) 5 km (d) 2 km

4. Six friends Shalu, Meera, Anjali, Rahul, Ashu and Kamini are standing in six different directions as shown below. In which direction is Anjali standing?

   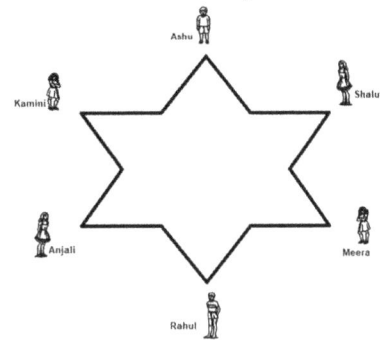

   (a) South (b) West
   (c) North-East (d) South-West

5. Shraddha is facing the Community centre. What will she be facing if she turns 270° clockwise?

   (a) Mall (b) School
   (c) Temple (d) Park

Direction Sense Test

Mirror and Water Images 7

Learning Objectives : In this chapter, students will learn about:
- Mirror Images of Capital Letters
- Mirror images of Small Letters
- Mirror images of Numbers
- Water Images of Capital Letters
- Water Images of Small Letters
- Water Images of Numbers
- Mirror Images of Certain Words and Numbers

CHAPTER SUMMARY

Mirror Images

The image of an object as seen into the mirror is called its mirror reflection or mirror image. Mirror image is also called as vertical plane. It is obtained by inverting an object laterally.

A mirror - image is therefore said to be laterally inverted and the phenomenon is called Lateral Inversion.

Mirror Images of Capital Letters

Letters	Mirror Images	Letters	Mirror Images	Letters	Mirror Images
A	A	J	ↄ	S	2
B	ꓭ	K	ꓘ	T	T
C	ꓛ	L	⌐	U	U
D	ꓷ	M	M	V	V
E	ꓱ	N	И	W	W
F	ꓞ	O	O	X	X
G	ꓨ	P	ꟼ	Y	Y
H	H	Q	Ꝺ	Z	Z
I	I	R	Я	-	-

International Mathematics Olympiad – 5

Mirror Images of Small Letters

Letters	Mirror Images	Letters	Mirror Images	Letters	Mirror Images
a	a	j	ɟ	s	ꙅ
b	d	k	ʞ	t	ƚ
c	ɔ	l	l	u	ᴜ
d	b	m	ɯ	v	v
e	ɘ	n	ᴎ	w	w
f	ʇ	o	o	x	x
g	ƅ	p	q	y	ʏ
h	ʜ	q	p	z	ƹ
i	i	r	ɿ	-	-

Mirror Images of Numbers

Numbers	Mirror Images	Numbers	Mirror Images	Numbers	Mirror Images
1	1	4	ᔭ	7	ᴦ
2	ƨ	5	ƨ	8	8
3	ƹ	6	ᓂ	9	ҽ

Note : The mirror image of number six '6' is same as the water image of number 9.

Water Images

The reflection of an object as seen in the water is called its water image. It is obtained by inverting an object vertically.

Water Images of Capital Letters

Letters	A	B	C	D	E	F	G	H	I
Water Images	∀	ᗺ	C	D	E	Ɛ	ც	H	I
Letters	J	K	L	M	N	O	P	Q	R
Water Images	ſ	K	⌐	W	И	O	ᑫ	Ò	ᖇ
Letters	S	T	U	V	W	X	Y	Z	-
Water Images	ƧS	⊥	∩	∧	M	X	ʎ	Σ	-

Mirror and Water Images

Water Images of Small Letters

Letters	a	b	c	d	e	f	g	h	i
Water Images	ɐ	b	c	q	ǝ	ɟ	ƃ	ɥ	¡
Letters	j	k	l	m	n	o	p	q	r
Water Images	ꞁ	k	l	ɯ	ᴜ	o	b	d	ɹ
Letters	s	t	u	v	w	x	y	z	-
Water Images	s	ʇ	ɲ	ʌ	ʍ	x	ʎ	ʐ	-

Water Images of Numbers

Letters	0	1	2	3	4	5	6	7	8	9
Water Images	0	ᴉ	ᄅ	ㄣ	ㄱ	ƻ	9	ㄥ	8	6

Mirror Images of Certain Words and Numbers

Words	Mirror Images	Letters	Mirror Images
PREDICTION	ИOITCIDERP	32596	32596
HOSPITAL	JATIPSOH	8932	8932
DARPAN	ИAPRAD	868	868
STRIGENT	TNEGIRTS	786	786
OPULENT	TNELUPO	10190	10190
SARCASM	MSACRAS	5693	5693
LIBERAL	LAREBIL	8964	8964
OFFENCE	ECNEFFO	7362	7362
ADVANCE	ECNAVDA	5893	5893
IMAGES	SEGAMI	7839	7839

MULTIPLE CHOICE QUESTIONS

1. Choose the correct mirror image of the given figure (X) from amongst the four alternatives.

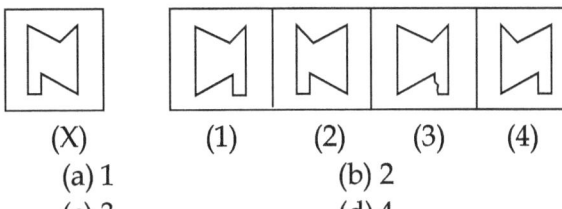

(X)   (1)   (2)   (3)   (4)
(a) 1   (b) 2
(c) 3   (d) 4

2. Choose the correct mirror image of the given figure (X) from amongst the four alternatives.

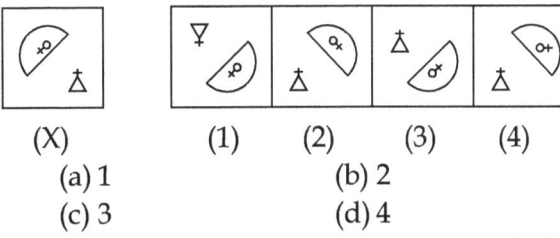

(X)   (1)   (2)   (3)   (4)
(a) 1   (b) 2
(c) 3   (d) 4

3. Choose the correct mirror image of the given figure (X) from amongst the four alternatives.

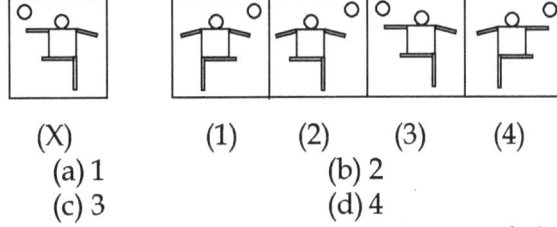

(X)   (1)   (2)   (3)   (4)
(a) 1   (b) 2
(c) 3   (d) 4

4. Choose the correct mirror image of the given figure (X) from amongst the four alternatives.

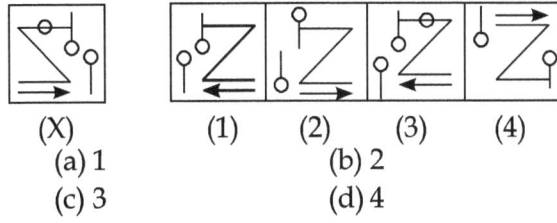

(X)   (1)   (2)   (3)   (4)
(a) 1   (b) 2
(c) 3   (d) 4

5. Choose the correct mirror image of the given figure (X) from amongst the four alternatives.

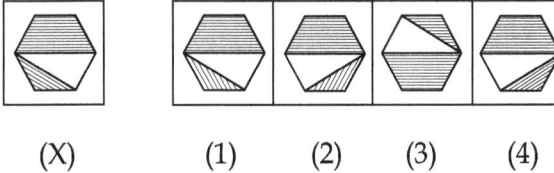

(X)   (1)   (2)   (3)   (4)
(a) 1   (b) 2
(c) 3   (d) 4

6. Choose the correct mirror image of the given figure (X) from amongst the four alternatives.

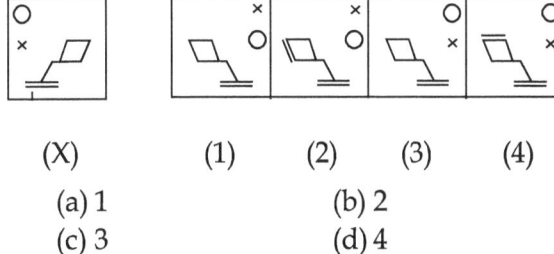

(X)   (1)   (2)   (3)   (4)
(a) 1   (b) 2
(c) 3   (d) 4

7. Choose the correct mirror image of the given figure (X) from amongst the four alternatives.

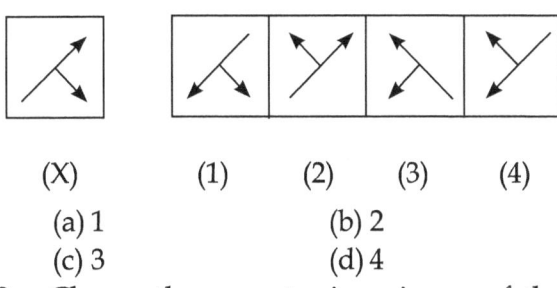

(X)   (1)   (2)   (3)   (4)
(a) 1   (b) 2
(c) 3   (d) 4

8. Choose the correct mirror image of the given figure (X) from amongst the four alternatives.

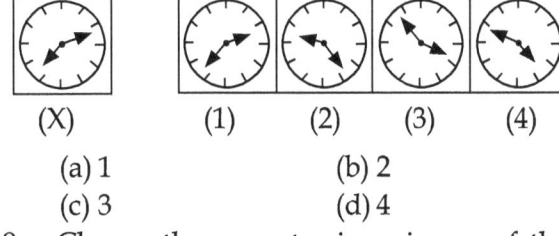

(X)   (1)   (2)   (3)   (4)
(a) 1   (b) 2
(c) 3   (d) 4

9. Choose the correct mirror image of the given figure (X) from amongst the four alternatives.

Mirror and Water Images

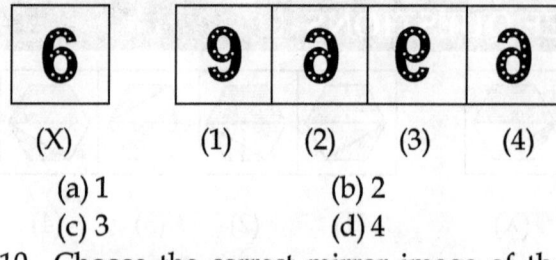

(X) (1) (2) (3) (4)

(a) 1 (b) 2
(c) 3 (d) 4

10. Choose the correct mirror image of the given figure (X) from amongst the four alternatives.

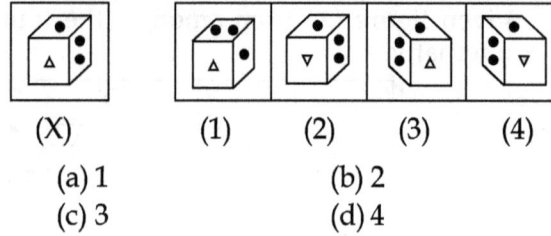

(X) (1) (2) (3) (4)

(a) 1 (b) 2
(c) 3 (d) 4

11. Choose the correct mirror image of the given figure (X) from amongst the four alternatives.

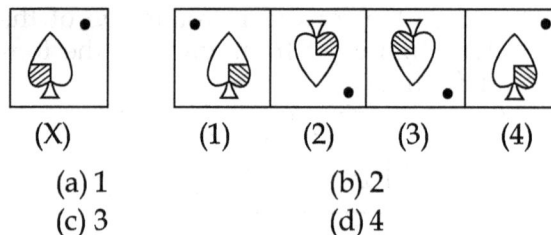

(X) (1) (2) (3) (4)

(a) 1 (b) 2
(c) 3 (d) 4

12. Choose the correct mirror image of the given figure (X) from amongst the four alternatives.

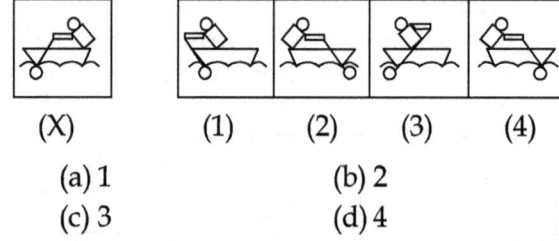

(X) (1) (2) (3) (4)

(a) 1 (b) 2
(c) 3 (d) 4

13. Choose the correct mirror image of the given figure (X) from amongst the four alternatives.

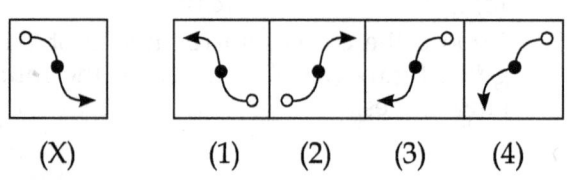

(X) (1) (2) (3) (4)

(a) 1 (b) 2
(c) 3 (d) 4

14. Choose the correct mirror image of the given figure (X) from amongst the four alternatives.

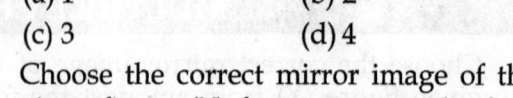

(X) (1) (2) (3) (4)

(a) 1 (b) 2
(c) 3 (d) 4

15. Choose the correct mirror image of the given figure (X) from amongst the four alternatives.

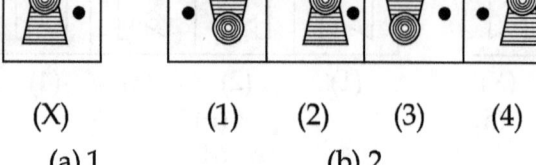

(X) (1) (2) (3) (4)

(a) 1 (b) 2
(c) 3 (d) 4

16. Choose the correct mirror image of the given figure (X) from amongst the four alternatives.

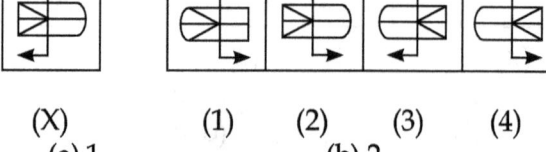

(X) (1) (2) (3) (4)

(a) 1 (b) 2
(c) 3 (d) 4

17. Choose the correct mirror image of the given figure (X) from amongst the four alternatives.

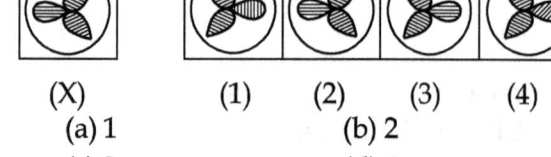

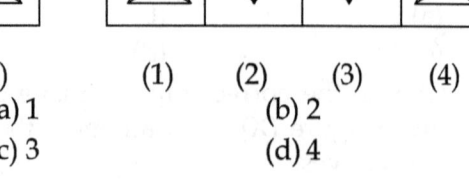

(X) (1) (2) (3) (4)

(a) 1 (b) 2
(c) 3 (d) 4

18. Choose the correct mirror image of the given figure (X) from amongst the four alternatives.

(X) (1) (2) (3) (4)
(a) 1 (b) 2
(c) 3 (d) 4

19. Choose the correct mirror image of the given figure (X) from amongst the four alternatives.

 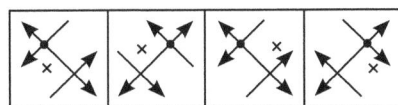

(X) (1) (2) (3) (4)
(a) 1 (b) 2
(c) 3 (d) 4

20. Choose the correct mirror image of the given figure (X) from amongst the four alternatives.

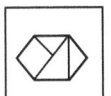 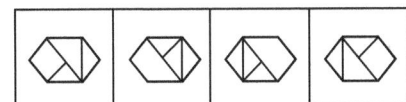

(X) (1) (2) (3) (4)
(a) 1 (b) 2
(c) 3 (d) 4

21. Choose the correct mirror image of the given figure (X) from amongst the four alternatives.

 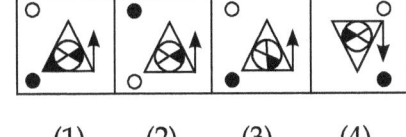

(X) (1) (2) (3) (4)
(a) 1 (b) 2
(c) 3 (d) 4

22. Choose the correct mirror image of the given figure (X) from amongst the four alternatives.

 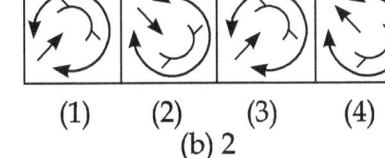

(X) (1) (2) (3) (4)
(a) 1 (b) 2
(c) 3 (d) 4

23. Choose the correct mirror image of the given figure (X) from amongst the four alternatives.

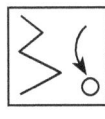 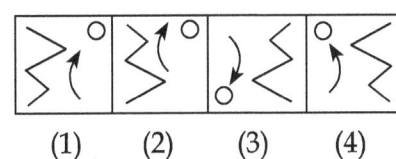

(X) (1) (2) (3) (4)
(a) 1 (b) 2
(c) 3 (d) 4

24. Choose the alternative which closely resembles the water-image of the given combination.

NUCLEAR

(1) ЯAEJCUN   (2) ИUCLEAR
(3) ИUCLEAR   (4) ИUCLEAR

(a) 1 (b) 2
(c) 3 (d) 4

Direction (25–27) : In each of the following questions, a figure marked (A) is followed by four figures (1), (2), (3) and (4) which shows the possible water images of figure (A). Choose one out of these four figures which shows the correct water image of the figure (A).

25.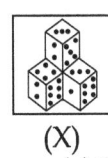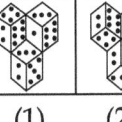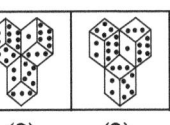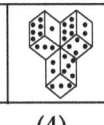

(X) (1) (2) (3) (4)
(a) 1 (b) 2
(c) 3 (d) 4

26.

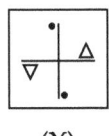

(X) (1) (2) (3) (4)

Mirror and Water Images

(a) 1   (b) 2
(c) 3   (d) 4

27.

(X)   (1)   (2)   (3)   (4)

(a) 1   (b) 2
(c) 3   (d) 4

Directions: In the following questions, a word is followed by four alternatives, (A) (B), (C) and (D) showing possible water images of that word. Choose the alternative which shows the correct water image of that word.

28. CLOSELY
    (a) CLOSELY   (b) CLOSELY
    (c) CLOSELY   (d) CLOSELY

29. IMAGES
    (a) IMAGES   (b) SEGAMI
    (c) IMAGES   (d) IMAGES

30. DARPAN
    (a) DARPAN   (b) DARPAN
    (c) DARPAN   (d) DARPAN

31. 5DOB6V2
    (a) 5DOB6V2   (b) 5DOB6V2
    (c) 5DOB6 V2   (d) 5DOB6V2

32. national
    (a) national   (b) national
    (c) national   (d) national

33. DL2CA34OO
    (a) DL2CA34OO   (b) DL2CA34OO
    (c) DL2CA 34OO   (d) DL2CA34 OO

34. D6Z7F4
    (a) D6Z7F4   (b) D9 Z7F4
    (c) D6Z7F4   (d) D6Z7F4

35. FRUIT
    (a) FRUIT   (b) FRUIT
    (c) FRUIT   (d) FRUIT

36. ACOUSTIC
    (a) ACOUSTIC   (b) ACOUSTIC
    (c) ACOUSTIC   (d) ACOUSTIC

37. FAMILY
    (a) FAMILY   (b) FAMILY
    (c) FAMILY   (d) FAMILY

38. RADIANT
    (a) RADIANT   (b) RADIANT
    (c) TNAIDAR   (d) RADIANT

39. MUNDANE
    (a) MUNDANE   (b) MUNDANE
    (c) MUNDANE   (d) MUNDANE

40. OBLITERATE
    (a) OBLITERATE   (b) OBLITERATE
    (c) OBLITERATE   (d) OBJITERATE

41. DETERRENT
    (a) DETERRENT   (b) DETERRENT
    (c) DETERRENT   (d) DETERRENT

42. QUESTION
    (a) QUESTION   (b) QUESTION
    (c) QUESTION   (d) QUESTION

43. SURFACE
    (a) SURFACE   (b) SURFACE
    (c) SURFACE   (d) SURFACE

44. DISCLOSE
    (a) DISCLOSE   (b) DISCLOSE
    (c) ESOLCSID   (d) DISCLOSE

45. OBLITERATE
    (a) ETARETILBO   (b) OBLITERATE
    (c) EBLITERATO   (d) OBLITERATE

46. TERMINATE
    (a) TERMINATE   (b) TERMINATE
    (c) TERMINATE   (d) TERMINATE

47. NIRMALA
    (a) ALAMRIN   (b) NIRMALA
    (c) NRILAMA   (d) INRMALA

48. VINAYAKA
    (a) INVAYAKA   (b) AKAYANIV
    (c) AKAYANIV   (d) NIVYAAKA

49. OBSTINATE
    (a) OBSTINATE (mirrored)
    (b) BOSTINATE
    (c) ETANITSBO
    (d) SOBTNIATE
50. PROCRASTINATE
    (a) ETANITSARCORP
    (b) PROCRASTINATE (mirrored)
    (c) RPORCASTNITAE
    (d) ETPROCRASTINA
51. PRECARIOUS
    (a) PRECARIOUS (mirrored)
    (b) SUOIRACERP
    (c) SUOPRECARI
    (d) SPRECARIOU
52. PERFECTION
    (a) NOITCEFERP
    (b) RPEFECTION
    (c) PERFECTION (mirrored)
    (d) ERPFECTION
53. FANTASY
    (a) FANTASY (mirrored)
    (b) FNTASAY
    (c) YSATNAF
    (d) YFANTSAY
54. INDULGENCE
    (a) ECNEGLUDNI
    (b) DNIULGENCE
    (c) ECNINDULGE
    (d) INDULGENCE (mirrored)
55. BENEDICTION
    (a) NOITCIDENEB
    (b) NEBEDICTION
    (c) BENEDICTION (mirrored)
    (d) NOIBENEDICT
56. VERBAL
    (a) LABREV
    (b) LRVEBA
    (c) REVBAL
    (d) VERBAL (mirrored)
57. STRENGTHEN
    (a) STRENGTHEN (mirrored)
    (b) NEHTGNERTS
    (c) TSRENGTHEN
    (d) NSTRENGTHE
58. RECALCITRANT
    (a) RECALCITRANT (mirrored)
    (b) NTARTICLACER
    (c) TNARTCILACER
    (d) CITRANTRECAL
59. OPPORTUNITY
    (a) YTINUTROPPO
    (b) YOPPORTUNIT
    (c) OPPORTUNITY (mirrored)
    (d) TYINUTROPPO
60. APPETITE
    (a) ETITEPPA
    (b) APPETITE (mirrored)
    (c) EPPAETIT
    (d) ETITAPPE
61. CRITICISM
    (a) MSICITIRC
    (b) MRCITICIS
    (c) CMSICITIR
    (d) CRITICISM (mirrored)
62. INSOMANIA
    (a) AINAMOSNI
    (b) AININSOMA
    (c) INSOMANIA (mirrored)
    (d) ASOINMANI
63. SEDATIVES
    (a) SEVITADES
    (b) SDAETIVES
    (c) SEVITADES (mirrored)
    (d) SEDATIVES (mirrored)
64. PANIPAT
    (a) TAPNIPA
    (b) PANIPAT (mirrored)
    (c) PANIPAT (mirrored)
    (d) QANIPAT
65. EMANATE
    (a) ETANAME
    (b) EMANATE (mirrored)
    (c) ENAMEAT
    (d) EATEMAN
66. CAR27aug
    (a) CAR27aug (mirrored)
    (b) CAR27aug (mirrored)
    (c) guaCAR27
    (d) gua72RAC
67. KALINGA261B
    (a) B162aGNILAK
    (b) KALINGA261B (mirrored)
    (c) KALINGA261B (mirrored)
    (d) KALINGA261B (mirrored)
68. JUDGEMENT
    (a) TNEMEGDUJ
    (b) TJUDGEMEN
    (c) JUDGEMENT (mirrored)
    (d) DJUGEMNET
69. MAHAVIR
    (a) RIVAHAM
    (b) RMAHAVI
    (c) RIVAHAM (mirrored)
    (d) HAMAVIR
70. CONSOLIDATE
    (a) ETADILOSNOC
    (b) CONSOLIDATE (mirrored)
    (c) TAECONSOLID
    (d) OCNSOLIDATE

HOTS

1. Find the mirror images of the given pictures.

2. Find the mirror images of the given pictures.

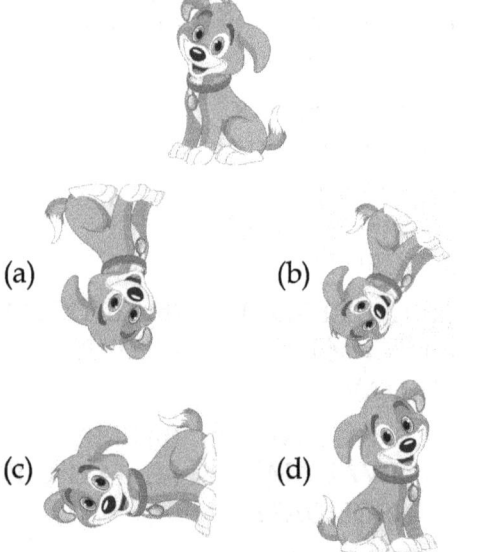

3. Find the mirror images of the given pictures.

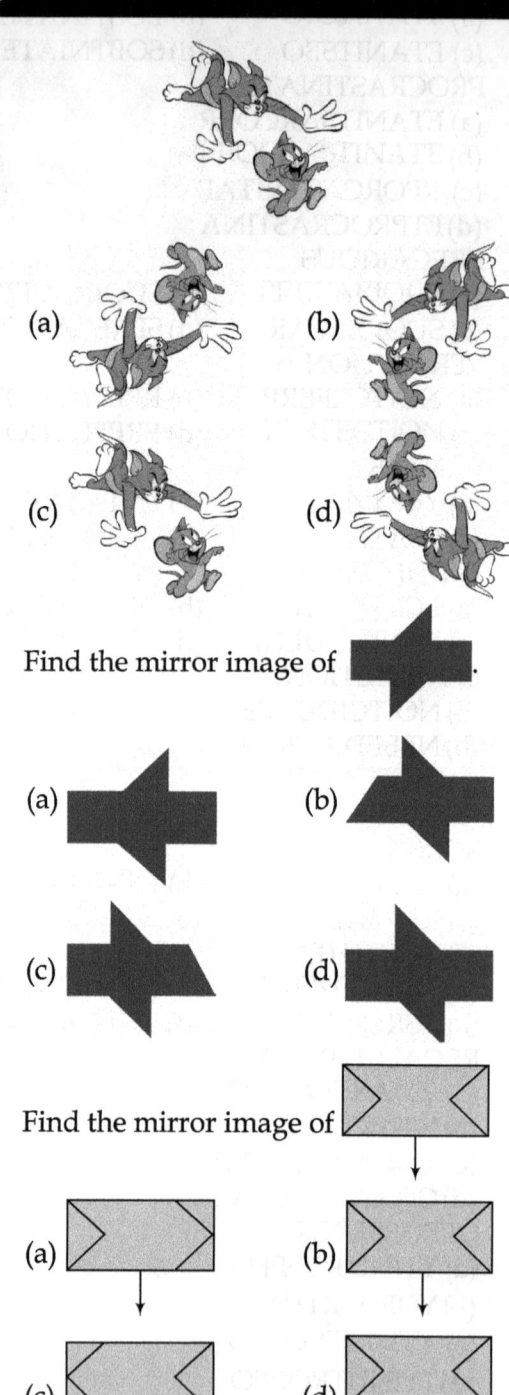

4. Find the mirror image of

5. Find the mirror image of

Data Handling 8

Learning Objectives: In this chapter, students will learn about:
- ✓ Qualitative and Quantitative Data
- ✓ Census or Sample

CHAPTER SUMMARY

Data
Collection of information is called data. It can be numbers, words, measurements, observations or even just descriptions of things.

Qualitative vs. Quantitative
Data can be qualitative or quantitative.
- (a) Qualitative data contains descriptive type information (i.e. it describes something)
- (b) Quantitative data contains numerical type information (i.e. it describes about numbers).

Quantitative data can also be Discrete or Continuous:

- **(i) Discrete Data**

  Discrete Data can only take certain values. It is counted.

  Example: The number of students in a class (you can't have half a student).

- **(ii) Continuous Data**

  Continuous Data can take any value (within a range). It is measured.

Examples:
- A person's height: could be any value (within the range of human heights), not just certain fixed heights,
- Time in a race: you could even measure it to fractions of a second,
- A dog's weight,
- The length of a leaf

Example: What do we know about Arrow the Dog?

Qualitative:
- He is brown and black.
- He has long hair.
- He has lots of energy.

Quantitative:
Discrete:
- Dog has 4 legs.
- He has 2 brothers.

Continuous:
- He weighs 25.5 kg.
- He is 565 mm tall.

Collecting of Data
Data are facts that are collected by counting things, objects or events.

Example: You want to find how many cars pass by a certain point on a road in a 10-minute interval.

So stand at that point on the road and count the cars that pass by in that interval.

You collect data by doing a Survey.

Census or Sample

Census : A Census is when you collect data for every member of the group (the whole "population").

Sample : A sample is when you collect data just for selected members of the group.

Example : There are 120 people in your local football club. You can ask everyone (all 120) what their age is. That is a census. Or you could just choose the people that are there this afternoon. That is a sample.

A census is accurate, but hard to do. A sample is not as accurate, but may be good enough, and is a lot easier.

Symbols, graphs and pictures are also used to represent information. When pictures are used to represent information, it is known as pictorial representation. Some methods of pictorial representation are (i) pictograph (ii) Bar charts (or bar graph)

Pictorial Representation of Data

Pictographs

A pictograph represents data through pictures of objects. A heading for the pictograph is also given which states what data is being represented by the pictograph.

Example : Which one of the following is quantitative data?

(a) She is black and white.
(b) She has two ears.
(c) She has long hair.
(d) She has a long tail.

Answer : Quantitative data is numerical information (numbers). The only one that is quantitative is (b) - two ears.

Example : Which one of the following is continuous data?

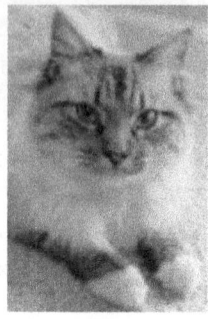

(a) She has two eyes.
(b) She has five kittens.
(c) She weighs 5.4 kg.
(d) She has four paws.

Answer : (c)

Discrete data can only take certain values (like whole numbers). Continuous data can take any value (within a range). The weight of a cat is continuous because it can take any value within certain limits.

Example : Which one of the following is discrete data?

(a) She is 45.2 cm long.
(b) She is 22.3 cm high.
(c) She weighs 5.4 kg.
(d) She has 30 teeth.

Answer : (d)

Discrete data can only take certain values (like whole numbers). Continuous data can take any value (within a range). The number of teeth has to be a whole number, so is discrete.

Example : A census collects information about:

(a) All members of the population.
(b) All adult members of the population.
(c) A large sample of the population.
(d) A small sample of the population.

Answer : (a)

A Census is when you collect data for every member of the group (the whole "population").

Example : Which one of the following is NOT quantitative data?

(a) The snake is 7 feet long.
(b) The snake has two eyes.
(c) The snake is green and yellow
(d) The snake has no legs.

Answer : (c)
The snake is green and yellow is qualitative because it is descriptive. The other three are all quantitative because they tell us about quantity. Even D tells us that the number of legs is zero, so is quantitative.

Bar Graphs

It is one of the simplest and the most common device used for the presentation of numerical data. In this form datum are represented by bars or rectangles of uniform width, which are drawn with equal spaces in between them either vertically or horizontally.

A Bar Graph (also called Bar Chart) is a graphical display of data using bars of different heights. Imagine you just did a survey of your friends to find which kind of movie they liked best :

Table: Favourite Type of Movie				
Comedy	Action	Romance	Drama	Science Fiction
4	5	6	1	4

This can be shown on a bar graph like this :

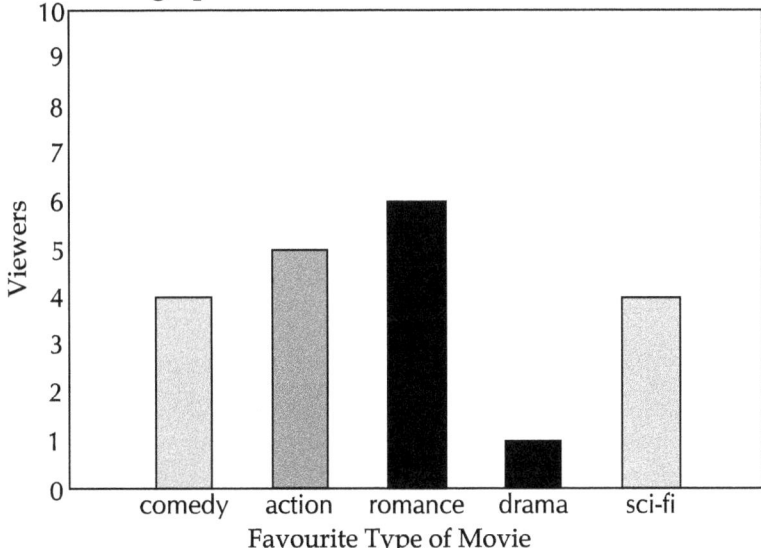

It is a really good way to show relative sizes : we can see which types of movie are most liked and which are least liked, at a glance.

Bar graphs can be used to show the relative sizes of many things, such as what type of bikes people have, how many customers a retail shop has on different days and so on.

Data Handling

Example : Most Popular Fruit
A survey of 145 people revealed their favourite fruit :

Fruit	Apple	Blueberry	Banana	Grapes	Kiwifruit	Orange
People	35	40	10	5	25	30

And here is the bar graph :

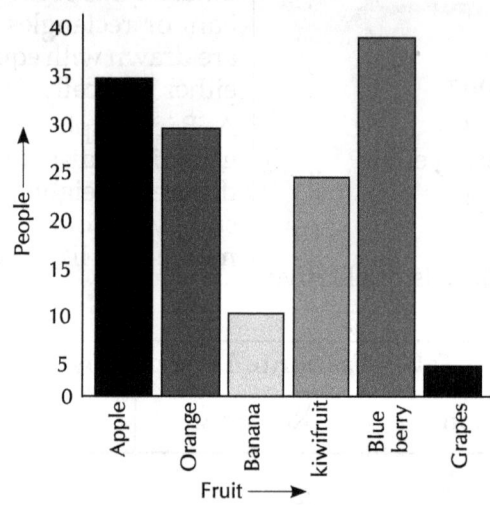

You can see that for this particular group, Blueberries are most popular and Grapes are the least popular among fruits.

Example : Student Grades
Following tables shows grades of 28 students :

Grade	A	B	C	D
Students	4	12	10	2

And here is its bar graph :

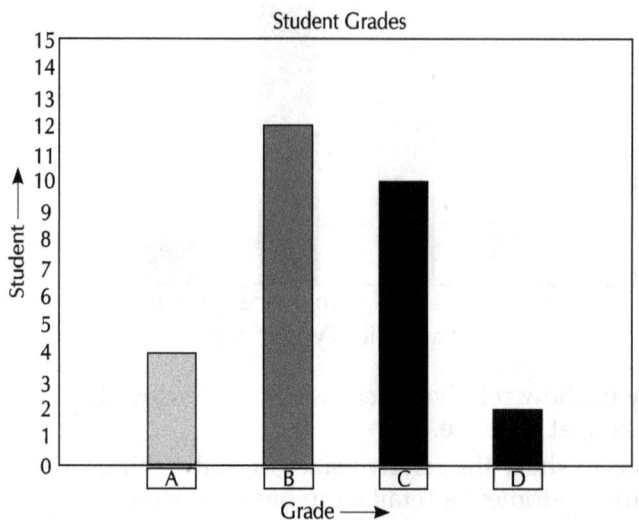

Pie Chart

These diagrams are used to study the relations between two or more articles with their component parts.

It is a special chart that uses "pie slices" to show relative sizes of data. Let us use the same favourite type of movie example discussed in bar chart earlier. For that example, here is the relevant pie chart:

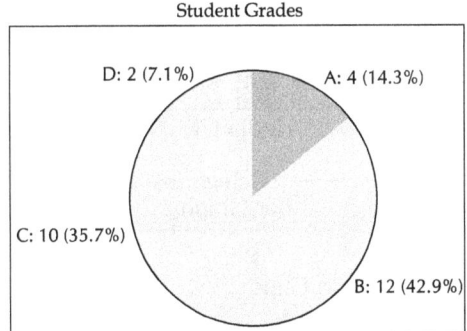
Favourite Type Movie

It is easy to see which movie types are most liked, and which are least liked, at a glance.

You can also use pie charts to show the relative sizes of many things, such as what type of bike people have, how many customers a retail shop has on different days, how popular are different breeds of dogs etc.

Example : Student Grades

For the student grade chart which we used for bar graph here is the pie chart:

Student Grades

Line Graphs

These diagrams are used to show how a quantity changes continuously. It is a graph that shows information that is connected in some way (such as change over time). Suppose, you are learning facts about dogs, and each day you do a short test to see how good you are. These are the results :

Facts I got Correct			
Day 1	Day 2	Day 3	Day 4
3	4	12	15

And here is the same data as a Line Graph :

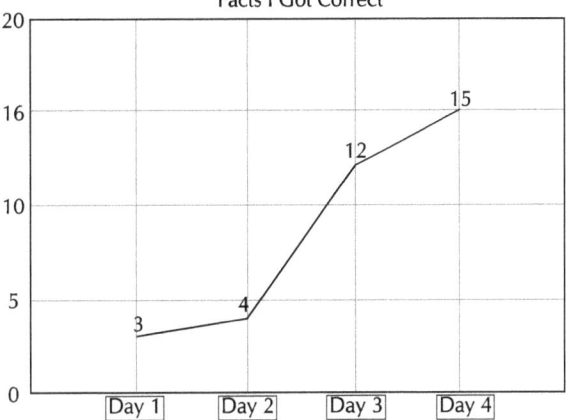

Histograms

It is most popularly used for graphical representation of a frequency distribution. A Histogram is a graphical display of data using bars of different heights. It is similar to a Bar Chart, but a histogram groups numbers into ranges. One sample histogram is shown in figure below:

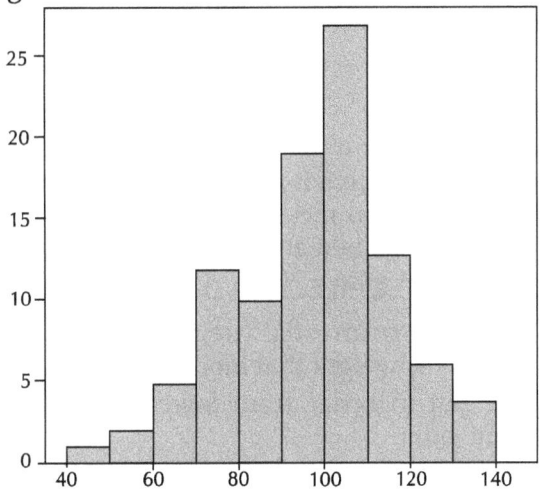

Example : Height of Orange Trees

Suppose you are measuring the height of every tree in the orchard in centimeters (cm).

Data Handling

The heights vary from 100 cm to 340 cm. You decide to put the results into groups of 50 cm as :
- The 100 to just below 150 cm range,
- The 150 to just below 200 cm range, etc.

So a tree that is 260 cm tall is added to the "250-300" range. And here is the resultant histogram :

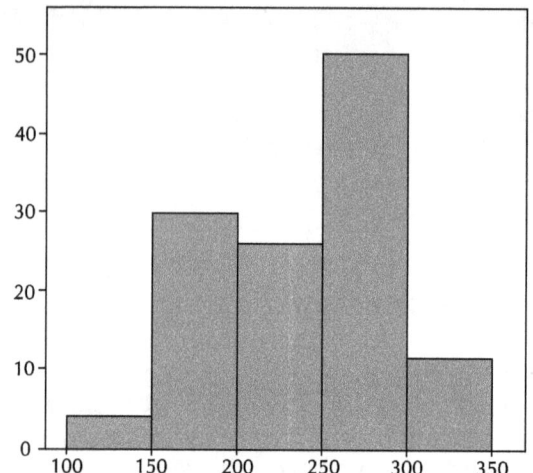

You can see (for example) that there are 30 trees from 150 cm to just below 200 cm tall The horizontal axis is continuous like a number line:

```
       continuous
◄──┬────┬────┬────┬────┬────┬──►
  100  150  200  250  300  350
```

Example : How much is a puppy growing?

Suppose you have a puppy named Tommy. Each month you measure how much weight Tommy has gained and here are results :

0.5, 0.5, 0.3, −0.2, 1.6, 0, 0.1, 0.1, 0.6, 0.4

They vary from −0.2 (negative indicates Tommy lost weight that month) to 1.6

Now, put in order from lowest to highest weight gain:

−0.2, 0, 0.1, 0.1, 0.3, 0.4, 0.5, 0.5, 0.6, 1.6

Let us put the results into groups of 0.5 as :
- The −0.5 to just below 0 range,
- The 0 to just below 0.5 range, etc.

So, you can see there are no values from 1 to just below 1.5. But we still show the space. The resultant histogram will be :

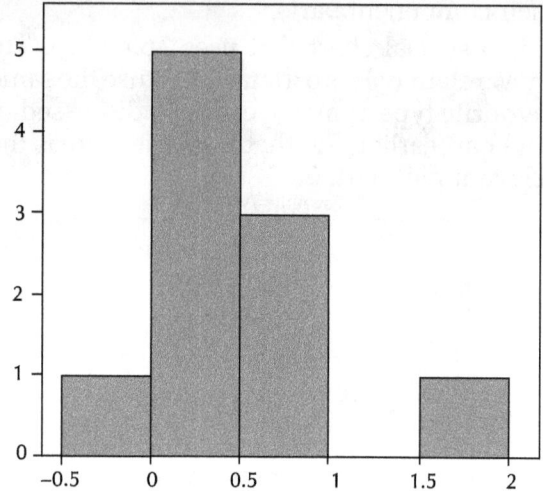

Histograms are a great way to show results of continuous data, such as weight, height, how much time, etc.

Remember, when the data is in categories (such as Country or Favourite Movie), you should use a Bar Chart.

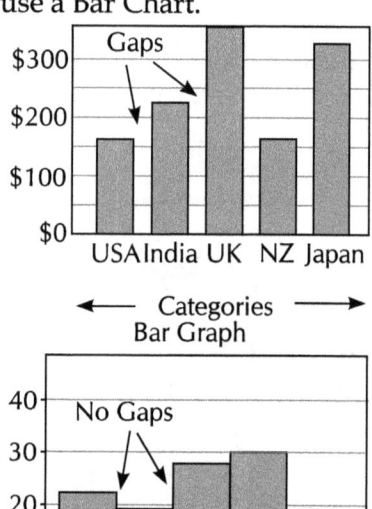

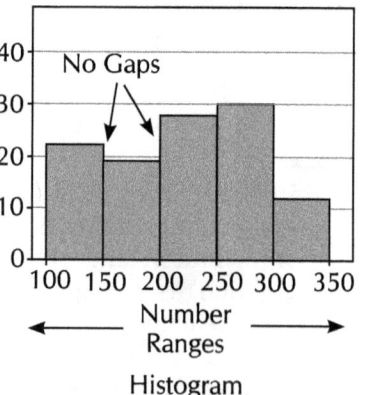

Frequency Distribution

Frequency distribution shows how often something occurs.

Example : Golu played football on Saturday Morning, Saturday Afternoon and Thursday Afternoon. The frequency was 2 on Saturday, 1 on Thursday and 3 for the whole week.

By counting frequencies we can make a Frequency Distribution table.

Example : Goals

Indian team has scored the following numbers of goals in recent games :

2, 3, 1, 2, 1, 3, 2, 3, 4, 5, 4, 2, 2, 3

Let us put the numbers in order, then added up :
- how often 1 occurs (2 times),
- how often 2 occurs (5 times), etc,

Now wrote them down as a Frequency Distribution table :

Scores
1,1,2,2,2,2,2,3,3,3,3,4,4,5

Score	Frequency
1	2
2	5
3	4
4	2
5	1

From the table we can see interesting things such as :
- getting 2 goals happens more frequently
- only once did they get 5 goals

So, Frequency Distribution gives you the values and their frequency (how often each value occurs).

Here is another example :

Example : Newspapers

These are the numbers of newspapers sold at a local shop over the last 10 days :

22, 20, 18, 23, 20, 25, 22, 20, 18, 20

Let us count how many of each number there is :

Papers Sold	Frequency
18	2
19	0
20	4
21	0
22	2
23	1
24	0
25	1

It is also possible to group the values. Here they are grouped in 5s :

Papers Sold	Frequency
15-19	2
20-24	7
25-29	1

Data Handling

MULTIPLE CHOICE QUESTIONS

1. The bar graph shows the results when a die was thrown a number of times.

   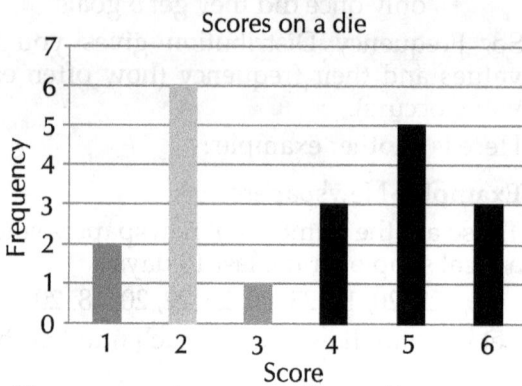

   How many sixes were thrown?
   (a) 2 (b) 3
   (c) 5 (d) 6

2. The bar graph shows the favourite colors of 20 students in a class.

   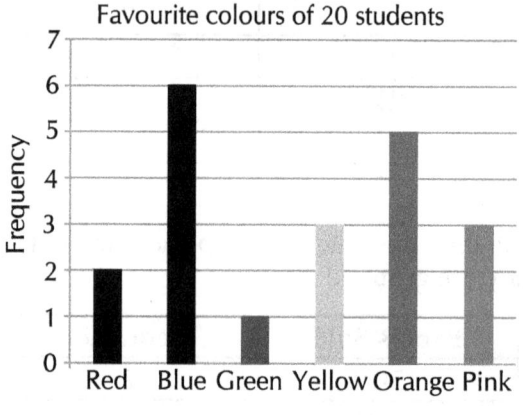

   How many more of them favoured orange than those who favoured green?
   (a) 2 (b) 3
   (c) 4 (d) 5

3. The bar graph shows the scores obtained by Shraddha in her end of year exams.

   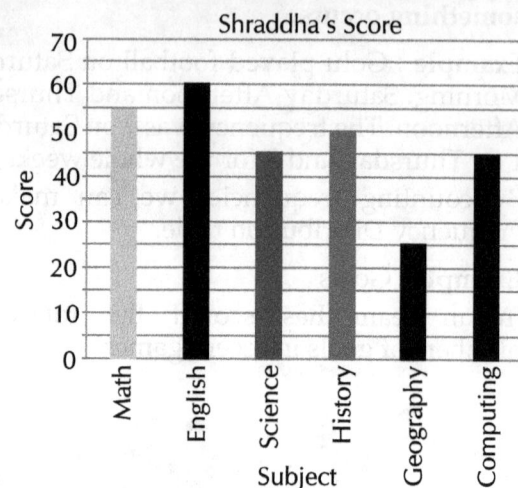

   How much more did Shraddha score in her best subject than in her worst subject?
   (a) 25 (b) 35
   (c) 45 (d) 60

4. The bar graph shows the scores obtained by Shraddha in her end of year exams.

   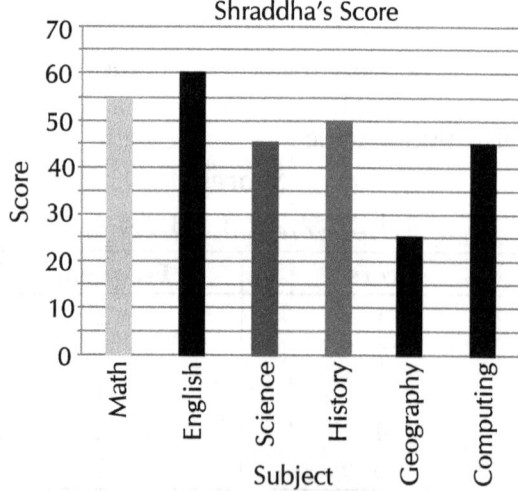

   Shubhra's score in English was 15% higher than Shraddha's score in English. What was Shubhra's score in English?
   (a) 89 (b) 79
   (c) 72 (d) 69

5. The pie chart shows the amount of time that Shraddha spends on various activities each day.

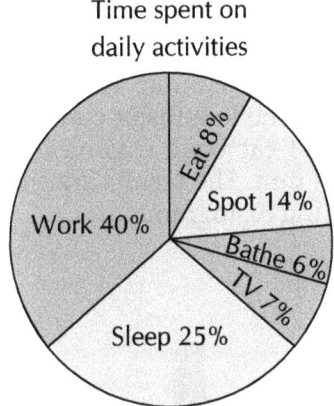

Time spent on daily activities

If this information were displayed using a bar graph with hours on the vertical axis, what would be the height of the bar for sleep?
(a) 8 hours (b) 7 hours
(c) 6 hours (d) 2.5 hours

6. Shraddha recorded the amount of time she spent on six activities over a twenty four hour period and drew a bar graph, as follows:

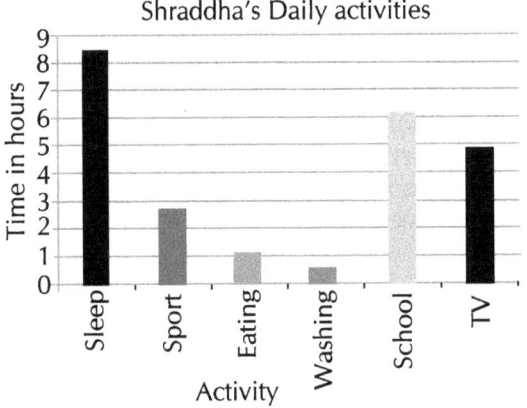

Approximately how many more hours did she spend sleeping than watching TV?
(a) About 3½ hours longer
(b) About 4 hours longer
(c) About 4½ hours longer
(d) About 5 hours longer

7. Shraddha recorded the temperature in her room (in Degrees Fahrenheit) every two hours over a 12 hour period from noon to midnight. The results are shown in the line graph.

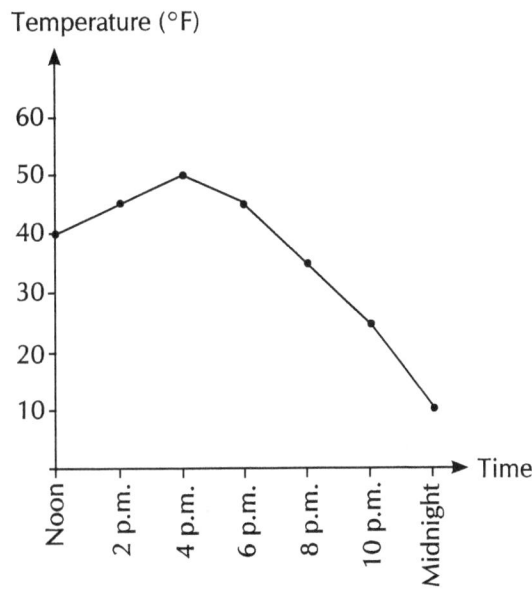

What was the approximate temperature in her room at 9 p.m.?
(a) 35°F (b) 30°F
(c) 25°F (d) 20°F

8. The line graph shows how the record time for the 100 m sprint changed from 1964 when Bob Hayes of the US held the record to 2012 when Usain Bolt of Jamaica held the record.

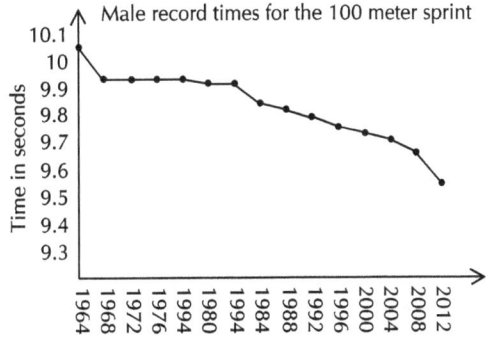

Male record times for the 100 meter sprint

Data Handling

From the graph, what was the maximum length of time for which the record remained unchanged?

(a) 3 years (b) 9 years
(c) 12 years (d) 16 years

9. The histogram shows the heights of 21 students in a class, grouped into 5-inch groups.

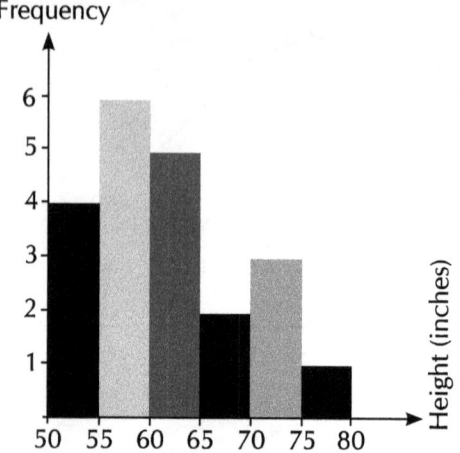

How many students were greater than or equal to 60 inches tall?

(a) 21 (b) 17
(c) 11 (d) 6

10. The histogram shows the heights of 21 students in a class, grouped into 5 inches groups.

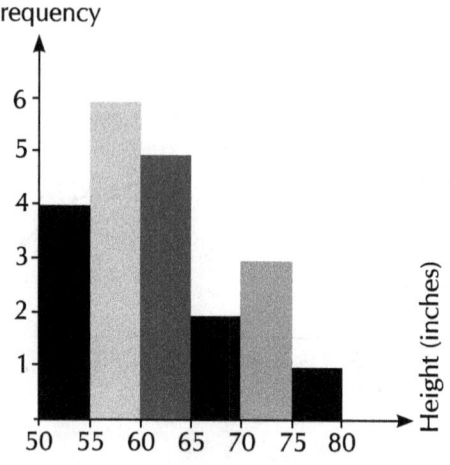

How many students were greater than or equal to 55 inches tall but less than 70 inches tall?

(a) 13 (b) 15
(c) 16 (d) 17

11. A class carried out an experiment to measure the lengths of cuckoo eggs. The length of each egg was measured to the nearest mm. The results are shown in the following histogram:

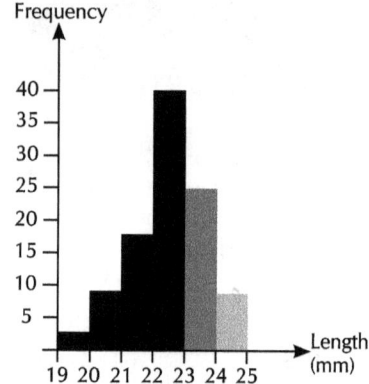

How many eggs were measured altogether in the experiment?

(a) 25 (b) 40
(c) 90 (d) 100

12. The histogram shows the birth weights of 100 new born babies. Babies who weigh less than 5 lb are considered to have a low birth weight. Babies who weigh 10 lb or more are considered to have a high birth weight.

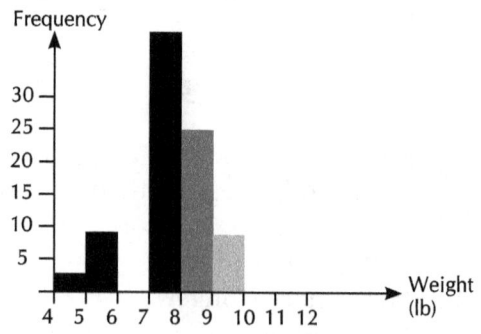

What percent of the babies had neither a low nor a high birth weight?
(a) 97%   (b) 91%
(c) 85%   (d) 83%

13. Which letter occurs the most frequently in the following sentence?

    THE SUN ALWAYS SETS IN THE WEST.
    (a) E   (b) S
    (c) T   (d) W

14. A fair die was thrown 100 times. The frequency distribution is shown in the following table:

Score	Frequency
1	16
2	18
3	11
4	15
5	19
6	21

    How many throws scored less than 3?
    (a) 11   (b) 34
    (c) 45   (d) 56

15. 60 students sat for a test. The frequency distribution is shown in the following table:

Mark	Frequency
0	1
1	3
2	6
3	9
4	8
5	11
6	8
7	7
8	4
9	1
10	2

    How many students scored 5 or more?
    (a) 11   (b) 22
    (c) 33   (d) 38

16. 60 students sat for a test. The frequency distribution is shown in the following table:

Mark	Frequency
0	1
1	3
2	6
3	9
4	8
5	11
6	8
7	7
8	4
9	1
10	2

    How many students scored greater than or equal to 4, but less than or equal to 7?
    (a) 19   (b) 26
    (c) 27   (d) 34

17. Shraddha did a survey of the number of pets owned by her classmates, with the following results:

Number of pets	Frequency
0	4
1	12
2	8
3	2
4	1
5	2
6	1

    How many of her classmates had less than 3 pets?
    (a) 16   (b) 20
    (c) 24   (d) 26

Data Handling

18. The children in a class did a survey of the number of siblings (brothers and sisters) each of them had. The results are recorded in the following table:

Number of siblings	Frequency
0	3
1	6
2	8
3	5
4	4
5	2
6	1
7	0
8	0
9	1

How many families had more than 4 children?
(a) 4   (b) 5
(c) 8   (d) 13

19. Which one of the following is discrete data?
(a) Sam is 160 cm tall
(b) Sam has two brothers and one sister
(c) Sam weighs 60 kg
(d) Sam ran 100 meters in 10.2 seconds

20. Lisa conducted a survey of the cars passing her house. How many cars passed in total?

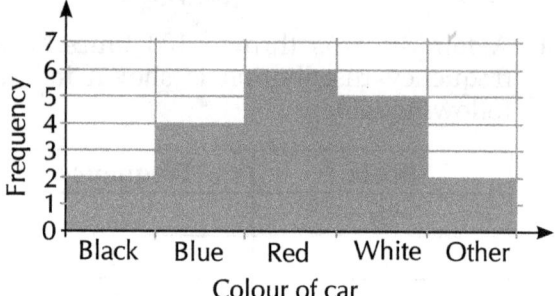

(a) 17   (b) 19
(c) 23   (d) 40

HOTS

Following pie chart shows the percentage of males and females in a city with population over 1,00,000.

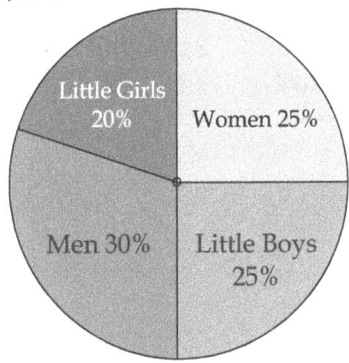

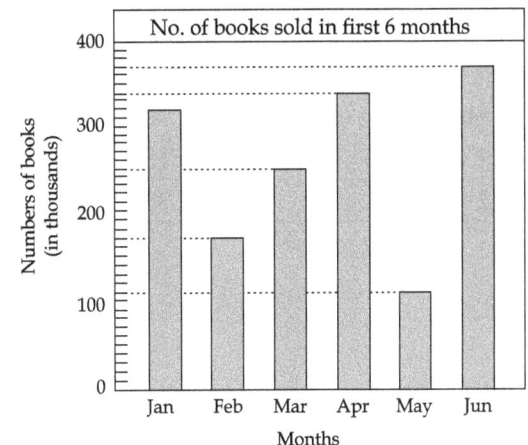

1. What is the sum of the numbers of little girls and women in the city?
   (a) 44,000 (b) 45,000
   (c) 45,500 (d) 42,100

2. Following bar graph represents the number of present students in class 5th in a particular week.

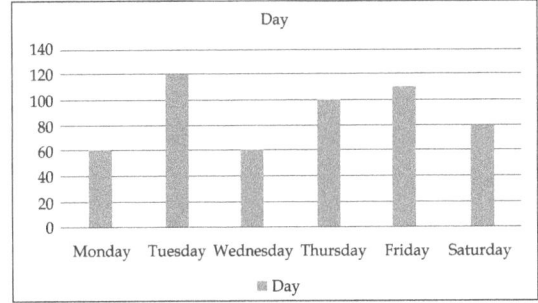

   If there are 150 students in the class 5th, how many students were absent on Friday?
   (a) 20 (b) 80
   (c) 30 (d) 40

3. The column graph shows the number of books (in thousands) sold by a shop owner during the first 6 months of a certain year.

   In which month is the number of books sold twice as many as those sold in February?
   (a) February (b) May
   (c) April (d) January

4. The incomplete pictograph shows the amount of money Dinesh spent on four days.

Day	Money spent
Monday	⬡⬡⬡⬡
Tuesday	⬡⬡
Wednesday	⬡⬡⬡
Thursday	⬡⬡⬡⬡⬡
Friday	⬡
Saturday	⬡⬡⬡⬡
Sunday	

   Each ⬡ stands for ₹ 50
   If Golu spent ₹ 500 in weekend (Saturday and Sunday), how many symbols must be drawn for Sunday?
   (a) 5 (b) 6
   (c) 9 (d) 10

Data Handling

5. The table shows how rabbits grew every year. After which year did the number of rabbits cross 1000?

Times	Numbers of rabbits
Start	10
1 year	18
2 year	32
3 year	58
4 year	105
5 year	
6 year	

(a) 5 years (b) 6 years
(c) 8 years (d) 10 years

SECTION 3
ACHIEVERS' SECTION

Key Charts

Greatest and smallest number
To find greatest number-arrange digits in descending number.
To find smallest number-arrange digits in ascending number except putting 0 to extreme left.

NUMBER SYSTEM

Comparing numbers
Number having more number of digits is larger.
Example: 500 < 5405
If number of digits are equal, start comparing digits from left.

Rounding number
Rounding number
Example: 45 rounded to 50 off to 10's
625 rounded to 600 off to 100's

Uses
1. In Clocks
2. Name of King/Queen like Queen Elizabeth II
3. Which class you study? V

ROMAN NUMERALS

Symbols
I–1 X–10
L–50 V–5
C–100 D–500
M–1000

Rules
V, L, D cannot be repeated
I,X,C,M can be repeated 3 times
If a symbol appears before a larger number it is subtracted
If a symbol appears after a larger number it is subtracted

OPERATIONS ON NUMERALS

Operations:
Addition +
Subtraction –
Multiplication ×
Division ÷

Properties:
Commutative:
$2 + 3 = 3 + 2, 2 \times 3 = 3 \times 2$
Associative:
$(2 + 3) + 4 = 2 + (3 + 4), (2 \times 3) \times 4 = 2 \times (3 \times 4)$
Identity
$2 + 0 = 2, 2 \times 1 = 2$
Multiplication 0 property
$2 \times 0 = 0, 0 \times 2 = 0$

Types of Fractions
Unit fractions: 1/3 , 1/5
Proper fractions (Numer < Denom): 5/9, 4/9 , 3/7
Improper fractions (Denom > Numer): 7/4, 9/4 , 7/3
Equivalent fractions: 2/3 , 4/6 , 6/9

DECIMALS AND FRACTIONS

Decimal Fractions
Fractions with denominator 10,100 etc.
5/10 = 0.5,   5/100 = 0.05

Comparing
10.2 > 5.7
5/10 > 3/10

Even numbers - Numbers divisible by 2
Odd numbers - Number not divisible by 2
Numbers having two factors - 1 and itself: 2,3,5,7

FACTORS AND MULTIPLES

Highest Common Factor
Factor of 12 - 1,2,3,4,6,12
Factor of 16 - 1,8,16,24
Common factor - 1,2,4
HCF - 4

Lowest Common Multiple:
Multiples of 4 - 4,8,12,16,20, 24
Multiples of 6 - 6,12,18,24
Common multiples - 12,24
LCM - 12

Key Charts

Different types of Quadrilateral

Properties	Rectangle	Square	Parallelogram	Rhombus	Trapezium
All Sides are equal	No	Yes	No	Yes	No
Opposite Sides are equal	Yes	Yes	Yes	Yes	No
Opposite Sides are parallel	Yes	Yes	Yes	Yes	Yes
All angles are equal	Yes	Yes	No	No	No
Opposite angles are equal	Yes	Yes	Yes	Yes	No
Sum of two adjacent angles is 180	Yes	Yes	Yes	Yes	No
Bisect each other	Yes	Yes	Yes	Yes	No
Bisect perpendicularly	No	Yes	No	Yes	No

Thoughtful Questions

1. You are walking in a dense forest and there is a tree with 5 apples (some are good and some are poisonous).

   There are two forest explorers, one of them always lie and another always say the truth, and it is not at all possible to differentiate between them. When somebody asked them which apple is safe to eat, they answered:

   Explorer 1: "The one on the left end".
   Explorer 2: "The one on the right end".
   So, determine which apple is safe?

   Solution: Since they can either lie or tell the truth and there is no way to differentiate between them. Hence, it cannot be determined.

2. There are six children, among which 5 are boys and 1 girl. Only one child among them lies and rest everyone speaks the truth.
   1st child says, " I am a boy".
   2nd child says, "I am a girl".
   3rd child says, "First child is lying and the second child is truthful".
   4th child says, "One of us is not a boy".
   5th child says, " The first child is a boy".
   6th child says, "There are 5 boys among us"
   Who is the liar?

Solution: Notice every statement carefully. Let us start from bottom, 6th child says there are 5 boys and that is true as there is only 1 girl. 5th child only gives one statement, but not sure if it is truth or a lie. 4th child also gives only one statement and is correct as one of them is a girl. Now notice the 3rd child statement, if it is truthful, then there would be 2 girls, which negates the given information. So, the 3rd child is the liar.

3. In a 400 meters race run between Navneet and Bunny, Bunny beats Navneet by 2020 meters.

When Navneet and Ankit run the same lap, Navneet beats Ankit by 40 meters. What will happen when Bunny and Ankit run the lap?

Assume that each runner maintained constant speed during their sprint.

Solution: See the last note mentioned in the question, that Bunny is consistently running faster than Navneet, who is consistently running faster than Ankit.

Given the above assumption of runners maintaining constant speeds, the gap between Navneet and Bunny is steadily increasing, as is the gap between Navneet and Ankit. By the time Navneet reaches the finish line, the gap between Navneet and Ankit will be 40 m.

However, this means that when Bunny reaches the finish line, 20 m ahead of Navneet, the gap between Bunny and Ankit will not yet become 60 m, and therefore he will beat Ankit by less than 60 m.

4. Golu's uncle is a cricket umpire who does umpiring seven days a week during the season. Because of his schedule, he can take his trouser to the cleaners only once a week. He takes them on Wednesday and picks them up on Thursday. If he wears only washed trousers every day of the week, what is the minimum number of trousers he would need to make it throughout the season?

Solution: He will in all need 9 trousers.

He will need the 8th trouser when he takes the 7 trousers to the cleaners on Wednesday. He'll need a 9th trouser to pick up 7 trousers on Thursday.

Then he can start the cycle all over again on Friday.

5. One day, my brother hid my wallet and put it inside a locker box. Then he laid out 5 coloured keys, only one of them can unlock the box. He promised to return wallet if I recognised the correct key. Also, these keys can talk about themselves. Using the clues below, can you find the correct key and find my wallet?

The green key is somewhere to the left of the key to the door.

The blue key is not at one of the ends.

The black key is three spaces away from the key to the door (2 between).

The pink key is next to the key to the door.

The orange key is in the middle.

Solution
- Green is to the left to the door key suggests that the green key is not the key to the door.
- The black key is 3 spaces away from the door key so the black key is also not the key to the door.
- The pink key is next to the door key hence the pink key is not the key to the door.

Now 50–50 chances says either the blue or orange key. Now since the black key is 3 spaces away from the right key, the right key cannot be the orange key as the orange key is at most 2 spaces away from any of the other keys. This leaves blue key as our answer.

6. Two men were being accused of a crime. The judges found one of them guilty and the other one as not guilty.

The judge turned to the guilty one and said:

"This is the strangest case I have come across! Though your guilt has been established beyond any doubt, the law forces me to set you free." What could be the reason for this?

Solution: The two defendants were Co-joined twins. Co-njoined twins are identical twins joined in utero. This is a rare phenomenon with the occurrence ratio is 1 in every 200,000 live births. As law says, even if hundred guilty people are acquitted, but one innocent should not be convicted. Hence, the judge is forced to let the guilty go even when his crime is proved.

Model Test Paper 1

1. The table shows the number of toys a factory made in March and April.

Toys Made at a Factory	
Month	Number Made
March	962, 458
April	879, 581

   How many more toys did the factory make in March than in April?
   (a) 117,123 (b) 82,977
   (c) 82,877 (d) 117,137

2. Harry had 500 coins in a jar. He sorted the coins into 25 different stacks. Each stack had the same number of coins. How many coins were there in each stack?
   (a) 20 (b) 45
   (c) 25 (d) 12

3. There are 914 students enrolled in Lakeview Elementary School. Frederich Elementary School has 276 fewer students enrolled. How many students are enrolled at Frederich Elementary School?
   (a) 642 (b) 762
   (c) 1,190 (d) 638

4. How is 4.026 written in words?
   (a) Four and twenty six thousandths
   (b) Four and twenty six hundredths
   (c) Four thousand, twenty six
   (d) Four hundred twenty six

5. Which of the following shows a reflection (flip) of the shaded shape across the heavy dotted line?

   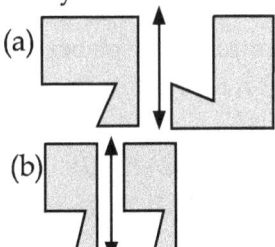

   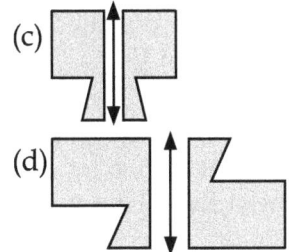

6. In the figure, point O is the center of the circle. Which two points appear to make a diameter when connected with a straight line?

   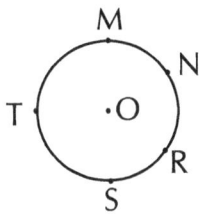

   (a) M and S (b) O and R
   (c) N and S (d) T and R
   (e) None of these

7. Which unit could be used for measuring the amount of liquid needed to fill a small teacup?
   (a) gram (b) kg
   (c) meter (d) milliliter
   (e) None of these

8. Which of the following has exactly 6 vertices?

   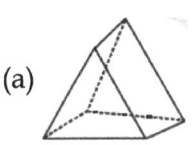 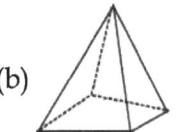

   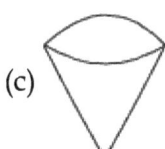 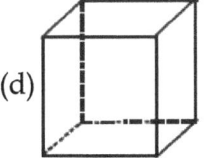

Model Test Paper

9. What number comes next in the sequence?
   8, 9, 10, 16, 17, 18, 24, 25, 26, ..?...
   (a) 35 (b) 32
   (c) 36 (d) 12
10. Symbol that can never be repeated is
    (a) I (b) V
    (c) X (d) C
11. Tom left home at 7:15 a.m. to go to work. He returned home at 4:45 p.m. What is the total amount of time Tom was away from home?
    (a) 7 hours, 30 minutes
    (b) 9 hours, 30 minutes
    (c) 3 hours, 30 minutes
    (d) 8 hours, 30 minutes
    (e) None of these
12. A rule was used to make the pattern shown below.
    51, 45, 39, 33, 27, 21 . . .
    Which could be the rule used to make the pattern?
    (a) Divide by 7 (b) Divide by 6
    (c) Subtract 7 (d) Subtract 6
    (e) None of these
13. Which of these could be solved by using the open sentence S – 7 =?
    (a) Rita collected 7 more seashells than Henry. If S is the number of seashells that Henry collected, how many did Rita Collect?
    (b) Bony collected 7 fewer seashells than Kamal. If S is the number of seashells Kamal collected, how many did Bony collect?
    (c) David needs 7 seashells more to complete his collection. If S is the number of seashells he has so far, how many will he have after he gets 7 more?
    (d) Amit filled 7 boxes with seashells. If S is the number of seashells he put in each box, how many seashells did he use in all?
14. Using the rule between IN numbers and OUT numbers, determine the missing number.
    IN : 121 146 183 175 192
    OUT: 1331 1752 2379 ? 2880
    (a) 1925 (b) 2275
    (c) 2450 (d) 2625
    (e) None of these
15. Simon and Julie need 72 paper flowers to complete a bulletin board. They have 19 paper flowers so far. Which operation should be used in the box below to find how many more paper flowers they need?
    72? 19 =
    (a) addition (b) division
    (c) multiplication (d) subtraction
16. Shelley is ordering a skirt from a catalog. She can choose one of two lengths: a short skirt or a long skirt. Then she can choose one of three fabric patterns: stripes, plaid, or flowers. How many different skirts could Shelley order choosing a length and a fabric pattern?

    Short   Long   Stripes Plaid Flowers
    Skirts   Fabric Patterns

    (a) 2 (b) 3
    (c) 5 (d) 6
17. There are about 20 times as many species of ants as there are species of bats. Let b represents the number of species of bats. Which expression represents the number of species of ants?
    (a) b + 20 (b) b − 20
    (c) 20 × b (d) 20 divide b

18. Which angle in the given figure is acute?

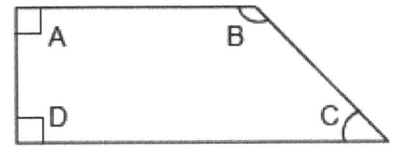

(a) Angle A (b) Angle B
(c) Angle C (d) Angle D

19. What number gives 234 when you multiply it by 45 and then divide by 20?
(a) 104 (b) 106
(c) 108 (d) 110

20. The following table shows the distance around four different planets. Which planet's distance has the numeral 3 in the ten thousands place?

DISTANCE AROUND

Planet	Distance Around (in miles)
Jupiter	88,732
Mars	4,213
Mercury	3,032
Neptune	30,603

(a) Jupiter (b) Mars
(c) Mercury (d) Neptune

21. Javed saved some notes which consist of ₹1, ₹10 and ₹20 notes. If his savings was ₹200, and he has ten ₹1 note and three ₹10 notes then how many ₹20 notes did he have?
(a) 8 (b) 10
(c) 12 (d) 9

22. Which set of numbers given below has a sum of 160 and a product of 5775?
(a) 55 and 105 (b) 60 and 100
(c) 65 and 95 (d) 70 and 90

23. Anu baked 1000 cookies. She sold 640 of them and gave the rest equally to 20 of her friends. How many cookies did each of her friends receive?
(a) 18 (b) 20
(c) 24 (d) 30
(e) None of these

24. Mr. Sharma bought 829 apples. 69 of them were rotten and thrown away. He sold 376 of them and packed the rest equally into bags each containing 12 apples. How many such bags of apples did he have?
(a) 42 bags (b) 21 bags
(c) 32 bags (d) 24 bags

25. Find the area of the shaded part of the rectangular strip of papers.

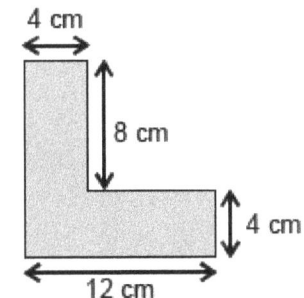

(a) 8 cm² (b) 32 cm²
(c) 72 cm² (d) 80 cm²

26. The average mass of 3 boys is 64 kg. If the total mass of 2 of them is 119 kg, how heavy is the third boy?
(a) 36 kg (b) 73 kg
(c) 160 kg (d) 192 kg

27. If 2/3 of a number is 10, what is 6 times the number?
(a) 15 (b) 30
(c) 45 (d) 90

28. There are 45 animals in a pet shop. 23 of them are puppies, 6 of them are parrots and the rest are kittens. How many kittens are in the pet shop?
(a) 10 (b) 16
(c) 8 (d) 7
(e) 5

29. The teacher pupil ratio in a school is 1 : 40. The number of boys is $4/5$ the number of girls. There are 2400 girls. How many teachers are there in the school?
    (a) 108 (b) 480
    (c) 1920 (d) 4320
    (e) None of these

30. There are 30 pupils in a class. Each boy brings 5 stickers and each girl brings 4 stickers. If the boys bring 60 stickers more than that by the girls, how many boys are there?
    (a) 10 (b) 15
    (c) 20 (d) 25
    (e) 5

31. The total mass of 3 adults Govind, Joy and Vineet is 219.4 kg. Govind is 6.9 kg lighter than Vineet. Vineet is 10.4 kg heavier than Joy. How heavy is Govind?
    (a) 68.5 kg (b) 70.4 kg
    (c) 72 kg (d) 78.9 kg
    (e) None of these

32. 40 kg of crystals are graded into 3 sizes: small, medium and large. The ratio by mass of large to medium to small crystals is 4 : 3 : 1. There are 15 large crystals per kg. The total numbers of large crystals are
    (a) 525 (b) 560
    (c) 300 (d) 570
    (e) None of these

33. A cylindrical tank with a capacity of 32 litres is 4/5 full of water. One quarter of the water is poured into a pail. How much water is left in the cylindrical tank?
    (a) $6\,2/5$ litres (b) $19\,1/5$ litres
    (c) $5\,3/17$ litres (d) $8\,4/5$ litres

34. Number X is a common multiple of 8 and 7. It is between 1100 and 1200. What is number X?
    (a) 1144 (b) 1197
    (c) 1120 (d) 1136

35. The decimal representation of $6 + 2\dfrac{21}{25} + \dfrac{9}{1000}$ is _____
    (a) 6.849 (b) 8.0849
    (c) 8.849 (d) 8.93

36. The sum of five numbers that are arranged in ascending order is 861. The sum of first three numbers is 466 and the sum of last three numbers is 579. What is the third number?
    (a) 184 (b) 157
    (c) 195 (d) 125

37. The difference in the area of a large square and the area of a small square is 56 cm². If the side of the small square is 5 cm, find the perimeter of the large square.
    (a) 25 cm (b) 36 cm
    (c) 20 cm (d) 81 cm

38. The adjoining figure is made up of 2 similar squares, A and B. Find the perimeter of the figure if the area of square A is 36 cm².

    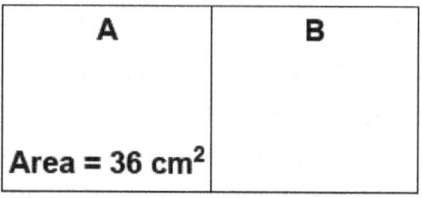

    (a) 24 cm (b) 48 cm
    (c) 30 cm (d) 36 cm

39. A number when rounded off to both the nearest hundred and nearest thousand is 235000. The smallest possible of such a number is _____
    (a) 234999 (b) 234950
    (c) 234990 (d) 234900

40. The numeral that represents three million, seventy eight thousand, four hundred and fourteen is _____
    (a) 3,00788,414 (b) 3,00078,414
    (c) 3,78,414   (d) 3,078,414

41. Sanjay has 10 pets. His pets are either birds or rabbits. All the birds have 16 legs lesser than all the rabbits. How many rabbits does he have?
    (a) 6   (b) 9
    (c) 4   (d) 2

42. Anil transferred eggs from 24 paper trays into plastic trays. Each paper tray could hold 30 eggs while each plastic tray held 20 less. How many plastic trays did he use?
    (a) 36   (b) 72
    (c) 84   (d) 108

43. 6 teachers took 3 classes to the bird park. Each class had 30 pupils. The entrance fee to the bird park was ₹ 15 for an adult. The teachers paid ₹ 600 and received a change of ₹ 60. What was the entrance fee per pupil?
    (a) ₹ 6   (b) ₹ 5
    (c) ₹ 8   (d) ₹ 10

44. Mohit read 1/4 of a book. If he read further 60 pages, he would have read 2/3 of the book. How many pages were there in the book?
    (a) 132   (b) 36
    (c) 96   (d) 144

45. 1 kg of rice costs as much as 1.25 kg of wheat flour. Leela paid ₹ 12.60 for 2 kg of rice and 5 kg of wheat flour. Find the cost of 5 kg of wheat flour.
    (a) ₹ 1.68   (b) ₹ 2.10
    (c) ₹ 8.40   (d) ₹ 10.50

46. 12 taps flowing at the same rate can fill a pool in 1 h. How long will it take 5 taps to fill the same pool?
    (a) 2 h 4 min   (b) 2 h 14 min
    (c) 2 h 24 min   (d) 2 h 34 min

47. Kavita can finish painting a house in 6 days and Anita can finish painting the same house in 10 days. On 1 April, they started painting the house together. After painting for 3 days, Kavita could not continue working and Anita had to finish painting the house alone. On which day will the house be fully painted?
    (a) 5 April   (b) 6 April
    (c) 7 April   (d) 8 April

48. Sumit wrote 3 numbers on three cards and covered two of the numbers. The number on Card A is 75% of the number on Card B. The number on Card C is 4 times the number on Card A.

    A   B   C
    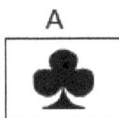 

    If the number on Card B is 124, the value of the number on Card C is
    (a) 372   (b) 90
    (c) 92   (d) 95

49. Deepak made the smallest possible cube by using rectangular blocks each measuring 6 cm by 4 cm by 3 cm. How many such blocks did he use to make the cube?
    (a) 12   (b) 20
    (c) 24   (d) 72
    (e) 18

50. Arpit cuts a piece of string, 60 cm long, into 12 equal pieces. The length of each piece of string, is
    (a) 6 cm   (b) 12 cm
    (c) 5 cm   (d) 7 cm
    (e) 10 cm

Model Test Paper

Model Test Paper 2

1. Three different positions of a triangle are given. Which of the following options describe its positions?

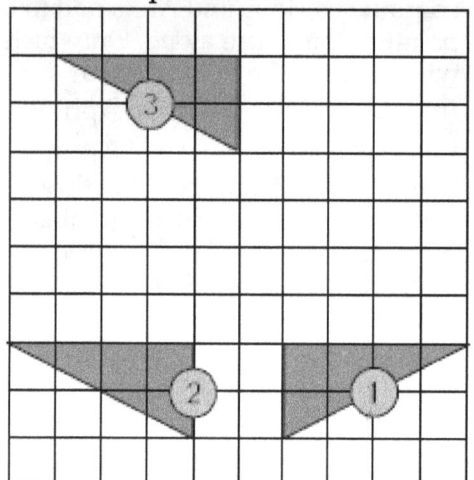

   (a) Rotation, then reflection
   (b) Reflection, then translation
   (c) Reflection, then rotation
   (d) None of these

2. In the given diagram, the girls who are athletic are indicated by which number?

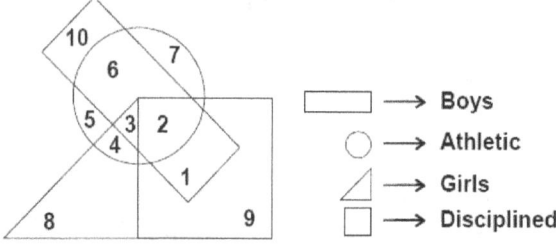

   (a) 1 (b) 3
   (c) 4 (d) 6

3. How many circles will be there in Pattern 20?

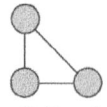 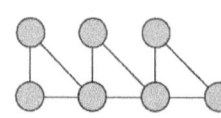
   Pattern 1   Pattern 2   Pattern 3

   (a) 41 (b) 42
   (c) 43 (d) 44

4. Raspberries cost more than Blueberries. Blueberries cost more than Strawberries. Raspberries cost more than both Strawberries and Blueberries. If the first two statements are true, the third statement is _____
   (a) True (b) False
   (c) Uncertain (d) None of these

5. Which number completes the puzzle? 25 36 49 64 81?

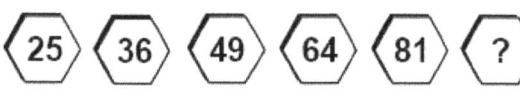

   (a) 121 (b) 400
   (c) 92 (d) 100

6. The water in Neha's watering bucket is boiling. What would most likely be the temperature of the water?
   (a) 0°C (b) 100°C
   (c) 4°C (d) 2°C

7. The given table shows that for science class, Mohit is ordering kits that contain bugs. Based on the data in the table, what will be the total number of bugs in 7 kits?

   Bug kits

Number of kits	3	4	5	6	7
Total number of bugs	18	24	30	36	?

   (a) 48 (b) 38
   (c) 40 (d) 42

8. Geeta put a CD in the CD player and pressed play. When she put the CD in, it looked like the picture shown here. After the song ended, Geeta opened the CD player and the CD looked like it had rotated (turned) 90° clockwise.

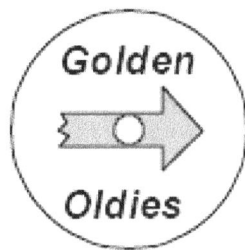

Which figure given below shows the CD after it rotated (turned) 90° clockwise?

(A) 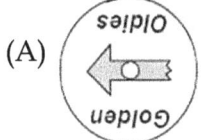 (B)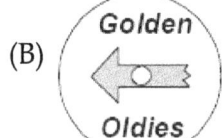

(C) 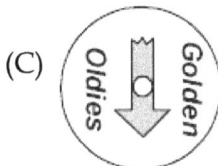 (D)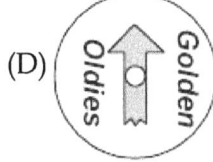

9. ? × 43 − 43 = 43 × 43 + 12 × 43

   The missing number is _____?
   (a) 12 (b) 54
   (c) 56 (d) 98

10. Shreya has a piece of ribbon which is 2 times as long as Sasha's ribbon. If Sasha's ribbon is 8.4 m long, how much longer is Shreya's ribbon?
    (a) 11.6 m (b) 16.8 m
    (c) 17.8 m (d) 14.4 m

11. Which digit will appear on the face opposite to the face with number 1?

    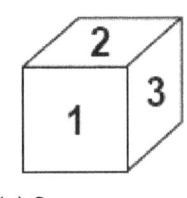 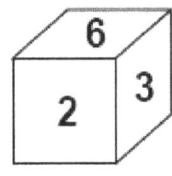

    (a) 3 (b) 5
    (c) 6 (d) 1

12. Which one will replace the question mark?

    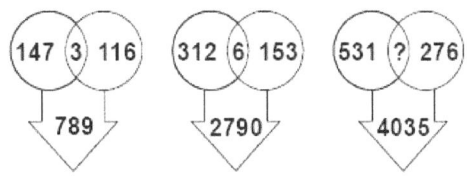

    (a) 18 (b) 5
    (c) 9 (d) 6

13. If "ICECREAM" is coded as "CICEERMA" then "CHOCOLATES" will be coded as
    (a) OHCLOCETAS
    (b) HCCOLOTASE
    (c) COHOCALTES
    (d) OCOHCTLASE

14. How many meaningful words can be formed using the letters A, R and T?
    (a) 3 (b) 4
    (c) 5 (d) 2

15. Which point is to the SouthEast of A?

    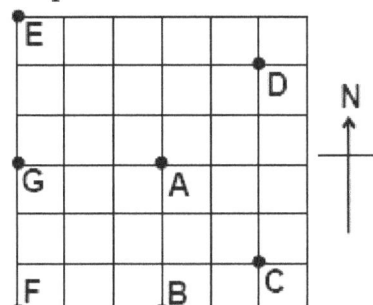

    (a) C (b) B
    (c) D (d) E

16. Find the odd one out.
    (a) C E D (b) F H G
    (c) I J K (d) L N M

17. Which one of the shapes below would not look the same after half a turn?

    (a) 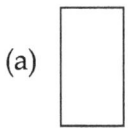 (b)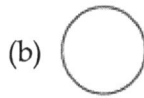

    (c) 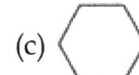 (D)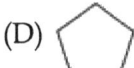

Model Test Paper

18. Today is Wednesday. What will be the day after 94 days?
    (a) Monday (b) Tuesday
    (c) Wednesday (d) Sunday

19. John has these coins. In how many different ways can he make up a sum of 80? (You do not have to use all the coins each time)

    (a) 1 (b) 3
    (c) 4 (d) 6

20. What will come in the place of ? to make the number sentence true?
    24748 − ? + 4239 × 3 = 33918
    (a) 3574 (b) 3754
    (c) 3457 (d) 3547

21. What should be the number in the START box?

    START ⟶ ÷ 25 ⟶ − 18 = 63

    (a) 2025 (b) 640
    (c) 1120 (d) 207360

22. Point P is the centre of the circular target shown in the picture. Which of the following appears to be the radius of the circle?

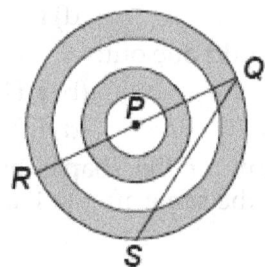

    (a) PQ
    (b) SQ
    (c) PR
    (d) Both (a) and (c)

23. Which given figure(s) does not have a line of symmetry?

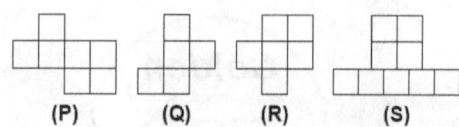

    (a) P only (b) Q only
    (c) R and S (d) P and Q

24. The value of 15 × (17 + 19) ÷ 4 − 35 ÷ 7 is _____
    (a) 100 (b) 120
    (c) 125 (d) 130

25. Peter is five times as old as his grandson, James. After six years, James will be 24 years old. How old is Peter now?
    (a) 80 years (b) 90 years
    (c) 100 years (d) 85 years

26. A watermelon is 10 times as heavy as two apples of equal mass. If the mass of each apple is 214 g, find the mass of 3 such watermelons.
    (a) 12840 g (b) 6420 g
    (c) 2140 g (d) 4280 g

27. Roman numeral for the difference of 6895 and 5287 is _____
    (a) DCVIII (b) MDCVIII
    (c) MCDVIII (d) XVICD

28. Which geometric figure has at least one triangular face?
    (a) Cube (b) Cone
    (c) Cylinder (d) Sphere

29. Tanya put one "S" on the calendar to show the date of her first basket ball game in January. Tanya's second basket ball game is exactly after 15 days. What is the date of her second basket ball game?

January						
S	M	T	W	T	F	S
						1
2	3	4	5	S 6	7	8
9	10	11	12	13	14	15
16	17	18	19	20	21	22
23	24	25	26	27	28	29
30	31					

(a) 20 (b) 23
(c) 22 (d) 21

30. Akriti saw different shapes of windows on cars and trucks in a parking lot. Four of the windows she saw are drawn below.

Window 1   Window 2   Window 3   Window 4

Which window appears to have only 1 line of symmetry?
(a) Window 1 (b) Window 2
(c) Window 3 (d) Window 4

31. What is 6050.287 rounded to the nearest tenth?
(a) 6050 (b) 6100
(c) 6050.29 (d) 6050.3

32. What number am I?
 • I am a two-digit even number.
 • I am a common multiple of 6 and 7.
 • I have a total of 8 factors.
(a) 35 (b) 42
(c) 36 (d) 84

33. When it is 10:30, what kind of angle is formed by the hands of the clock?

(a) Acute (b) Obtuse
(c) Right (d) Straight

34. Which point on the number line best represents 1.35?
(a)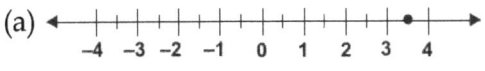
(b)
(c)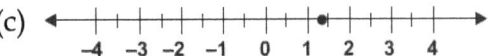
(d)

35. What is the missing value in the given pattern?
0.25 × 12 = 0.25 × 3 + 0.25 × 3 + 0.25 × ___.
(a) 2 (b) 3
(c) 6 (d) 8

36. Girish is making a math puzzle. He writes that 'w' is an even number which has 12 as a factor. Which of the following could represent the variable 'w'?
(a) 2156 (b) 1728
(c) 1429 (d) 1256

37. A shopkeeper mixed 3.6 kg of hazelnuts with 0.75 kg of raisins. He packed the mixture equally into 5 boxes. What is the weight of each box?
(a) 14.25 kg (b) 4.35 kg
(c) 0.87 kg (d) 0.72 kg

38. Every week Suhana saves ₹ 10 on Monday and ₹ 15 on Friday. If this is her total weekly savings, how many weeks would she take to save enough to buy a ₹ 175 wireless phone?
(a) 52 weeks (b) 46 weeks
(c) 7 weeks (d) 14 weeks

39. There are 9 rows of seats in a theatre. Each row has the same number of seats. If there is a total of 162 seats, how many seats are in each row?
(a) 17 (b) 18
(c) 19 (d) 20

40. Arjun's snack shop sells small, medium and large sodas. Yesterday, they sold 3 large sodas and 8 more medium sodas than large sodas. Arjun's snack shop also sold 8 small sodas yesterday. Totally how many sodas did Arjun's snack shop sell yesterday?
    (a) 31 (b) 13
    (c) 22 (d) 33

41. Abhilasha made cake for a party. She put the cake into the oven at twenty-five past four and took it out thirty minutes later. What time was it when Abhilasha took out the cake?
    (a) Five past eight (b) Five o'clock
    (c) Five to five   (d) Five past four

42. The temperature of water in a swimming pool is 51°F. Since the freezing point of water is 32°F, how many degrees would the temperature of the water have to drop to reach the freezing point?
    (a) 9°F   (b) 21°F
    (c) 2°F   (d) 19°F

43. There are 26 birdhouses made at a factory each hour. What is the total number of birdhouses made at the factory in 8 hours?
    (a) 34   (b) 64
    (c) 202 (d) 208

44. Rehana drank 5/8 glass of lemonade. Roshni drank 1/4 glass of lemonade. If the glasses held the same amount of lemonade, how much more lemonade did Rehana drink than Roshni?
    (a) 3/8 (b) 1/8
    (c) 3/4 (d) 1/2

45. A car can travel 315 km on 30 litres of petrol. How far can the car travel if it has 50 litres of petrol in its petrol tank?
    (a) 10.5 km (b) 189 km
    (c) 525 km   (d) 840 km

Answer Keys

Scan the QR Code to see the Hints and Solutions

Access Content Online on Dropbox: https://www.dropbox.com/scl/fi/1ytekiwscpktjdl0dbu9o/IMO-5-Math-Olympiad-Hints-Solution-Dropbox.pdf?rlkey=qnw9lcelb5g1yg523pl02tthz&dl=0

SECTION 1: MATHEMATICAL REASONING

1. NUMBER SYSTEM

Answer Key

1. (c)	2. (a)	3. (a)	4. (b)	5. (c)	6. (b)	7. (b)	8. (b)	9. (b)	10. (c)
11. (b)	12. (c)	13. (b)	14. (d)	15. (b)	16. (c)	17. (d)	18. (b)	19. (b)	20. (b)

HOTS

1. (b)	2. (b)	3. (c)	4. (c)	5. (d)

2. ROMAN NUMBERS

Answer Key

1. (d)	2. (b)	3. (a)	4. (c)	5. (a)	6. (c)	7. (c)	8. (a)	9. (b)	10. (d)
11. (c)	12. (a)	13. (d)	14. (c)	15. (c)	16. (d)	17. (c)	18. (b)	19. (c)	20. (c)
21. (a)	22. (a)	23. (b)	24. (c)	25. (a)					

HOTS

1. (d)	2. (b)	3. (b)	4. (b)	5. (c)

3. OPERATIONS ON NUMBERS

Answer Key

1. (d)	2. (d)	3. (b)	4. (b)	5. (b)	6. (a)	7. (d)	8. (d)	9. (a)	10. (a)
11. (b)	12. (b)	13. (a)	14. (a)	15. (a)	16. (b)	17. (c)	18. (b)	19. (a)	20. (a)
21. (b)	22. (a)	23. (b)	24. (a)	25. (b)	26. (c)	27. (c)	28. (b)	29. (c)	30. (d)
31. (a)	32. (b)	33. (a)	34. (c)	35. (a)	36. (c)	37. (c)	38. (b)	39. (d)	40. (c)
41. (b)	42. (a)	43. (b)	44. (d)	45. (a)					

HOTS

1. (b)	2. (a)	3. (b)	4. (a)	5. (b)	6. (d)	7. (d)	8. (a)	9. (b)	10. (c)

4. DECIMALS AND FRACTIONS

Answer Key

1. (c)	2. (d)	3. (c)	4. (a)	5. (d)	6. (d)	7. (b)	8. (c)	9. (b)	10. (d)
11. (c)	12. (a)	13. (a)	14. (c)	15. (a)	16. (d)	17. (c)	18. (b)	19. (b)	20. (c)
21. (a)	22. (a)	23. (b)	24. (c)	25. (c)	26. (d)	27. (c)	28. (a)	29. (c)	30. (b)
31. (a)	32. (a)	33. (b)	34. (c)	35. (b)	36. (c)	37. (b)	38. (a)	39. (a)	40. (a)
41. (d)	42. (d)	43. (d)	44. (d)	45. (b)					

HOTS

1. (b)	2. (d)	3. (b)	4. (b)	5. (b)

5. ALGEBRA

Answer Key

1. (a)	2. (b)	3. (a)	4. (d)	5. (c)	6. (b)	7. (d)	8. (a)	9. (c)	10. (c)
11. (d)	12. (b)	13. (b)	14. (a)	15. (a)					

HOTS

1. (c)	2. (a)	3. (b)	4. (c)	5. (b)

6. LCM AND HCF

Answer Key

1. (a)	2. (a)	3. (c)	4. (c)	5. (b)	6. (c)	7. (a)	8. (b)	9. (c)	10. (c)
11. (d)	12. (b)	13. (d)	14. (c)	15. (c)	16. (d)	17. (a)	18. (c)	19. (c)	20. (b)
21. (a)	22. (a)	23. (d)	24. (c)	25. (c)	26. (b)	27. (c)	28. (b)	29. (d)	30. (c)
31. (b)	32. (d)	33. (d)	34. (c)	35. (d)					

HOTS

1. (c)	2. (c)	3. (c)	4. (c)	5. (a)

7. RATIO AND PROPORTION

Answer Key

1. (a)	2. (b)	3. (a)	4. (a)	5. (c)	6. (b)	7. (a)	8. (a)	9. (a)	10. (b)
11. (b)	12. (b)	13. (c)	14. (a)	15. (c)	16. (b)	17. (b)	18. (b)	19. (c)	20. (a)
21. (c)	22. (d)	23. (b)	24. (b)	25. (a)	26. (c)	27. (b)	28. (d)	29. (c)	30. (d)
31. (a)	32. (a)	33. (d)	34. (b)	35. (d)	36. (c)	37. (b)	38. (d)	39. (b)	40. (c)
41. (a)	42. (d)	43. (a)	44. (b)	45. (b)					

HOTS

| 1. (c) | 2. (a) | 3. (b) | 4. (c) | 5. (c) |

8. MEASUREMENT

Answer Key

1. (c)	2. (a)	3. (c)	4. (a)	5. (b)	6. (c)	7. (d)	8. (a)	9. (c)	10. (b)
11. (d)	12. (a)	13. (c)	14. (c)	15. (d)	16. (b)	17. (d)	18. (b)	19. (d)	20. (c)
21. (b)	22. (b)	23. (c)	24. (a)	25. (d)	26. (c)	27. (a)	28. (c)	29. (b)	30. (a)

HOTS

| 1. (d) | 2. (d) | 3. (d) | 4. (d) | 5. (a) |

9. TEMPERATURE

Answer Key

| 1. (d) | 2. (b) | 3. (b) | 4. (c) | 5. (a) | 6. (d) | 7. (b) | 8. (c) | 9. (a) | 10. (a) |
| 11. (c) | 12. (a) | 13. (b) | 14. (a) | 15. (a) | 16. (b) | 17. (a) | 18. (c) | 19. (c) | 20. (a) |

HOTS

| 1. (d) | 2. (a) | 3. (c) | 4. (a) | 5. (c) |

10. MONEY

Answer Key

1. (a)	2. (b)	3. (b)	4. (c)	5. (b)	6. (c)	7. (c)	8. (b)	9. (a)	10. (d)
11. (c)	12. (d)	13. (d)	14. (d)	15. (d)	16. (a)	17. (b)	18. (c)	19. (b)	20. (d)

HOTS

1. (d)	2. (a)	3. (b)	4. (c)	5. (a)

11. AREA, PERIMETER AND VOLUME

Answer Key

1. (b)	2. (c)	3. (b)	4. (d)	5. (a)	6. (d)	7. (c)	8. (b)	9. (c)	10. (a)
11. (a)	12. (c)	13. (a)	14. (b)	15. (c)	16. (d)	17. (d)	18. (a)	19. (c)	20. (a)

HOTS

1. (c)	2. (a)	3. (d)	4. (c)	5. (c)

12. GEOMETRICAL SHAPES AND ANGLES

Answer Key

1. (a)	2. (d)	3. (b)	4. (c)	5. (c)	6. (b)	7. (a)	8. (d)	9. (a)	10. (b)
11. (c)	12. (d)	13. (b)	14. (d)	15. (c)	16. (b)	17. (c)	18. (c)	19. (a)	20. (c)
21. (c)	22. (c)	23. (a)	24. (d)	25. (a)	26. (b)	27. (d)	28. (b)	29. (c)	30. (b)

HOTS

1. (c)	2. (b)	3. (c)	4. (c)	5. (c)

SECTION 2: LOGICAL REASONING

1. SERIES AND PATTERN

Answer Key

1. (c)	2. (d)	3. (d)	4. (c)	5. (a)	6. (d)	7. (c)	8. (b)	9. (a)	10. (c)
11. (b)	12. (c)	13. (c)	14. (c)	15. (c)	16. (c)	17. (d)	18. (c)	19. (d)	20. (a)
21. (b)	22. (d)	23. (a)	24. (c)	25. (c)	26. (b)	27. (a)	28. (c)	29. (b)	30. (a)
31. (c)	32. (b)	33. (d)	34. (d)	35. (a)	36. (d)	37. (c)	38. (d)	39. (d)	40. (b)

	HOTS			
1. (c)	2. (c)	3. (a)	4. (b)	5. (d)

2. ANALOGY

Answer Key

1. (c)	2. (c)	3. (b)	4. (c)	5. (a)	6. (d)	7. (b)	8. (c)	9. (b)	10. (c)
11. (d)	12. (c)	13. (b)	14. (d)	15. (a)	16. (a)	17. (d)	18. (d)	19. (c)	20. (c)
21. (d)	22. (b)	23. (a)	24. (b)	25. (c)	26. (d)	27. (c)	28. (d)	29. (d)	30. (b)
31. (c)	32. (d)	33. (b)	34. (c)	35. (b)	36. (b)	37. (a)	38. (c)	39. (a)	40. (c)
41. (b)	42. (b)	43. (b)	44. (c)	45. (d)	46. (c)	47. (b)	48. (d)	49. (c)	50. (b)

	HOTS			
1. (b)	2. (d)	3. (d)	4. (a)	5. (d)

3. ODD ONE OUT

Answer Key

1. (d)	2. (d)	3. (d)	4. (d)	5. (c)	6. (c)	7. (a)	8. (b)	9. (c)	10. (d)
11. (d)	12. (d)	13. (a)	14. (d)	15. (b)	16. (a)	17. (d)	18. (d)	19. (a)	20. (d)
21. (d)	22. (a)	23. (a)	24. (d)	25. (a)	26. (c)	27. (d)	28. (b)	29. (d)	30. (a)
31. (b)	32. (d)	33. (b)	34. (d)	35. (c)					

	HOTS			
1. (b)	2. (a)	3. (c)	4. (d)	5. (b)

4. CODING AND DECODING

Answer Key

1. (c)	2. (a)	3. (c)	4. (b)	5. (b)	6. (c)	7. (a)	8. (b)	9. (b)	10. (b)
11. (a)	12. (a)	13. (d)	14. (c)	15. (c)	16. (a)	17. (c)	18. (a)	19. (a)	20. (b)
21. (a)	22. (b)	23. (a)	24. (b)	25. (c)	26. (b)	27. (a)	28. (b)	29. (c)	30. (b)
31. (a)	32. (b)	33. (c)	34. (a)	35. (b)	36. (c)	37. (e)	38. (c)	39. (b)	40. (b)
41. (e)	42. (e)	43. (c)	44. (e)	45. (c)	46. (a)	47. (c)	48. (e)	49. (b)	50. (b)

	HOTS			
1. (d)	2. (b)	3. (c)	4. (d)	5. (c)

5. NUMBER RANKING AND ALPHABET TEST

Answer Key

1. (c)	2. (a)	3. (a)	4. (c)	5. (d)	6. (d)	7. (d)	8. (d)	9. (d)	10. (a)
11. (c)	12. (b)	13. (a)	14. (b)	15. (a)	16. (c)	17. (e)	18. (d)	19. (d)	20. (c)
21. (c)	22. (a)	23. (c)	24. (d)	25. (b)	26. (b)	27. (e)	28. (c)	29. (c)	30. (a)
31. (c)	32. (e)	33. (b)	34. (c)	35. (c)					

HOTS

1. (b)	2. (d)	3. (a)	4. (b)	5. (d)

6. DIRECTION SENSE TEST

Answer Key

1. (a)	2. (c)	3. (b)	4. (d)	5. (b)	6. (d)	7. (d)	8. (d)	9. (a)	10. (c)
11. (d)	12. (a)	13. (d)	14. (d)	15. (a)	16. (d)	17. (b)	18. (c)	19. (c)	20. (a)

HOTS

1. (c)	2. (a)	3. (d)	4. (d)	5. (c)

7. MIRROR AND WATER IMAGES

Answer Key

1. (d)	2. (b)	3. (d)	4. (c)	5. (d)	6. (c)	7. (c)	8. (d)	9. (b)	10. (c)
11. (a)	12. (d)	13. (c)	14. (d)	15. (d)	16. (c)	17. (a)	18. (a)	19. (b)	20. (d)
21. (a)	22. (b)	23. (c)	24. (d)	25. (b)	26. (c)	27. (c)	28. (c)	29. (d)	30. (b)
31. (d)	32. (d)	33. (a)	34. (c)	35. (b)	36. (b)	37. (d)	38. (d)	39. (c)	40. (a)
41. (b)	42. (a)	43. (d)	44. (b)	45. (b)	46. (c)	47. (b)	48. (c)	49. (a)	50. (b)
51. (a)	52. (c)	53. (a)	54. (d)	55. (c)	56. (d)	57. (a)	58. (a)	59. (c)	60. (b)
61. (d)	62. (c)	63. (d)	64. (c)	65. (b)	66. (b)	67. (c)	68. (c)	69. (c)	70. (b)

HOTS

1. (a)	2. (d)	3. (b)	4. (d)	5. (b)

8. DATA HANDLING

Answer Key

1. (b)	2. (c)	3. (b)	4. (d)	5. (c)	6. (a)	7. (b)	8. (c)	9. (c)	10. (a)
11. (d)	12. (b)	13. (b)	14. (b)	15. (c)	16. (d)	17. (c)	18. (c)	19. (b)	20. (b)

HOTS

| 1. (b) | 2. (d) | 3. (c) | 4. (b) | 5. (c) |

MODEL TEST PAPERS – 1

Answer Key

1. (c)	2. (a)	3. (d)	4. (a)	5. (c)	6. (a)	7. (d)	8. (a)	9. (b)	10. (b)
11. (b)	12. (d)	13. (b)	14. (c)	15. (d)	16. (d)	17. (c)	18. (c)	19. (a)	20. (d)
21. (a)	22. (a)	23. (a)	24. (c)	25. (d)	26. (b)	27. (d)	28. (b)	29. (a)	30. (c)
31. (c)	32. (c)	33. (b)	34. (c)	35. (c)	36. (a)	37. (b)	38. (d)	39. (d)	40. (d)
41. (a)	42. (b)	43. (b)	44. (d)	45. (c)	46. (c)	47. (a)	48. (a)	49. (c)	50. (c)

MODEL TEST PAPERS – 2

Answer Key

1. (b)	2. (c)	3. (a)	4. (a)	5. (d)	6. (b)	7. (d)	8. (c)	9. (c)	10. (b)
11. (c)	12. (b)	13. (b)	14. (a)	15. (a)	16. (c)	17. (d)	18. (d)	19. (c)	20. (d)
21. (a)	22. (d)	23. (d)	24. (d)	25. (b)	26. (a)	27. (b)	28. (b)	29. (c)	30. (d)
31. (d)	32. (b)	33. (b)	34. (c)	35. (c)	36. (b)	37. (c)	38. (c)	39. (b)	40. (c)
41. (c)	42. (d)	43. (d)	44. (a)	45. (c)					

Appendix

There are different organizations that conduct these examinations and covering all of them is not needed as the focus should be to understand the main type of exams conducted. They are similar for these organizations with the difference being the change in name of the exam.

	Science Olympiad Foundation (SOF)	
S. No.	Name of Exam	Grade
1.	National Science Olympiad (NSO)	Class 1-10
2.	National Cyber Olympiad (NCO)	Class 1-10
3.	International Mathematics Olympiad (IMO)	Class 1-10
4.	International English Olympiad (IEO)	Class 1-10
5.	International Commerce Olympiad (ICO)	Class 1-10
6.	International General Knowledge Olympiad (IGKO)	Class 1-10
7.	International Social Studies Olympiad (ISSO)	Class 1-10
	Indian Talent Olympiad (ITO)	
S. No.	Name of Exam	Grade
1.	International Science Olympiad (ISO)	Class 1-12
2.	International Math Olympiad (IMO)	Class 1-12
3.	English International Olympiad (EIO)	Class 1-12
4.	General Knowledge International Olympiad (GKIO)	Class 1-12
5.	International Computer Olympiad (ICO)	Class 1-12
6.	International Drawing Olympiad (IDO)	Class 1-12
7.	National Essay Olympiad (NESO)	Class 1-12
8.	National Social Studies Olympiad (NSSO)	Class 1-12
	EduHeal Foundation	
S. No.	Name of Exam	Grade
1.	Eduheal International Cyber Olympiad (ICO)	Class 1-12
2.	Eduheal International English Olympiad (IEO)	Class 1-12
3.	National Interactive Math Olympiad (NIMO)	Class 1-12
4.	National Interactive Science Olympiad (NISO)	Class 1-12
5.	International General Knowledge Olympiad (IGO)	Class 1-12
6.	National Space Science Olympiad (NSSO)	Class 1-12

S. No.	Humming Bird Education	
	Name of Exam	Grade
1.	Humming Bird Commerce Competency Olympiad (HCC)	Class 1-12
2.	Humming Bird Cyber Olympiad (HCO)	Class 1-12
3.	Humming Bird English Olympiad (HEO)	Class 1-12
4.	Humming Bird General Knowledge Olympiad (HGO)	Class 1-12
5.	Humming Bird Hindi Olympiad (HHO)	Class 1-12
6.	Humming Bird Mathematics Olympiad (HMO)	Class 1-12
7.	Humming Bird Science Olympiad (HSO)	Class 1-12
8.	Humming Bird Aptitude and Reasoning Olympiad (ARO)	Class 1-12
9.	Humming Bird Spelling Competition (Spell BEE)	Class 1-12
10.	Humming Bird Language Olympiad	Class 1-12

S. No.	International Assessments for Indian Schools (IAIS) (MacMillan and EEA Collaboration)	
	Name of Exam	Grade
1.	IAIS Maths Olympiad	Class 3-12
2.	IAIS ScienceOlympiad	Class 3-12
3.	IAIS English Olympiad	Class 3-12
4.	IAIS Digital Technologies Olympiad	Class 3-12

S. No.	SilverZone Foundation	
	Name of Exam	Grade
1.	International Informatics Olympiad	Class 1-12
2.	International Olympiad of Mathematics	Class 1-12
3.	International Olympiad of Science	Class 1-12

S. No.	Unified Council	
	Name of Exam	Grade
1.	Unified Council Cyber Exam	Class 1-12
2.	Unified International English Olympiad.	Class 1-12
3.	Unified International Mathematics Olympiad (UIMO)	Class 1-12

S. No.	Unicus	
	Name of Exam	Grade
1.	Unicus Non-Routine Mathematics Olympiad (UNRMO)	Class 1-11
2.	Unicus Mathematics Olympiad (UMO)	Class 1-11

3.	Unicus Science Olympiad (USO)	Class 1-11
4.	Unicus English Olympiad (UEO)	Class 1-11
5.	Unicus Cyber Olympiad (UCO)	Class 1-11
6.	Unicus General knowledge Olympiad (UGKO)	Class 1-11
7.	Unicus Critical Thinking Olympiad (UCTO)	Class 1-11
CREST (Online Mode)		
S. No.	Name of Exam	Grade
1.	Mathematics (CMO)	Classes KG-10
2.	Science (CSO)	Classes KG-10
3.	English (CEO)	Classes KG-10
4.	Computer (CCO)	Classes 1-10
5.	Reasoning (CRO)	Classes 1-10
6.	Spell Bee Summer (CSB)	Classes 1-8
7.	Spell Bee Winter (CSBW)	Classes 1-8
8.	Mental Maths (MMO)	Classes 1-12
9.	Green Warrior Olympiad (GWO)	Classes 1-12

How To Apply?

Anyone willing to participate in the Olympiad exam can follow these steps to apply for the exam:

- Log in to the official website of the conducting organization.
- Find the Registration Option to register
- Fill up the details such as Student Name, Parent Name, School Name, Class, Postal Address, E-mail Address, Password, etc.
- Select the subjects you want to apply for. Pay the necessary registration fees and you are done.
- You will receive necessary details on your email id.

There are no minimum marks required by the Olympiad conducting organizations to apply for the exam.

Awards

Based on the organization rules, students as well as schools participating in these exams are awarded with several recognitions based on the marks they score.

www.ingramcontent.com/pod-product-compliance
Lightning Source LLC
Chambersburg PA
CBHW062128160426
43191CB00013B/2232